Supercharging

MS DOS®

Supercharging

MS DOS®

The Microsoft Guide to High Performance Computing for the Experienced PC User

By VAN WOLVERTON
author of
RUNNING MS-DOS®

Microsoft®
PRESS

PUBLISHED BY

Microsoft Press

A Division of Microsoft Corporation

16011 N.E. 36th Way, Box 97017, Redmond, Washington 98073–9717

Copyright © 1986 by Van Wolverton

Library of Congress Cataloging in Publication Data
Wolverton, Van, 1939–
  Supercharging MS-DOS
  Includes index.
  1. MS-DOS (Computer operating system) I. Title.
QA76.76063W655 1986 005.4′46 86-21775
ISBN 0-914845-95-0

Printed and bound in the United States of America.

        8 9 FGFG 8 9 0 9 8

Distributed to the book trade in the
United States by Harper and Row.

Distributed to the book trade in
Canada by General Publishing Company, Ltd.

Distributed to the book trade outside the
United States and Canada by Penguin Books Ltd.

Penguin Books Ltd., Harmondsworth, Middlesex, England
Penguin Books Australia Ltd., Ringwood, Victoria, Australia
Penguin Books N.Z. Ltd., 182-190 Wairau Road, Auckland 10, New Zealand

British Cataloging in Publication Data available

For Edward, Katherine, and Andrew,
Inheritors of the Faith, Keepers of the Flame,
Guardians of the Trust:
You'll never know just how much
I love you.

CONTENTS

Introduction   ix

Section I

Going Beyond the Basics   1

Chapter 1
Let's Get Technical: Of Bytes,
ASCII, and Hexadecimal   3

Chapter 2
Using the Extended Character Set   9

Chapter 3
Taking Control of Your Screen and
Keyboard with ANSI.SYS   17

Chapter 4
Learning Your Printer's
Language   35

Chapter 5
Debug: A Special Sort of Editor   47

Chapter 6
Advanced Batch-File Techniques   71

Chapter 7
Designing an Interactive
Menu System   89

Section II

Customizing Your System   103

Chapter 8
Controlling the Environment
and CONFIG.SYS   105

Chapter 9
Setting Up and Using
a RAM Disk   117

Chapter 10
Display It Your Way   131

Chapter 11
Print It Your Way   149

Chapter 12
Increasing Your Keyboard's IQ   181

Chapter 13
Playing It Smart with
Files and Disks   193

Chapter 14
Putting It All Together:
Your Own Menu System   219

Chapter 15
The Care and Feeding of
Your Computer   241

Section III   **Quick Reference   251**

Appendix A
A Quick Reference to
ANSI.SYS Commands   253

Appendix B
Epson-Compatible Printer
Commands   259

Appendix C
The ASCII and IBM Extended
Character Sets   263

Appendix D
ANSI.SYS Key and Extended
Key Codes   269

Appendix E
Converting Hexadecimal Numbers
to Decimal   273

Appendix F
A Sample Menu System   277

Glossary   285

Index   291

INTRODUCTION

If you have used your computer for a few months, you know there's more to DOS than A>. But do you know how *much* more? This book shows you how, using nothing more than DOS, you can:

- Design your own screens, using bold, reverse video, and color, to display menus, help information, or instructions.

- Create, examine, or change *any* file, no matter what it contains — even a program.

- Set up a customized menu system that lets you run any of your application programs just by pressing one or two keys.

You'll see how to do all that, and more. But this book doesn't describe routine uses of DOS; it assumes that you have used DOS long enough to be familiar with its commands, have written some batch files, and want to know more. *Running MS-DOS,* also published by Microsoft Press, introduces MS-DOS and shows you how to use its commands. If you're new to computers, you should start with that book; this book picks up where *Running MS-DOS* leaves off.

Like *Running MS-DOS,* however, this book still doesn't assume that you want to become a programmer; it assumes that your goal is to take advantage of these advanced capabilities of DOS in order to use the computer more productively. In keeping with this goal, the book is written in plain English and uses real-life examples as often as possible.

About the Batch Files and Programs

The book describes many batch files and several programs. Some are short, most contain 10 to 20 lines, and a few are longer. It takes some time to type and test them, but you should find several that will make your life easier. Except for one program in Chapter 12 that works only with the IBM PC/AT and compatible computers, the batch files and programs work with any IBM or IBM-compatible computer.

Although you can buy special-purpose utility programs that provide many of the capabilities covered by the batch files and programs in this book, you may find that you don't need them. And you can easily tailor the batch files shown here to your own needs or preferences. Not only can this make your computer a more efficient tool, but you also get the satisfaction of knowing that you did it yourself and the comfort of knowing that, if the need arises, you can change it again.

And it's all — well, *almost* all — DOS.

What's in the Book and Where

Part 1 includes Chapters 1 through 7. These chapters describe some general techniques for advanced DOS uses. Chapter 1 defines *byte, hexadecimal,* and *ASCII.* Chapter 2 shows you how to use the IBM extended character set, and Chapter 3 shows you how to use the ANSI.SYS device driver to control the display and keyboard. Chapter 4 shows you how to use printer commands. Chapter 5 shows you how to use the Debug program. Chapters 6 and 7 show you some advanced batch-file techniques, then apply these techniques to creating a menu system.

Part 2 includes Chapters 8 through 15. These chapters apply the techniques described in Part 1 to specific parts of your computer system; they show you how to create and use a number of batch files and programs. Chapter 8 shows you how to control the environment and configuration, and Chapter 9 shows you how to set up and use a RAM disk. Chapters 10, 11, and 12 cover the display, printer, and keyboard, and Chapter 13 covers files and disks. Chapter 14, drawing on techniques described in most of the preceding chapters, shows you how to create a complete menu system tailored to the application programs you use. Chapter 15 concludes Part 2 by suggesting some ways to make your environment safer and more comfortable for both your computer and yourself.

Appendices A through F provide additional reference material. Appendices A and B are quick references to ANSI.SYS commands and the more common printer commands. Appendices C and D are quick references to the ASCII and IBM extended character set and the key codes used with ANSI.SYS commands. Appendix E gives a bit more detail about hexadecimal numbers, and Appendix F shows the contents of all the files needed for the menu system described in Chapter 14.

How You Can Use the Book

Read Part 1 first. It provides a foundation of techniques used in the specific batch files and programs in Part 2. You needn't read the chapters in Part 2 in order. If you're especially interested in the printer, for example, try Chapter 11 first. Where knowledge of something in a previous chapter is required, a cross-reference is provided.

The menu system described in Chapter 14 draws from almost every other chapter; more than anything else in the book, it demonstrates how much you can do with DOS. If you tailor the menu system to the programs you use, you can run any application in any directory just by pressing one or two keys.

The menu system requires more effort than any other batch file in the book but, once you set it up, you may never again type a command to change the directory or start an application program. But because Chapter 14 draws so heavily on the other chapters in the book, it would probably be better to wait until you have gone through most of the book before tackling the menu system.

Differences Between Versions 2 and 3

DOS has been revised several times. A change in the number following the decimal point—3.10 to 3.20, for example—marks a minor change that leaves DOS substantially the same as the previous version. A change in the number preceding the decimal point, however, marks a major change. Version 2.00, for example, includes almost three times as many commands as Version 1.10.

Unless otherwise noted, the commands and responses in this book are based on Version 3.10 of DOS, but the book can be used with all versions of DOS since 2.00 and all models of IBM and IBM-compatible computers. For simplicity, all 2.xx versions of DOS are referred to as as Version 2, and all 3.xx versions are referred to as Version 3. The examples in this book cannot be used with Version 1.

Chapter 15 urges you to get Version 3 if you're still using Version 2. The following list shows the significant additions made by each of the minor versions of Version 3:

Version 3.0

File sharing for network and multitasking systems
Share command
Attrib command
VDISK device driver
<drive>:<path> allowed before program name
<path> allowed before file name in IF EXIST <filename>

Version 3.1

Support for the IBM PC Network
Join command
Subst command

Version 3.2

Xcopy command
Replace command
Append command
DRIVER.SYS, which assigns a second letter to a disk drive
Support for 3.5-inch drives

What to Type and When

This book uses the following conventions to show what you type and how DOS responds:

- Hands-on examples are shown in different type, on separate lines, just as you would see them on your display. The characters you type are printed in lowercase. Here is an example that shows this convention:

```
A>path
PATH=A:\;A:\DOS
```

- Occasionally, similar information appears in the text. In these instances, the interaction between you and the computer is printed in italics to distinguish it from the surrounding text. For example, you may see: "the commands are *prompt $e[1;36m* for high-intensity cyan and *$prompt $e[m* to return the display attributes to normal."

- The names of keys in the examples are shown in angle brackets <> to distinguish them from characters that you type; <Ctrl-Break>, for example, means hold down the Ctrl key and press the Break key.

- The book shows the system prompt as *A>*, as in the first example. DOS displays something different if your system disk is not in drive A, or if you have defined your own system prompt. Whenever you see *A>* in the book, assume that it refers to your system prompt.

- Many commands include parameters that allow you to specify a particular disk drive, device, or other option. Options are shown in angle brackets <> when they represent a variable entry, such as the name of a file. When they must be entered exactly, they are shown in the form you must use. For example, here are the parameters of the Copy command:

```
copy <file1> <file2>
```

The word *copy* is required and must be entered as shown. *<file1>* represents the name of the source file, and *<file2>* represents the name of the target file.

Enough preparation; it's time to dig into DOS. Turn on your computer and turn to Chapter 1.

SECTION

I

Going Beyond
the Basics

CHAPTER

1

Let's Get Technical: Of Bytes, ASCII, and Hexadecimal

You can use most application programs and DOS commands without knowing about bytes, ASCII codes, or hexadecimal numbers, so why should you care about them? Well, because knowing something about these subjects will help you to become more adept at using DOS. And this book describes a few DOS commands and programs that require at least a familiarity with these concepts. Even if you never use your computer for anything but running the same few application programs, the techniques that are covered in this book can make your system easier to use or more productive.

What Is a Byte?

You know that computer memory and disk capacity are measured in bytes, and that a byte can store a character, but just what is a byte?

Computer memory is made up of thousands of electronic switches (usually transistors). Because these switches can be either on or off, they are used to represent the numbers 1 and 0. The base-2 number system — whose digits are 1 and 0 — is called *binary*, so each switch represents one *binary digit*, or *bit*. A *byte* is a group of eight of these switches, or bits.

We're talking about small switches here. A typical memory chip has 262,144 of them, giving it a capacity of 32,768 bytes. A computer with 640K bytes of memory has 5,242,880 switches.

Eight on-off switches can be arranged in 256 different combinations, so a byte can have 256 possible values ranging from 0 (all switches off) to 255 (all switches on). DOS can quickly locate any byte in its memory and either check the position of the eight switches (*read* the byte) or set the switches (*write* the byte).

When you save a file on a disk, DOS reads the position of the switches in memory where the file is stored, then records the state of these switches on the disk. When you load a file from a disk, DOS reads the state of the switches from the disk, then sets the switches in memory to match. Although the binary value of a byte can represent a character, a numeric value, or even a program instruction, its meaning as a character is most important to this book. Almost all microcomputers throughout the world use the same code to translate byte values to the familiar letters, numbers, and symbols we humans use.

The ASCII Code

The term ASCII (rhymes with *passkey*) frequently crops up in manuals, books, and articles about computers. Like many other computer terms, ASCII is an acronym—it stands for American Standard Code for Information Interchange. The key word here is *code*: Like the Morse code used in radio and telegraphy, ASCII is an internationally accepted code for representing characters in computers and telecommunications.

Because the value of a byte can range from 0 through 255, a byte can represent one of 256 possible characters. The ASCII standard defines the code for the first 128 characters (codes 0 through 127). With few exceptions, any microcomputer in any country uses the same code to translate byte values to characters; the exceptions are usually characters that vary from country to country, such as the currency symbol ($ in the United States, £ in the United Kingdom, ¥ in Japan, and so forth).

The first 128 characters can be divided into two groups: The first 32 (codes 0 through 31) are *control characters,* which define some action such as a carriage return or tab. The remaining 96 (codes 32 through 127) are the standard characters you normally see in text.

There is no formal standard for the second 128 characters (codes 128 through 255). The extended character set that's used by IBM and most IBM-compatible computers, however, is almost universally followed by computers that use DOS, so for your purposes it is a standard.

The 128 characters in the IBM extended character set fall into four groups:

- International characters (codes 128 through 175), mostly accented characters such as ç (code 135) and ñ (code 164).

- Line- and box-drawing characters (codes 176 through 223), such as ╔ (code 201) and ╝ (code 188).

- Greek letters (codes 224 through 237), such as ∝ (code 224) and φ (code 237).

- Mathematical symbols (codes 238 through 253), such as ± (code 241) and √ (code 251).

Books and manuals, such as the IBM BASIC manual and the IBM Technical Reference manual, frequently include charts of the ASCII code, showing each byte value and its corresponding character. Your printer's manual may include more than one chart, because many printers let you choose from several character sets that offer different combinations of international characters, fonts, or graphics characters. Appendix C in this book shows the full IBM-compatible character set, including the ASCII standard characters and IBM extended character set. The code for each character is given in both decimal and hexadecimal.

Hexadecimal Numbers

Hexadecimal, or *hex,* is the name of the base-16 number system, just as decimal is the name of the base-10 number system we commonly use. We use decimal numbers because we have ten fingers. Who uses a base-16 number system, and why?

Not surprisingly, the reason is related to the base-2 number system used by computers. Because 2 and 16 are both powers of 2, hexadecimal is a short-cut way of working with binary numbers. The decimal number 178, for example, is 10110010 in binary, but only B2 in hexadecimal. Programmers, engineers, and others who work with computers use hexadecimal to avoid all those ones and zeroes.

There are 16 hexadecimal digits: 0 through 9, plus A through F for the decimal values 10 through 15. This means that a hexadecimal number can look like F, which is 15 in decimal, or 10F (271 in decimal), or even FACE (64,206 in decimal).

Using a computer doesn't mean you have to learn hexadecimal, but it's difficult to avoid hexadecimal completely as you explore more advanced uses of DOS. The Compare command (FC if you're not using an IBM PC), for example, reports the location and value of differing bytes in hexadecimal. The Debug program uses hexadecimal numbers exclusively, and printer commands that control graphics also require hexadecimal values.

But you needn't learn hexadecimal arithmetic. The most you'll have to do in this book is recognize that a hexadecimal number is, indeed, a number, and perhaps type a few hexadecimal numbers. But if you're interested, Appendix E describes hexadecimal numbers in a bit more detail, including a table that simplifies converting hexadecimal numbers to decimal.

Chapter Summary

A byte:

- Is made up of eight binary digits, or bits.

- Can hold a value from 0 through 255.

The ASCII code:

- Is used to represent letters, numbers, and symbols.

- Covers the first 128 characters (codes 0 through 127).

- Is extended by IBM and compatible computers to cover the other 128 characters (codes 128 through 255).

- Is shown in Appendix C, which also shows the IBM extended character set.

Hexadecimal:

- Is the name of the base-16 number system.

- Is used by programmers because it's a shortcut way to use binary, the base-2 numbers that computers use.

- Is described in more detail in Appendix E, which also includes a hexadecimal-to-decimal conversion table.

CHAPTER
2

Using the Extended
Character Set

Your computer displays many characters besides the letters, numbers, and punctuation marks on the keyboard. These additional characters belong to the IBM extended character set. This chapter shows you how you can enter and use these non-keyboard characters.

As Chapter 1 explains, character codes 0 through 31 represent control functions, codes 32 through 127 represent the standard ASCII text characters, and (on IBM and IBM-compatible computers) codes 128 through 255 represent international characters, line- and box-drawing symbols, and mathematical symbols. The figures in Appendix C show both the standard ASCII character set and the IBM extended character set.

Using the Alt Key to Enter a Non-Keyboard Character

You can't type the non-keyboard characters because the keyboard doesn't have keys for all 256 codes. But there is a way on most IBM-compatible computers to enter any of these characters directly from the keyboard: Hold down the key labeled *Alt,* type the character's code on the numeric keypad, then release the Alt key.

Throughout this chapter—throughout the book, in fact—you'll use this technique to enter non-keyboard characters. Give it a try: Hold down the Alt key, type *171* on the numeric keypad (*not* the top row of number keys), then release the Alt key. DOS should respond by displaying the fraction ½ in a single character position; this is character 171.

This book uses the convention Ctrl-C to represent holding down the key labeled Ctrl and pressing C; it uses a similar convention to represent holding down the Alt key, typing a number on the keypad, and releasing the Alt key. The example in the previous paragraph would be shown as Alt-171.

Backspace to erase the fraction and enter more non-keyboard characters:

```
A>⟨Alt-232⟩⟨Alt-233⟩⟨Alt-234⟩
```

DOS should display three Greek letters.

The Alt key-plus-number technique works for any character, not just the non-keyboard characters. Press Escape to clear the screen and type:

```
A>⟨Alt-100⟩⟨Alt-105⟩⟨Alt-114⟩
```

100 is the code for d; typing Alt-100 is the same as typing *d.* 105 is the code for i, and 114 is the code for r. What you just typed looks like a Directory command. Press Enter. It *is* a Directory command.

If you really had to, you could type everything using just the Alt key and numeric keypad. Happily, you don't, but being able to type any character, whether or not it appears on the keyboard, will prove to be quite useful.

Using the International Characters

You can use the Alt-key technique to enter characters from another language. Press Escape to erase the line and type:

`A>⟨Alt-168⟩Por qu⟨Alt-130⟩?`

DOS displays a question in Spanish:

`A>¿Por qué?`

Entering the Control Characters

You can use the Alt key to type control codes—characters 1 through 31 in the ASCII code—as well as characters. For example, a carriage return is character 13. Type another Directory command, but, instead of pressing the Enter key, type Alt-13:

`A>dir⟨Alt-13⟩`

The result is the same as if you had pressed the Enter key.

How Many Ways Are There to Type Something?

You press Ctrl-C (or Ctrl-Break) to cancel a command, Ctrl-Z (or F6) to mark the end of a file, Ctrl-S (or Ctrl-NumLock) to temporarily halt the display. There are three ways to type the control characters that correspond to the action keys:

Action Key	Ctrl-	Alt-
Ctrl-Break	Ctrl-C	Alt-3
Backspace	Ctrl-H	Alt-8
Tab	Ctrl-I	Alt-9
Enter	Ctrl-M	Alt-13
Ctrl-PrtSc	Ctrl-P	Alt-16
Ctrl-NumLock	Ctrl-S	Alt-19
F6	Ctrl-Z	Alt-26

Because most manuals and books use the Ctrl-key technique of entering these characters—and because DOS echoes the control characters as a caret followed by the corresponding letter, regardless of how they are entered—this book, too, uses the Ctrl-key technique to represent typing character codes 1 through 26 (Ctrl-A through Ctrl-Z). The Alt-key technique is used to represent typing all other non-keyboard characters.

Note: Edlin, like DOS, lets you enter the control characters with either the Ctrl key or Alt key, but always echoes with a caret followed by the appropriate letter. Some word processors and text editors, however, accept only one of these techniques. Microsoft Word, for example, ignores Ctrl-A through Ctrl-Z, so you must use the Alt-key technique. You'll have to experiment with your program to see which method it accepts.

Besides the control functions just listed, the first 26 ASCII characters have other uses. Most printers, for example, accept commands to control the type of printing or line spacing in a document. So that the printer can distinguish a command from text to be printed, the commands start with non-printing characters. You can control your printer by including these commands in the text.

For example, character 14 (Ctrl-N) tells an Epson-compatible printer to print one line in large type; make sure your printer is on and type:

```
A>echo <Ctrl-N>This line is large. > prn
```

The line should be printed in large type.

Searching for Control Characters with a Word Processor

In some instances, using the Alt-key technique may be the only way of achieving what you want. It's sometimes difficult or impossible, for example, to search for or replace control characters in a document using a word-processing program, even though it may be just what you want to do. Suppose that you want to search for a tab or carriage return; many word processors use those characters to select an option of the search command, or even to end the command, so you can't tell the program to search for them by pressing the Tab key or Enter key.

Some word processors, however, such as Microsoft Word, let you search for a tab (character 9) by entering Alt-9 as the search character. When you enter the search characters, the word processor may display the corresponding characters shown in Appendix B (a small o for the tab), but it will search for the correct character.

The Character Code You Can't Enter with the Alt Key

Of the 256 possible character codes, there's one you can't enter with the Alt-key method: character 0, sometimes called the *null* character because many programs ignore it. (This is not the number 0, which is character 30; if this seems confusing, check Figure C-1 in Appendix C.) As the chart in

Appendix C shows, no character corresponds to character 0. To enter character 0 into a file, press F7 while copying from the console or using Edlin, or using the Debug program (described in Chapter 5).

Characters for Drawing Lines and Boxes

Many application programs draw lines or boxes on the screen. The lines and boxes are made up of individual characters whose codes are between 179 and 223. There are four sets of corners and straight lines for drawing with double lines, single lines, and combinations. You can use these characters to draw your own lines or boxes. Using the numbers on the numeric keypad, type:

```
A><Alt-201><Alt-205><Alt-187>
```

DOS displays the top half of a small box:

```
A>⌐¬
```

Press the Escape key to clear the line and type:

```
A><Alt-200><Alt-205><Alt-188>
```

DOS shows you the bottom:

```
A>└┴┘
```

There are some possibilities here. Press Escape to clear the command line, then press Enter to get back to the system prompt.

The next example is meant to give you some ideas about how to use these non-keyboard characters. You'll create a small file named MENU.DOC by copying from the console (keyboard) to a file. In the lines to be typed, note that the third and seventh lines are blank. Further, *F1* in the fifth line means *F* and *1,* not the first function key, and the same is true of *F2* in the ninth line. Finally, ^Z in the last line means press the function key labeled F6, or type Ctrl-Z. Type the following:

```
A>copy con menu.doc
Function Keys

<Alt-201><Alt-205><Alt-205><Alt-187>
<Alt-186>F1<Alt-186> Word Processing
<Alt-200><Alt-205><Alt-205><Alt-188>

<Alt-201><Alt-205><Alt-205><Alt-187>
<Alt-186>F2<Alt-186> Communications
<Alt-200><Alt-205><Alt-205><Alt-188>
^Z
        1 File(s) copied
A>_
```

The screen should look like Figure 2-1.

```
A>copy con menu.doc
Function Keys
```

 Word processing

 Communications
```
^Z
        1 File(s) copied
A>_
```

Figure 2-1. How DOS echoes the line- and box-drawing characters.

You can display MENU.DOC, just as you can display any other text file, with the Type or Copy commands. For better effect, use a batch file so that you can clear the screen first. Type the following to create and test a short batch file named SHOWMENU.BAT:

```
A>copy con showmenu.bat
echo off
cls
type menu.doc
^Z
        1 File(s) copied

A>showmenu
```

DOS clears the screen and displays your short function-key menu:

```
Function Keys
```

 Word processing

 Communications

```
A>_
```

These line- and box-drawing characters are used throughout the book. If your word processor or text editor accepts these characters, you can enter them using the Alt-key technique, then copy, move, or delete them just as you can any other character. As you'll see in Chapter 4, if your printer accepts the extended characters, you can print them, too.

Chapter Summary

- Non-keyboard characters are the characters that can't be typed just by pressing a key. Their codes are 0 through 31 and 127 through 255.

- You can enter any character code except 0 (zero) by holding down the Alt key, typing the code number on the numeric keypad, then releasing the Alt key. To enter character 0, press F7 while copying from the console or using Edlin.

- Codes 0 through 31 are defined by the ASCII standard as control characters, such as carriage return or tab, not as printable characters. The IBM extended character set, however, does define characters for them.

- Codes 128 through 168 represent international characters; 169 through 178 are miscellaneous graphic characters; 179 through 223 are the line- and box-drawing characters; and 224 through 253 are the Greek and mathematical symbols.

- If your word processor accepts non-keyboard characters, you can work with them just as you work with the standard characters. If your word processor doesn't accept them, you can use Edlin.

Taking Control of Your Screen and Keyboard with ANSI.SYS

M ost application programs take pains to make themselves attractive and easy to use. They don't simply display one line after another, scrolling old lines off the top of the screen; they display their messages and results in specific areas of the screen. They also control the color and brightness of what they display, and often they assign special meanings to certain keys. You can use a DOS program called ANSI.SYS to employ these same techniques to make your batch files and system prompt more attractive and easier to use.

This chapter shows you how to control the display and keyboard with ANSI.SYS commands. After going through the examples in this chapter, and using the ANSI.SYS command summary in Appendix A, you'll be ready to design your own screens. Using a few additional techniques described in other chapters, you can design a menu system tailored to your computer and the people who use it. Chapter 14 shows one example of such a menu system that uses batch files and ANSI.SYS commands to guide you—or anyone else who uses your computer—through routine use of application programs and batch files.

ANSI.SYS Is a Device Driver

Every device that is attached to your computer must be controlled by a program. DOS itself controls the disk drives and provides a limited amount of control for the keyboard, display, and printer. For more precise control, a program called a *device driver* is required to tell DOS how to use (or *drive*) a specific device.

Some device drivers are stored in files with the extension SYS. You may have programs on your system disk, such as VDISK.SYS (included with Version 3 of DOS), which defines and controls a virtual disk in memory; MOUSE.SYS, which controls a mouse; or HARDDISK.SYS, which controls a fixed disk. In order for DOS to use such a program, the CONFIG.SYS file must include a Device command that names the device driver (for example, *device = vdisk.sys or device = mouse.sys*).

ANSI.SYS provides much more detailed control of the console device—the display and keyboard—than the basic control provided by DOS.

Preparing for the Examples

Before you can use the ANSI.SYS commands, make sure the following files and commands are on your system disk:

- CONFIG.SYS must be in the root directory of your system disk, and must contain the configuration command *device = ansi.sys.*

- ANSI.SYS must be on your system disk. If it isn't, copy it from your original DOS disk.

If ANSI.SYS isn't in the root directory of your system disk, the Device command must specify its path name. For example, if your system disk is drive C and ANSI.SYS is in the directory \DOS, you would put *device = c: \dos \ansi.sys* in CONFIG.SYS.

If you made changes to meet these requirements, restart DOS by pressing Ctrl-Alt-Del before continuing; DOS reads CONFIG.SYS only when it starts.

ANSI.SYS Commands

Using the ANSI.SYS display commands, you can position the cursor, tell DOS to display something in high intensity, change colors, or clear the screen. Combining ANSI.SYS commands with text gives you near-total control over the appearance of the display.

Using the ANSI.SYS Define Key command, you can change the effect of pressing a key, causing a key to produce a different character or even a series of characters, such as a command.

ANSI.SYS commands are sometimes called *escape sequences* because they all begin with the Escape character (ASCII code 27) followed by a left bracket. Most commands include a numeric or alphabetic code, and each command ends with a different letter. The general form, then, of an ANSI.SYS command is:

{ESC}[<code><letter>

The ending *<letter>* identifies the command. For example, the command to move the cursor down five rows is *{ESC}[5B*; the code is *5* and the ending letter is *B*. Some codes are more than one number or string, separated by semicolons. For example, the command to move the cursor to row 10, column 20 is *{ESC}[10;20H*.

The case of the final letter is important. For example, *H* identifies the command that moves the cursor, but *h* identifies the command that sets the display mode.

Because ANSI.SYS commands control the console device, they must be typed at the keyboard or sent to the display. If you could type *{ESC}[2J*, for example, DOS would clear the screen. But there's a catch: When you press the Esc key, DOS cancels the line you're typing. Happily, there's a way around this, using the Prompt command. For a quick preview of what you can do with ANSI.SYS commands, type the following Prompt command:

```
A>prompt $e[7m$e[2J
```

You should be looking at a blank screen in reverse video; if not, enter the Prompt command again. The system prompt you just defined is actually two ANSI.SYS commands: *$e[7m* sets the display to reverse video, and *$e[2J* clears the screen.

Note that there is no system prompt. You defined the prompt to be the ANSI.SYS commands, which affect the appearance of the screen but don't actually display anything. Type the following commands to restore the normal screen and standard DOS system prompt (the second Prompt command restores the standard system prompt):

```
prompt $e[m
```

```
prompt
```

```
A>cls
```

Your screen should be back to normal.

Sending ANSI.SYS Commands to the Console

Because all ANSI.SYS commands start with an Escape character, but DOS cancels the command line when you press the Escape key, you can't type an ANSI.SYS command. You have three alternatives:

- Put the ANSI.SYS commands in a file and display the file with the Type or Copy command.

- Use the Prompt command to send the ANSI.SYS commands to the console.

- Put the Escape sequences into a batch file and use Echo commands to send the ANSI.SYS commands to the console. (See Chapter 7 for examples of this method.)

Creating a File That Contains ANSI.SYS Commands

Creating a file that contains ANSI.SYS commands isn't difficult. Some text editors (such as Edlin) and word processors (such as Microsoft Word) let you enter an Escape character. You could also use the DOS Debug program, described in Chapter 5. Be sure that the program you use also lets you save a file with no formatting codes (such as *unformatted* in Microsoft Word or *non-document* mode in WordStar).

Once you have created the file and stored it on disk, carry out the ANSI.SYS commands it contains by displaying the file with the Type or Copy commands. This technique is best for all but the simplest use of ANSI.SYS commands. It is used in this chapter and elsewhere in the book for the longer examples.

Using the Prompt Command to Carry Out ANSI.SYS Commands

For simpler uses of ANSI.SYS commands, you can enter an ANSI.SYS command without using a text editor or word processor: The Prompt command tells DOS what to display for the system prompt, and it lets you specify an Escape character without pressing the Escape key. You can include an ANSI.SYS command in the system prompt, or even make an ANSI.SYS command the entire system prompt.

A Brief Review of the Prompt Command

To let you tailor your system prompt, the Prompt command accepts special codes beginning with a dollar sign that cause certain information to be included in the system prompt. The current drive, for example, is represented by *$n*, and the greater-than sign (>) is represented by *$g*, so you could specify the standard system prompt with *prompt ng*.

What does all this have to do with ANSI.SYS commands? One of the special codes you can specify with the Prompt command—*$e*—represents the Escape character. This is the troublesome character that DOS won't allow you to type. So, by using *$e* with a Prompt command, you can send an ANSI.SYS command to the display.

If this isn't entirely clear, have faith: You'll enter an ANSI.SYS command with the Prompt command in a moment, which should clear up any uncertainties.

Preparing for the Examples

The short examples in this chapter use a Prompt command that defines the system prompt as an ANSI.SYS command. Most of the examples result in no visible system prompt. If you wish, you can restore the standard prompt after each example by typing *prompt*.

If you have defined your own system prompt—perhaps with a Prompt command in your AUTOEXEC.BAT file—you might want to create a batch file now that contains the Prompt command you use to define your system prompt. That way, after each example you can restore your system prompt simply by typing the name of the batch file.

Controlling the Display

The ANSI.SYS commands for controlling the display fall into three groups:

- *Cursor control* commands, which let you move the cursor up, down, left, right, or to a specific position; save the current cursor position; and restore the cursor to the saved position.

- *Erase* commands, which let you erase the entire display or part of a line.

- *Attribute and mode* commands, which let you control the number of columns (40 or 80), graphics and color modes, and attributes such as high intensity, blinking, foreground color, and background color.

Appendix A is a complete summary of ANSI.SYS commands, with descriptions of each command and brief examples of the most common uses. This chapter shows you how to use a few of the ANSI.SYS commands; several other commands are used in other chapters of the book. The general form of each command is the same, so after finishing the examples here you can use any of the commands described in Appendix A.

The Set Attribute Command

The Set Attribute command lets you control display attributes such as high intensity, blinking, or color. Color attributes (other than black and white) are simulated on a monochrome display, and some combinations of background and foreground colors are difficult to read. Some combinations are difficult to read even on a color display; you may want to experiment a bit to find a combination that is both pleasing and easy to read.

A Set Attribute command affects everything displayed after it is entered. Figure 3-1 shows a complete list of the attributes and colors.

The Set Attribute command has one parameter, the attribute code:

{ESC}[<attr>m

<attr> is a number that specifies the attribute to be turned on. If you omit <attr>, all attributes are turned off. You can include more than one <attr>, separated by semicolons. Figure 3-1 shows the display attributes and the corresponding values for <attr>.

m is the ending letter that identifies the Set Attribute command.

Non-Color Attributes

0   All attributes off
1   High intensity (bold)
4   Underline (monochrome display only)
5   Blink
7   Reverse video
8   Invisible

Foreground Color		Background Color	
30	Black	40	Black
31	Red	41	Red
32	Green	42	Green
33	Yellow	43	Yellow
34	Blue	44	Blue
35	Magenta	45	Magenta
36	Cyan	46	Cyan
37	White	47	White

Figure 3-1. Display attribute codes.

Changing the Display to Reverse Video

The screen normally displays light characters on a dark background. Displaying dark characters on a light background is called *reverse video*. As Figure 3-1 shows, the attribute code for reverse video is 7. To change your display to reverse video, type the following Prompt command to send a Set Attribute command with the attribute code 7 to the display:

```
A>prompt $e[7m
```

Remember, all ANSI.SYS commands begin with an Escape character followed by a left bracket, and end with a letter. The parameter for the Prompt command begins with $e, which represents the Escape character, followed by a left bracket. The 7 is the attribute code for reverse video, and *m* is the ending letter that identifies the Set Attribute command. Each time DOS would normally display the system prompt, it sends this Set Attribute command to the display.

Because of all the brackets and numbers, an ANSI.SYS command can get pretty hard to read, so it's not unusual to make a mistake when you type one. If any part of the ANSI.SYS command you just typed as a parameter to the Prompt command is echoed, you probably made a typing error; if *7m* is displayed, for example, you probably forgot the *e* or the left bracket. Just type the Prompt command again.

If nothing seems to happen, everything's OK. There's no system prompt on the line that contains the cursor because you defined the prompt to be just an ANSI.SYS command. Clear the screen by typing:

```
cls
```

The screen has changed to reverse video (dark characters on a light background). But there's no prompt, because the Prompt command didn't specify anything to be displayed (you'll restore the prompt in a moment). To put something on the screen, type a Directory command:

```
dir
```

There's some text in reverse video. To change back, enter another Set Attribute command that specifies no attribute code. This turns off all attributes, restoring the display to normal. Type the following Prompt command:

```
prompt $e[m
```

Again, if any part of the Prompt command is echoed, type it again. Now restore the system prompt by typing either a Prompt command with no parameters or the batch command that restores your system prompt:

```
prompt
```

Notice that what you typed is displayed normally (light characters on a dark background), but the rest of the screen still shows a light background. Restore the entire screen by typing another Clear Screen command:

```
A>cls
```

Everything is back to normal.

The Move Cursor Command

The Move Cursor command moves the cursor to a specific row and column location. Anything displayed after a Move Cursor command starts at the new cursor location.

The Move Cursor command has two parameters:

```
{ESC}[<row>;<col>H
```

$<row>$ specifies the row where the cursor is to be moved. It can be from 1 through 25. If you omit $<row>$, DOS assumes 1; if you omit $<row>$ and want to include $<col>$, enter the semicolon so that DOS will know that $<row>$ is missing.

$<col>$ specifies the column where the cursor is to be moved. It can be from 1 through 80. If you omit $<col>$, DOS assumes 1.

H is the ending letter that identifies the Move Cursor command.

Displaying Something at a Specific Location

Suppose you want to display "Middle of the screen" at row 12, column 30. Type the following Prompt command to send a Move Cursor command to the display:

```
A>prompt $e[12;30HMiddle of the screen
```

Middle of the screen should be displayed near the middle of the screen. If it isn't, or if part of the Prompt command is echoed, type the Prompt command again.

Restore the system prompt by typing *prompt* or the batch command (if you've created one) that restores your system prompt (the command you type will follow *screen*, because that's the end of the system prompt).

Displaying at a Specific Location with Attributes

You can combine the features of the first two examples by displaying something at a specific location, specifying the display attributes to be used. For example, you could display the words *Bold Blink Normal* starting at row 15, column 1, in attributes that match the words. If you have a color monitor, you can change the color of each word, too.

Two versions of this example are shown, one for monochrome and one for color. Follow the instructions under either "If You Have a Monochrome Monitor" or "If You Have a Color Monitor," then go on to the heading "Did It Work?". Each example includes four ANSI.SYS commands in a single Prompt command, so type carefully; guard especially against leaving out one of the left brackets. As before, if part of the command is echoed, you'll have to type it all again.

If You Have a Monochrome Monitor

If you have a monochrome monitor, you'll send the following ANSI.SYS commands to the display:

Command	Description
$e[15H	Move the cursor to row 15, column 1 (the column parameter is omitted, so DOS assumes 1).
$e[1mBold	Set attribute 1 (high intensity) and display the word *Bold*.
$e[5mBlink	Set attribute 5 (blink) and display the word *Blink*.
$e[mNormal	Turn all attributes off and display the word *Normal*.

Type the following Prompt command:

```
A>prompt $e[15H$e[1mBold $e[5mBlink $e[mNormal
```

Go on to the heading "Did It Work?".

If You Have a Color Monitor

If you have a color monitor, you'll send the following ANSI.SYS commands to the display:

Command	Description
$e[15H	Move the cursor to row 15, column 1 (the column parameter is omitted, so DOS assumes 1).
$e[1;31mBold	Set attributes 1 (high intensity) and 31 (red foreground), and display the word *Bold*.
$e[5;32mBlink	Set attribute 5 (blink) and 32 (green foreground), and display the word *Blink*.
$e[mNormal	Turn all attributes off and display the word *Normal*.

Type the following Prompt command:

```
A>prompt $e[15H$e[1;31mBold $e[5;32mBlink $e[mNormal
```

Did It Work?

The word *Bold* should be bold (high-intensity), *Blink* should be blinking and high-intensity, and *Normal* should be in standard letters. If you don't see *Bold Blink Normal* in the intended attributes and colors, type the Prompt command again.

Notice that turning on an attribute doesn't turn off any existing attributes, so *Blink* is both blinking and high intensity. If you wanted *Blink* not to be in high intensity, you would have to turn off all attributes with code 0, then turn on blink with code 5. You can intermix ANSI.SYS commands anywhere in text, changing attributes or color between each character.

Restore the system prompt by typing *prompt* or the batch command (if you've created one) that restores your system prompt.

In addition to quick demonstrations of ANSI.SYS commands, you can use the Prompt command and ANSI.SYS commands to define quite elaborate system prompts, complete with reminders of the current drive, directory, time, and date, all boxed in colored windows if you like. Chapter 9 shows several examples of system prompts that go a bit farther than the usual *A>*.

Putting ANSI.SYS Commands in a File

The previous example really stretched the use of the Prompt command to enter ANSI.SYS commands. When you need this many commands, it's usually better to put them in a file and display the file with the Type or Copy command.

Combining ANSI.SYS commands with text, as in the previous example, lets you design your own screens. For example, suppose your office prepares a monthly report. The procedure is fairly simple, but it happens only once a month, so people sometimes forget how to do it. You decide you need a help screen that anyone can quickly display to get instructions. The help screen tells the user that preparing the report requires three steps:

1. Enter the monthly data into a spreadsheet.

2. Update a word-processing document named REPORT. DOC.

3. Type the command *doreport*.

In addition, you want to remind the user that all printer output should be sent to the department office.

Using Edlin—or any other editing program that allows you to enter the Escape character—you can put these instructions, plus a few ANSI.SYS commands, in a file named MONTHRPT.HLP that will display the help screen. To see the help screen, simply display the file with the Type or Copy command.

Entering the Escape Character in a File

The next example requires you to enter a series of ANSI.SYS commands in a file using a word processor or text editor that can save a file without formatting codes. Some word processors, such as Microsoft Word, allow you to enter non-text characters such as the Escape character by using the Alt-key and numeric-keypad technique described in Chapter 2. Other programs may offer a different technique; check the manual to see whether you can enter these characters and, if so, how. If you don't have such a program, you can use Edlin, the DOS text editor. For a description of how to use Edlin, see your DOS manual or Chapters 11 and 12 of *Running MS-DOS*.

Using Microsoft Word or other programs that permit the Alt-key and numeric-keypad technique, to enter an Escape character you hold down the Alt key, type the 2 and 7 keys on the keypad (*not* the number keys at the top of the keyboard), then release the Alt key. The program will probably display a left arrow (←), the character that IBM and most compatible computers define for code 27.

Using Edlin, to enter an Escape character you type Ctrl-V, then a left bracket; Edlin echoes this as ^V[, its way of representing the Escape character. This left bracket is *not* the left bracket that follows the Escape character at the beginning of an ANSI.SYS command; you must type another left bracket, then the rest of the command. When you're entering an ANSI.SYS command with Edlin, the beginning of each command looks like ^V[[; if you use the Edlin List or Page command to display the file, however, the carat and bracket at the beginning are reversed: [^[with versions 3.0 and 3.1 of DOS.

Again, different versions of this example are shown for monochrome and color monitors. Follow the instructions under "If You Have a Monochrome Monitor" or "If You Have a Color Monitor."

If You Have a Monochrome Monitor

Use your editing program to create a file named MONTHRPT.HLP and enter the lines shown in Figure 3-2. The line numbers shown here are for reference only; start each line with the first Escape character.

```
1: {ESC}[2J
2: {ESC}[5;10H{ESC}[1mPREPARING THE MONTHLY REPORT
3: {ESC}[10;20H{ESC}[m1. Enter data into spreadsheet
4: {ESC}[12;20H2. Update WP document named REPORT.DOC
5: {ESC}[14;20H3. Type {ESC}[1mdoreport
6: {ESC}[20;10H{ESC}[7mSend printer output to department office
7: {ESC}[m
```

Figure 3-2. Monochrome help-screen text and commands.

The following explanations of the ANSI.SYS commands refer to the line numbers shown in Figure 3-2:

1. *{ESC}[2J* clears the screen.

2. *{ESC}[5;10H* moves the cursor to row 5, column 10.
   {ESC}[1m turns on the high-intensity attribute.

3. *{ESC}[10;20H* moves the cursor to row 10, column 20.
   {ESC}[m turns off all display attributes.

4. *{ESC}[12;20H* moves the cursor to row 12, column 20.

5. *{ESC}[14;20H* moves the cursor to row 14, column 20.
   {ESC}[1m turns on the high-intensity attribute.

6. *{ESC}[20;10H* moves the cursor to row 20, column 10.
   {ESC}[7m turns on the reverse-video attribute.

7. *{ESC}[m* turns off all display attributes.

Proofread the file carefully, save it, and go on to the heading "Displaying the Help Screen."

If You Have a Color Monitor

Use your editing program to create a file named MONTHRPT.HLP and enter the lines shown in Figure 3-3. The line numbers shown here are for reference only; start each line with the first Escape character.

```
1: {ESC}[46m
2: {ESC}[2J
3: {ESC}[5;10H{ESC}[31mPREPARING THE MONTHLY REPORT
4: {ESC}[10;20H{ESC}[34m1. Enter data into spreadsheet
5: {ESC}[12;20H2. Update WP document named REPORT.DOC
6: {ESC}[14;20H3. Type {ESC}[1mdoreport
7: {ESC}[20;10H{ESC}[33;41mSend printer output to department
   office
8: {ESC}[m
```

Figure 3-3. Color help-screen text and commands.

The following explanations of the ANSI.SYS commands refer to the line numbers shown in Figure 3-3:

1. *{ESC}[46m* sets the background color to cyan.

2. *{ESC}[2J* clears the screen.

3. *{ESC}[5;10H* moves the cursor to row 5, column 10.
   {ESC}[31m sets the foreground color to red.

4. *{ESC}[10;20H* moves the cursor to row 10, column 20.
   {ESC}[34m sets the foreground color to blue.

5. *{ESC}[12;20H* moves the cursor to row 12, column 20.

6. *{ESC}[14;20H* moves the cursor to row 14, column 20.
   {ESC}[1m turns on the high–intensity attribute.

7. *{ESC}[20;10H* moves the cursor to row 20, column 10.
   {ESC}[33;41m sets the foreground color to yellow and the background color to red.

8. *{ESC}[m* turns off all display attributes.

Proofread the file carefully and save it. Be sure to save the file without formatting codes.

Displaying the Help Screen

To display the help screen, type:

```
A>type monthrpt.hlp
```

Your screen should look like Figure 3-4. If not, load MONTHRPT.HLP with your editing program and proofread against the instructions. Then, correct any errors, save the file, and enter the Type command once again.

```
PREPARING THE MONTHLY REPORT



    1. Enter data into spreadsheet

    2. Update WP document named REPORT.DOC

    3. Type doreport
```

Send printer output to department office

Figure 3-4. Help screen.

If you have a monochrome display, the title should be in high intensity, the numbered items normal, *doreport* in high intensity, and the bottom line (*Send printer output . . .*) in reverse video.

If you have a color display, the background should be cyan, the title in red, the numbered items in blue, *doreport* in high-intensity blue, and the bottom line (*Send printer output . . .*) in high-intensity yellow on a red background.

To make displaying this help screen even quicker, you could put the Type command in a batch file named MONTH.BAT; anyone could then display the help screen by typing *month*. As you'll see in a moment, you can make it even easier to display a help screen by using the ANSI.SYS command that assigns a string (series of characters) to a key.

Controlling the Keyboard

All the examples thus far have dealt with controlling where and how text is displayed, or the *output* part of the console device. ANSI.SYS has one other major capability that deals with the keyboard, or the *input* part of the console device: You can change the characters produced when a key is pressed.

The Define Key Command

The Define Key command lets you specify one or more characters to be produced when a key is pressed. You can redefine almost every key on the keyboard, including the function keys. You can even redefine combinations of the Shift, Ctrl, and Alt keys with most other keys.

The Define Key command has two parameters: the identification code of the key, and the character or characters to be produced when the key is pressed:

{ESC}[<key code>;<result>p

<key code> is a number that identifies the key you're defining. For the main typewriter portion of the keyboard, <key code> is the same as the ASCII code for that character. Unshifted k, for example, is 107, and shifted K is 75 ; Appendix D contains the complete chart of key codes for the Define Key command. As you'll see in a moment, you can use two numbers separated by a semicolon to specify other keys, such as the function keys, numeric keypad, and combinations of keys.

<result> is the character or characters to be produced when the key specified in <key code> is pressed. <result> can be any combination of ASCII codes and strings enclosed in quotation marks, separated by semicolons. All the characters that are specified in <result> are produced each time the key is pressed.

To restore a key to its original meaning, specify a <result> identical to <key code>.

p is the ending letter that identifies the Define Key command.

Redefining a Key

Because the Define Key examples are fairly short, you'll use the Prompt command to enter them, just as you did earlier in this chapter.

Suppose you don't use the reverse-apostrophe (') key, but would like to be able to type the fraction ½ directly from the keyboard. The key code for the reverse-apostrophe key is 96, the same as its ASCII code; the character code for the fraction ½ is 171 (you can find both these numbers in the table in Appendix C).

To make the reverse-apostrophe key produce ½, type the following Prompt command:

A>prompt $e[96;171p

Now press the key labeled with the reverse apostrophe (on an IBM PC keyboard, it's at the right side of the typewriter portion of the keyboard, between the quotation mark and Enter keys); DOS should display ½. This redefinition stays in effect until you restart DOS.

If you wished, you could redefine any or all of the keys to include graphics characters or characters from other languages. You could even arrange the entire keyboard in some other layout, such as the Dvorak keyboard. By putting the Define Key commands into a batch file, and by putting another set of Define Key commands (to restore the original keyboard) into a second batch file, you could redefine or restore your keyboard by typing a single command.

To restore the original meaning of the reverse-apostrophe key, you enter a Define Key command that specifies a result code identical to the key code. As you saw in the previous example, the key code for the reverse apostrophe is 96, so both numbers in the Define Key command should be 96. Backspace to erase any characters on the command line and type the following Prompt command:

```
A>prompt $e[96;96p
```

Press the reverse-apostrophe key again; now DOS should display the reverse apostrophe. Backspace to erase any characters on the command line and restore the system prompt by typing *prompt* or the batch command that restores your system prompt.

Using the Extended Key Codes

As the previous example showed, the key code for the standard typewriter keyboard characters is the ASCII code for the character. But what about the rest of the keyboard, the function keys and keypad arrows, the combinations of the Shift, Ctrl, and Alt keys with other keys? You specify these keys by entering an *extended code,* which is two numbers separated by a semicolon. The first number of the extended code is always 0 ; the second number is an identification code that ANSI.SYS assigns to each key or combination of keys that can be redefined. Appendix D gives the extended key code for each key and combination of keys (on an IBM or IBM-compatible keyboard) that you can redefine with ANSI.SYS.

Function key F1, for example, is represented by 0;59, Alt-A by 0;30, and the right-arrow key by 0;116. Combinations that cannot be redefined—such as Ctrl-Up Arrow—are noted in Appendix D. If a key, such as the keypad + or −, doesn't appear in Appendix D at all, it cannot be redefined.

Assigning a Command to a Key

If you enter the same command fairly often, you can save yourself time by assigning the entire command to a single key. Suppose you frequently find yourself typing *dir|sort*; you can assign a string to a key by entering the string, enclosed in quotation marks, in the Define Key command. Because this is a sort of Directory command, assign it to the combination of the Alt key and D (referred to as Alt-D). The identification code for Alt-D is 0;32, so type the following Prompt command:

```
A>prompt $e[0;32;"dir | sort";13p
```

Hold down the Alt key and press D; DOS should display the Directory and Sort commands, then carry them out. As far as DOS is concerned, each time you press Alt-D it's just as if you typed the Directory and Sort commands.

In the Define Key command you just typed, notice that a semicolon and the number 13 follow the string in quotation marks. Since 13 is the ASCII code for a carriage return, including it in the result code makes the effect the same as if you pressed the Enter key. If you didn't include the 13, it would be as if you typed the commands without pressing Enter: DOS would display the string and leave the cursor at the end of the line. You would have to press Enter to carry out the command.

To restore Alt-D to its original meaning, type the following Prompt command:

```
A>prompt $e[0;32;0;32p
```

Now try pressing Alt-D again; nothing should happen. Restore the system prompt either by typing *prompt* or the batch command that restores your system prompt.

Displaying the Help Screen with One Keystroke

Earlier in this chapter, you created the file called MONTHRPT.HLP that contained instructions for preparing a monthly report, then displayed the file with the Type command. Now you can use the Define Key command to display the help screen with a single keystroke by assigning the Type command to a key.

Suppose you decide that Shift-F1 should display the help screen. Type the following Prompt command:

```
A>prompt $e[0;84;"type monthrpt.hlp";13p
```

Now hold down either Shift key and press the key labeled F1; DOS should display the help file just as it did before.

To restore Shift-F1 to its original meaning, type the following:

```
A>prompt $e[0;84;0;84p
```

Press Shift-F1 again; nothing should happen. Restore the system prompt by typing *prompt* or the batch command that restores your system prompt.

Using this technique, along with others presented in this chapter, you could create a whole series of help screens (or other screens tailored to your system) and display each simply by pressing a single key. A word of caution: Be sure not to redefine a key that has special meaning to DOS. If you redefine Ctrl-C (ASCII code 3), for example, its original meaning is lost and you won't be able to cancel a command unless you restore the original meaning. If you redefine the Enter key (ASCII code 13), you won't be able to enter another command to undo the redefinition, and must restart DOS. To be on the safe side, avoid redefining any key whose key code is less than 32 unless you're confident that you know what the result will be.

Also, keep in mind that many application programs assign their own meanings to keys, and these redefinitions may override your redefinitions. This usually isn't a problem, because you can't enter DOS commands while you're using the other program, and your redefinitions become effective again when you leave the program and return to DOS.

Chapter Summary

- ANSI.SYS is a device driver that lets you control the display and keyboard.

- To use ANSI.SYS commands, the files CONFIG.SYS and ANSI.SYS must be on your system disk. CONFIG.SYS must contain the command *device = ansi.sys*.

- The ANSI.SYS display commands let you control the cursor, display mode and attributes, and erase part or all of the screen.

- The ANSI.SYS Define Key command lets you redefine the effect of pressing a key.

- All ANSI.SYS commands start with {ESC}[and end with a letter. Most also include a code (one or more numbers or strings).

- ANSI.SYS commands must be sent to the display. Because you can't type the Escape character, you must either put the commands in a file and display the file, or use the Prompt command.

- Appendix A shows a summary of all ANSI.SYS commands. Appendix C shows the full ASCII and IBM-compatible character set. Appendix D shows the extended codes for all non-ASCII keys and combinations.

CHAPTER

4

Learning Your Printer's Language

If you use a word processor, you use its commands to specify whether you want something printed in boldface or italics, to change the margins, or to force the start of a new page. When you print the document, the word-processing program sends the necessary commands to the printer. If you use a graphics program, you use its commands to describe the chart or image, and the program sends the necessary commands to the printer.

But you can control the printer without using one of these application programs. This chapter shows you how to control the way a file is printed on an Epson or Epson-compatible dot-matrix printer by sending commands to the printer yourself. The commands shown here don't apply to letter-quality printers.

Printer Commands

Like the ANSI.SYS commands described in Chapter 3, printer commands aren't words, but consist of letters, numbers, and non-keyboard characters. Also like the ANSI.SYS commands, all but a few printer commands begin with an Escape character, which means you can't type most of these commands directly from DOS.

Printer commands fall into four general categories:

- *Typeface* commands control the type of print to be used, which may include normal, bold, extended, compressed, elite, and italic.

- *Format* commands control such characteristics as the space between lines, skipping to a new line or page, page size, margins, and tabs.

- *Graphics* commands control the printing of graphics images.

- *Printer control* commands reset the printer to its standard settings, sound the bell, cause the paper-out detector to be ignored, set the direction and speed of printing, and control other machine-related functions.

Printer manufacturers are free to design their own commands, but most dot-matrix printers available today use the same commands and character set as Epson printers. This chapter shows you how to use some of the commands common to Epson and Epson-compatible printers, but it doesn't cover all the commands; there are simply too many, and most of the commands are seldom needed or used.

You'll also learn in this chapter whether your printer can use the IBM extended character set, shown in Appendix C.

This chapter introduces you to the printer commands and shows you how to use a few of them. Chapter 10 shows several ways you can use your printer to do more than simply print word-processing documents and spreadsheets, and describes more printer commands. Appendix B is a quick reference to the more commonly used commands of the Epson-compatible printers.

Sending Commands to the Printer

You've probably already used DOS commands that communicate with your printer. For example, when you use a Mode command to print small characters (*mode lpt1:132*), DOS, in turn, sends a command to the printer. There are more direct ways, however, to send commands to the printer. In the next few pages, for example, you will:

- Redirect an Echo command to the printer. This is a quick way to enter short commands that don't begin with an Escape character.

- Copy from the console to the printer. This is a good way to enter a few commands that don't require the Escape character.

- Copy a file to the printer. This is the best way to enter a longer series of commands.

Sending Printer Commands with the Echo Command

The Echo command is most commonly used in batch files to display messages, but you can also enter it at the system prompt like any other command. If you redirect the output of the Echo command to the printer, you can use it to print a line or send a command to the printer.

It's easy to test. The printer command for compressed (small) print is character 15. This doesn't correspond to any key on the keyboard, but you can get it by typing Ctrl-O. Make sure your printer is turned on, and type the following Echo command (DOS echoes Ctrl-O as ^O):

`A>echo <Ctrl-O>This is small. > prn`

The line should be printed in compressed type. You could have entered the compressed-print command by holding down the Alt key and typing the numbers 1 and 5 on the numeric keypad (referred to as Alt-15, and described in Chapter 2), but Ctrl-O is quicker and DOS echoes the character as ^O no matter how you enter it.

After you enter a command for compressed print, the printer continues to use compressed print until you either enter a command to stop compressed print or reset the printer. To see this, print another line by typing:

`A>echo This line, too, is small. > prn`

The printer is still using compressed print.

You can enter a command anywhere in a line. The command to stop compressed print is character 18, or Ctrl-R. Type:

`A>echo <Ctrl-R>This is a <Ctrl-O>small<Ctrl-R> word. > prn`

The result should look like this:

`This is a small word.`

The command to start expanded (large) print is character 14, or Ctrl-N, and the command to stop expanded print is character 20, or Ctrl-T. Type:

`A>echo This is a <Ctrl-N>large<Ctrl-T> word. > prn`

The word *large* should be in expanded type:

`This is a large word.`

The printer cancels the command to start expanded print after one line, because it assumes that you would use the large letters only for one-line headings. Type these two Echo commands:

`A>echo <Ctrl-N>This line is large. > prn`
`A>echo This line is normal. > prn`

The second line is normal, even though you didn't enter a command to stop expanded print; the printer automatically returned to normal type after printing the first line:

`This line is large.`
`This line is normal.`

You can combine printer commands. Combining compressed and expanded print yields a darker print, similar to the bold you'll use in a moment, but somewhat wider. Type the following Echo command:

`A>echo <Ctrl-N><Ctrl-O>This is both expanded and small.<Ctrl-R> > prn`

You entered Ctrl-R at the end of the line because compressed print doesn't turn itself off automatically as expanded print does.

Sending Printer Commands by Copying from the Console

This example lets you see the effect of the commands you have used so far. Type:

```
A>copy con prn
This is normal.
<Ctrl-N>This is expanded.
<Ctrl-O>This is small.
<Ctrl-N>This is small and expanded.
<Ctrl-R>This is normal.
^Z
        1 File(s) copied

A>_
```

You should see five lines that look like this:

```
This is normal.
This   is   expanded.
This is small.
This is small and expanded.
This is normal.
```

These two techniques—redirecting the Echo command and copying from the console to the printer—work only for commands that don't begin with the Escape character because, as was explained earlier in Chapter 3, you can't type the Escape character. The commands you used are the most common printer commands that don't begin with Escape:

Command	Result
Ctrl-N	Expanded print (one line only)
Ctrl-O	Start compressed print
Ctrl-R	Stop compressed print
Ctrl-T	Stop expanded print

Putting Printer Commands in a File

Most of the remaining printer commands start with the Escape character. You must put them in a file using a word processor or text editor that permits the entry of non-text characters.

Suppose you want to convince someone that using a dot-matrix printer to print simple graphics figures would save time and money compared to having them done by a graphic artist. The following example uses the printer commands shown in Figure 4-1, plus some of the line-drawing characters from the IBM extended character set, to print something you could use to support your proposal.

Command	Result
{ESC}@	Reset the printer to its standard settings.
{ESC}E	Start boldface (much darker).
{ESC}F	Stop boldface.
{ESC}G	Start double printing (slightly darker).
{ESC}H	Stop double printing.
{ESC} – 1	Start underlining.
{ESC} – 0	Stop underlining.
{ESC}4	Start italics.
{ESC}5	Stop italics.

Figure 4-1. Commands used in a sample chart.

Printing this example also lets you see how closely your printer follows the Epson-compatible commands and IBM extended character set.

Printing the IBM Extended Character Set

All printers can print the standard ASCII character set (codes 32 through 126). Many printers can also print the IBM extended character set (codes 128 through 255) shown in Appendix C. This example uses eight characters from the extended set, shown in Figure 4-2, to draw a box.

Code	Character	Character	Code
Alt-201	╔	╗	Alt-187
Alt-204	╠	╣	Alt-185
Alt-200	╚	╝	Alt-188
Alt-205	═	║	Alt-186

Figure 4-2. Box-drawing characters used in a sample chart.

Creating the Sample Chart File

Use a text editor, a word processor, or Edlin to create a file named PSAMP.DOC and enter the lines shown in Figure 4-3. (See the heading "Entering the Escape Character in a File" in Chapter 3 for a description of how to enter the Escape character with a word processor or Edlin.) As usual, don't type the line numbers; they're only for reference.

Some tips on entering the lines:

- The periods in Figure 4-3 stand for spaces. Press the spacebar once for each period.

- In lines 3, 4, 5, and 9, don't type the italicized words; follow the instructions they give. In lines 3, 5, and 9, enter the character whose code is 205 (shown as *Alt-205*) twenty times.

- Use the Cut and Paste or Copy command of your word processor or text editor to avoid typing Alt-205 sixty times in three lines.

- In line 6 there are two spaces before the final *Alt-186*, in line 7 there is one space, and in line 8 there are three spaces.

- The right edge of the box that appears when you type lines 4, 6, 7, and 8 is four columns to the right of the other lines because the printer commands in those lines take up space on the display. When you print the file, however, the commands will be carried out, not printed, and the edge of the box will be smooth.

```
 1: {ESC}@
 2: Sample chart:
 3: <Alt-201> type <Alt-205> 20 times <Alt-187>
 4: <Alt-186>.......{ESC}GWe Can{ESC}H.......<Alt-186>
 5: <Alt-204> type <Alt-205> 20 times <Alt-185>
 6: <Alt-186>.<Alt-254>.Improve {ESC}4quality{ESC}5..<Alt-186>
 7: <Alt-186>.<Alt-254>.Increase {ESC}4revenue{ESC}5.<Alt-186>
 8: <Alt-186>.<Alt-254>.Decrease {ESC}4costs{ESC}5...<Alt-186>
 9: <Alt-200> type <Alt-205> 20 times <Alt-188>
10:
11: These charts {ESC}-1take less time{ESC}-0
12: These charts {ESC}-1cost less{ESC}-0
13: And we can make these charts {ESC}-1{ESC}4ourselves{ESC}-0{ESC}5
```

Figure 4-3. Contents of a sample chart file.

After you have entered the lines into PSAMP.DOC, proofread the file against Figure 4-3 and save it. Exit to DOS and print the file by typing the following Copy command:

```
A>copy psamp.doc prn
```

Your sample chart should look like Figure 4-4.

```
Sample chart:
┌────────────────────────┐
│        We Can          │
├────────────────────────┤
│ • Improve quality      │
│ • Increase revenue     │
│ • Decrease costs       │
└────────────────────────┘
```

```
These charts take less time
These charts cost less
And we can make these charts ourselves
```

Figure 4-4. Sample chart from a compatible printer.

If your printer output looks like Figure 4-4, your printer closely follows the Epson-compatible commands and IBM extended character set. Even if your word-processing program prints all these different fonts and lets you use the extended characters, you can still make good use of knowing how to control the printer yourself. If you have a compatible printer, skip the next topic and go on to the heading "Changing the Sample Chart with One Command."

If Your Printer Isn't Compatible

If your printer doesn't follow the IBM extended character set, your output may look something like Figure 4-5. If your printer doesn't follow the Epson-compatible commands, the boldface and italic words in Figure 4-4 may appear in normal print, or the output may differ in some other way.

```
Sample chart:
IMMMMMMMMMMMMMMMMMMMMMM;
:        We Can         :
LMMMMMMMMMMMMMMMMMMMMMM9
: ˜ Improve quality   :
: ˜ Increase revenue  :
: ˜ Decrease costs    :
HMMMMMMMMMMMMMMMMMMMMMM<
```

```
These charts take less time
These charts cost less
And we can make these charts ourselves
```

Figure 4-5. Sample chart from a non-compatible printer.

The characters used to draw the box (*I ; L 9 H < M and :*) are the characters whose code is 128 less than the characters you entered (compare Figure 4-5 to Figure 4-4). Figure 4-6 shows the relationship of these characters to the characters you entered. This is how some printers handle characters they can't print.

Character Entered	Code	Less 128	Character Printed
╔	201	73	I
╗	187	59	;
╠	204	76	L
═	205	77	M
║	186	58	:
╣	185	57	9
╚	200	72	H
╝	188	60	<
■	254	126	~

Figure 4-6. Effect of subtracting 128 from extended character codes.

Other printers define a totally different extended character set for codes 128–255. If this is the case, your printer's output won't look like either Figure 4-4 or Figure 4-5. You may be able to use these characters, however; look in your printer's manual for the character-set chart (probably in an appendix) and follow that chart instead of Appendix C.

It's possible that your printer can print the IBM extended character set, but that a switch must first be set correctly. Check your printer's manual to see if this is the case—the switch may be called a *DIP switch*, because it's one of four or eight tiny switches in a small plastic case called a *Dual Inline Package*. If you need to, change the switch setting and copy PSAMP.DOC to the printer again.

Similarly, just because your printer doesn't use the same commands as Epson-compatible printers doesn't mean that you can't control the printer. Again, you'll have to go to your printer's manual and find a summary of the printer commands (probably another appendix). You can most likely use the preceding examples, substituting your printer's commands for the ones shown.

If your printer doesn't follow the Epson-compatible commands and you haven't found corresponding commands in your printer's manual, skip the following two topics and go to the heading "Experimenting with Your Printer."

Changing the Sample Chart with One Command

Dot-matrix printers are remarkably versatile. Once you have entered some text into a file, you can quickly change its appearance. The following changes, for example, require adding or changing just one printer command, yet each changes the appearance of the entire file. Taking the few minutes it requires to try these three alternate versions of PSAMP.DOC (the file you created earlier) should give you an even better feeling for what your printer can do. Load PSAMP.DOC with your editing program, make the described change, save the revised version, exit to DOS, and copy PSAMP.DOC to the printer:

- Insert a line that contains {ESC}E after the first line. This prints the file in boldface.

- Change the {ESC}E you just inserted to {ESC}M. This prints the file in Elite type (a smaller type—12 characters per inch—than the standard 10 characters per inch).

- Change the {ESC}M in the second line to character 15 (type Alt-15 or Ctrl-O, whichever your editing program accepts). This prints the file in compressed print (17 characters per inch).

Using the summary of printer commands in Appendix B and the character set charts in Appendix C, you may want to try some other changes.

Be Judicious with the Reset Command

The Printer Reset command—{ESC}@—cancels all outstanding commands and returns the printer to the settings in effect when you first turned it on. These include normal, or draft-quality print, six lines per inch, and 66 lines per page. But the Reset command also resets such characteristics as the page-depth counter (where the printer keeps track of how many lines it has printed), the left margin, and even the printer's *buffer*, where the printer stores the data to be printed. This can cause unexpected results; if you put a Reset command at the end of a line, for example, the line probably won't be printed because the Reset command causes the line to be cleared from the printer buffer before the printer has a chance to print the line.

Because of the possible side effects, you should put a Reset command only at the beginning of a file, where you want to guarantee the standard settings. And it's best to avoid putting a Reset command in a file to be printed with a word processor. The word-processing program itself keeps track of the printer's state, and resetting all the conditions to the standard settings can cause strange results, such as the wrong type of print, irregular margins, or page breaks in the wrong place.

Experimenting with Your Printer

This chapter covered only a few of the printer commands. Chapter 10, which shows several interesting (and potentially useful) ways to use your printer, covers a few more commands, and Appendix B summarizes the common printer commands. But there are still more, dozens in all; some printers have more than 100 commands. There isn't room enough in this book to describe all the printer commands and still cover the other topics.

Besides installation instructions and summary tables, many printer manuals contain excellent descriptions of each command, complete with an example and sample output. It's definitely worth a look—you may never need most of these commands, but spending some time putting commands in files and printing the results might give you several ideas for new ways to use your printer.

Chapter Summary

- Printer commands control print attributes such as type of print, line spacing, starting a new page, and graphics.

- Most printer commands start with the Escape character (code 27). Because you can't type the Escape character, you must put these commands in a file and print the file.

- You can enter printer commands that don't start with the Escape character by redirecting the output of an Echo command, or by copying from the console to the printer.

- You can put commands in a file using any text editor or word processor that accepts non-keyboard characters.

- Use the Printer Reset command with care; it can cause unexpected results, especially if you put it in a file that is to be printed with a word-processing program.

- Chapter 10 shows some useful applications of your printer and describes a few more printer commands.

- Appendix B summarizes the most frequently used Epson-compatible printer commands.

CHAPTER
5

Debug:
A Special Sort of
Editor

Debug is a DOS program designed to help programmers find errors, or *bugs,* in their programs. It's a special-purpose editing program with some features especially suited to working with programs in assembly language. But Debug isn't limited to program files; you can use it to examine and change *any* file, no matter what it contains or what application program created it.

Debug doesn't look at a file as a collection of words, sentences, and paragraphs, but simply as a series of bytes. It includes no features for composing or formatting text, so it's not suitable for routine editing of text files. But because Debug makes so few assumptions about what a file contains, sometimes it's just the tool you need.

This chapter shows how to use many of Debug's capabilities. Some of these features are used in other parts of the book.

Bytes, Hexadecimal, and ASCII

Debug lets you work with the individual bytes of a file, and understands only hexadecimal numbers. If you haven't yet read Chapter 1, which describes a byte, hexadecimal numbers, and the ASCII code, you should take the time now to do so, because Debug requires some understanding of all three. A brief review:

- A *byte* is the basic unit of computer memory and disk storage. It is an area large enough to hold a number from 0 through 255.

- *Hexadecimal* is the base-16 number system normally used to keep track of memory addresses and other computer-related numbers. It uses the same digits as the familiar decimal (base 10) system for the numbers 0 through 9, but uses the letters A through F to represent the decimal numbers 11 through 15. Remember, 10 in hexadecimal is 16 in decimal; to keep your number systems straight, try reading it as "one-zero" rather than "ten."

- *ASCII* is a code that computer manufacturers and users have agreed to use to represent certain functions, letters, numbers, and other symbols. Because one byte can hold a number from 0 through 255, it can represent any of 256 possible characters; the ASCII code specifies the characters for only the lower 128 (codes 0 through 127), but the IBM PC and most compatibles also define characters for the upper 128 (codes 128 through 255). Appendix C shows the correlation of decimal numbers, hexadecimal numbers, and ASCII codes.

Working with Files

Like a word processor or text editor, Debug lets you examine a file, change it, and store the revised version. As you'll see, however, Debug shows you the file quite differently; although many of its commands perform functions similar to other editing programs, they, too, have a different look and feel. But there are enough similarities that you can quickly learn to use some of Debug's important capabilities.

Most word processors let you move the cursor anywhere on the screen to make changes; for this reason, these programs are often called *full-screen editors*. Simpler text editors, such as Edlin, don't let you use the cursor to move through the file, and limit you to working on one line at a time; such an editor is often called a *line editor*. Although a line-editor program does much less than a word processor, it's usually smaller and faster than the word processor, and well suited for small jobs such as batch files.

Like a line editor, Debug doesn't let you use the cursor to move through the file. It doesn't even let you work on lines, in fact, because it doesn't recognize lines. Debug treats a file as nothing but a series of bytes; you work on the file a byte at a time. It would be painstaking to edit a text file with Debug, but its approach is quite useful when working with other types of files such as programs, command strings for the screen or printer, or data files for programs.

A quick tour of Debug doesn't take long, and will show you both its similarities and differences compared to other editing programs. The simplest approach is to create a small text file and use Debug to examine and change it.

First, create a text file by copying from the console to a file named TEST.DOC:

```
A>copy con test.doc
This is item 1.
This is item 2.
And this is the last item.
^Z
        1 File(s) copied
A>_
```

Display the file with the Type command to confirm its contents:

```
A>type test.doc
This is item 1.
This is item 2.
And this is the last item.
A>_
```

You Need the File DEBUG.COM

Like other DOS external commands such as Diskcopy or Edlin, Debug's command file, DEBUG.COM, must be in either the current directory or a directory you have named in a Path command. If the file isn't in any directory, copy it to the appropriate directory on your working disk from the DOS supplemental disk.

Using Debug to Examine and Change a File

To start Debug, you enter its name, followed by the name of the file you want to examine or change. The test file is named TEST.DOC, so type:

```
A>debug test.doc
-
```

Debug responds by displaying a hyphen followed by the cursor. The hyphen is Debug's command prompt, like the DOS system prompt or the asterisk displayed by Edlin. Debug is waiting for you to enter one of its commands.

Displaying a File with the Dump Command

To display the file, you enter *d,* which is short for *Dump* (not display). Despite its slightly unsavory name, dump doesn't reflect on the usefulness of the command or its output; like other computer terms, dump acquired its own computer-related meaning in the dawn of computing, around 30 years ago. When a program went awry on one of those ancient, room-filling machines, sometimes the only way to find the problem was to print everything in the machine's memory, byte-by-byte, in hexadecimal, then search through hundreds of pages of these numbers. These mammoth printouts weren't formatted to make them easier for humans to read; they looked as if the computer had been tipped on its side and the data dumped on the floor. Hence *dump.*

Debug's Dump command displays the contents of the computer's memory byte-by-byte in two forms: the number contained in each byte in hexadecimal (remember, it can vary from 0 through FF, which is 255 decimal), and the ASCII character that number represents. If you load a file into memory with Debug, the display shows the contents of the file.

To display the memory where Debug loaded TEST.DOC, type:

```
-d
```

Debug responds by displaying the first 128 bytes starting at the address where it loaded TEST.DOC, as shown in Figure 5-1.

```
xxxx:0100  54 68 69 73 20 69 73 20-69 74 65 6D 20 31 2E 0D   This is item 1..
xxxx:0110  0A 54 68 69 73 20 69 73-20 69 74 65 6D 20 32 2E   .This is item 2.
xxxx:0120  0D 0A 41 6E 64 20 74 68-69 73 20 69 73 20 74 68   ..And this is th
xxxx:0130  65 20 6C 61 73 74 20 69-74 65 6D 2E 0D 0A xx xx   e last item...xx
xxxx:0140  xx xx xx xx xx xx xx xx-xx xx xx xx xx xx xx xx   xxxxxxxxxxxxxxxx
xxxx:0150  xx xx xx xx xx xx xx xx-xx xx xx xx xx xx xx xx   xxxxxxxxxxxxxxxx
xxxx:0160  xx xx xx xx xx xx xx xx-xx xx xx xx xx xx xx xx   xxxxxxxxxxxxxxxx
xxxx:0170  xx xx xx xx xx xx xx xx-xx xx xx xx xx xx xx xx   xxxxxxxxxxxxxxxx
```

Figure 5-1. Dump command output.

This isn't as formidable as it looks, although the file certainly isn't as easy to read as when you display it with the DOS Type command. But the right side of the screen contains some reassuringly familiar words, and there is a certain regularity to the entire display.

The last four lines of the display are shown in Figure 5-1 as *xx* because their contents depend on factors such as how much memory is installed in your system and the programs that you used before you entered the Debug command, so they would differ from whatever was shown here. Throughout this chapter, in fact, lowercase *x* is used to represent parts of the display that may vary and aren't significant to the immediate topic.

Each line of the Dump command's output shows 16 bytes of memory (the decimal number 16 is 10 in hexadecimal; you'll see the significance of that in a moment). The Directory command showed you that TEST.DOC is 62 bytes long, so the file takes up three full lines and 14 bytes of the fourth line.

Each line is divided into three groups: the *address* of the beginning of the line; the *byte values* of the 16 bytes starting at the address; and the *ASCII characters* that correspond to the byte values. Figure 5-2 shows the three groups of the first line of the preceding display.

Address	Byte values	ASCII characters
xxxx:0100	54 68 69 73 20 69 73 20-69 74 65 6D 20 31 2E 0D	This is item 1..

Figure 5-2. The three groups of a Dump command output line.

The Address

The left group (the first nine columns) contains the *address* of the first byte displayed in the line. The address consists of two parts: The first four digits (up to the colon) broadly define the location of the address in the computer's memory, much as an area code broadly defines the location of a telephone exchange; this number depends on how much memory is installed in your system and how much memory was available when you entered the Debug command. For this brief look at Debug, you can ignore these numbers, just as you can ignore the area code if you're dealing with local telephone numbers. To emphasize that you can ignore these numbers, they are shown as *xxxx* throughout this chapter. For example, the address in the first line of the preceding Dump command output is shown as *xxxx:0100*, but an actual number is shown on your screen; it could be 5195:0100, or 3DF8:0100, or almost any other four-digit number.

The second part of the address, the last four digits, contains the information that is most useful to you. For your purposes, the address of the first byte of the first line is 100, the address of the second byte is 101, of the third byte is 102, and so on to the sixteenth and last byte, whose address is 10F. The address of the fourth byte in the fifth line of Figure 5-1 (which begins with *xxxx:0140*) is 143. The address of the last byte in the file is 13D (its value is 0A hexadecimal, or 10 decimal). As you can see in Figure 5-1, the address of the first byte of each line is 10 (hexadecimal) higher than the previous line. Hexadecimal 10 is 16 decimal, so each line contains 16 bytes.

The Byte Values

The middle group, separated from the address by two spaces, contains 16 pairs of numbers that show the value, in hexadecimal, of the 16 bytes that start at the address at the beginning of the line. For example, the address of the first byte of the second line is 110, and the byte contains 0A hexadecimal (10 decimal); the address of the second byte is 111, and it contains 54 hexadecimal (84 decimal); and so on through the sixteenth and last byte of the second line, whose address is 11F, which contains 2E hexadecimal (46 decimal). The hyphen breaks the 16 bytes in a line into two groups of eight for easier reference.

The ASCII Translations

The right group (the last 16 columns) is separated from the byte values by three spaces. It shows the ASCII equivalent of the corresponding byte value in the middle group. For example, the first character on the first line is *T*, which is the ASCII character for 54 hexadecimal (84 decimal); the second character is *h,* the ASCII character for 68 hexadecimal (104 decimal). Debug shows only text characters, numbers, and punctuation marks from the space, whose ASCII code is 20 hexadecimal, or 32 decimal, through the tilde (~), whose ASCII code is 7E hexadecimal, or 126 decimal; any other character is shown as a period. For example, the carriage return, which is the last character in the first line (its value is 0D hexadecimal, or 13 decimal), is shown as a period because it's outside the range of the standard text characters.

The Carriage-Return and Line-Feed Characters

TEST.DOC contains three lines. Although it's pretty easy to tell from the text where each line begins, you can also find the lines by looking for the hexadecimal values of two special ASCII characters:

0D (13 decimal). This character is called *carriage return* in the ASCII character set, even though most of today's computers and computer terminals have nothing that resembles a carriage. The term is a carryover from the time when most of the computer terminals in use were Teletype terminals or other typewriter-like devices with carriages that had to be returned at the end of a line. The analogous operation on a display terminal is moving the cursor back to the beginning of the line.

0A (10 decimal). This character is called *line feed* in the ASCII character set. This term, too, is a carryover from the days of typewriter-like terminals; feeding paper into the machine rolled the paper up to print the next line. The analogous operation on a display terminal is moving the cursor down to the next line.

DOS uses both characters, in the sequence 0D 0A, to mark the end of a line. The carriage-return character moves the cursor back to the beginning of the line, and the line-feed character moves the cursor down one line. This sequence of characters appears at addresses 10F-110, 120-121, and 13C-13D, the ends of the three lines.

Getting Familiar with Dump Command Output

Once you understand how the Dump command displays a file, the rest of Debug comes pretty easily. Spend a bit of time now studying the Dump command output on your screen, referring to Figures 5-1 and 5-2 and comparing the ASCII characters on the right with the corresponding byte value in the middle group, until you can find the byte at a particular address or the address of a particular byte.

Here are a few questions you can use to test your understanding; you might want to cover the answers at the right (remember, all the numbers are hexadecimal):

1. What is the value of the byte at address 119?	69
2. What character does it represent?	i
3. What is the address of the beginning of the word *last*?	132
4. What address is six bytes past the beginning of the word *item* in the first line?	10E
5. What is the value of that byte?	2E
6. What character does it represent?	Period (.)
7. What is the address of the next-to-last byte in the file?	13C
8. What is its value?	0D
9. What character does it represent?	Carriage return

The Dump Command

The Dump command displays the contents of a portion of the computer's memory in the format just described. The Dump command has two parameters that let you tell Debug where to start dumping memory and, if you wish, where to stop dumping memory:

d<start><stop>

<*start*> is the hex address where Debug starts dumping memory.

<*stop*> is the hex address where Debug stops dumping memory. If you omit <stop>, Debug dumps 128 bytes (eight rows of 16 bytes each) beginning with <start>.

If you omit both <start> and <stop> (enter just *d*), Debug starts dumping memory with the byte that follows the memory dumped by the most recent Dump command. This lets you page through memory, 128 bytes at a time, just by entering *d*. If you don't tell Debug where to start dumping memory in the very first Dump command you use with a file, Debug starts at address 100.

For example, the Dump command you entered a while ago displayed the 128 bytes from 100 through 17F. Type another Dump command with no parameters:

-d

Debug displays the 128 bytes of memory from 180 through 1FF. The output isn't shown here, because the contents depend on how much memory is installed in your computer and what programs you ran before you started Debug.

To display just the area of memory from 122 through 130, type the following Dump command:

```
-d 122 130
xxxx:0120        41 6E 64 20 74 68-69 73 20 69 73 20 74 68    And this is th
xxxx:0130  65                                                 e
```

Debug displays only the bytes in the range you specified, from address 122 through address 130.

Changing an Area of Memory

Although looking at a file is sometimes all you want to do—and Debug lets you see exactly what is in a file in a way that most word processors can't match—you often want to change the file, too. Debug lets you enter data into the computer's memory, replacing whatever was there before. If you load a file into memory, enter new data into that memory, then write the memory back to the file, you have changed the file.

The Enter Command

The Enter command lets you enter data into memory as byte values or as a string of characters. It has two parameters, the address where the data is to be entered and the data itself:

e <address><data>

<address> is the address where memory is to be changed. If you enter just one byte, the byte at <address> is changed. If you enter more than one byte, the changes begin at <address>.

<data> is the data to be entered in memory. To change one byte, type the two-digit hexadecimal value to be entered or a character in quotation marks (a one-character string). To change more than one byte, you would type a series of two-digit hexadecimal numbers separated by spaces, or a multi-character string (two or more characters enclosed in quotation marks).

Changing a Series of Bytes

To change the beginning of TEST.DOC, type:

```
-e 100 "Changed by Debug."
```

To verify the change, display memory again with the Dump command. TEST.DOC occupies the 62 bytes of memory from 100 through 13D; dump that memory by typing:

```
-d 100 13d
xxxx:0100  43 68 61 6E 67 65 64 20-62 79 20 44 65 62 75 67   Changed by Debug
xxxx:0110  2E 54 68 69 73 20 69 73-20 69 74 65 6D 20 32 2E   .This is item 2.
xxxx:0120  0D 0A 41 6E 64 20 74 68-69 73 20 69 73 20 74 68   ..And this is th
xxxx:0130  65 20 6C 61 73 74 20 69-74 65 6D 2E 0D 0A         e last item...
```

The memory where Debug loaded TEST.DOC doesn't start with *This is item 1.* anymore; it starts with *Changed by Debug.* Equally important (as you'll see in a moment), the carriage-return and line-feed characters (0D and 0A) at 10F and 110 have been replaced. The rest of the memory occupied by the file remains unchanged.

Instead of specifying the data to be entered (*Changed by Debug.*) as a string, you could have made the same change by typing *E 100 43 68 61 6E 67 65 64 20 62 79 20 44 65 62 75 67 2E*. Obviously, the string method is easier when you're entering data that can be typed from the keyboard. When you're changing non-text data, however, you may find it quicker to change a series of bytes by entering the two-digit hexadecimal numbers.

Changing a Single Byte

The byte at address 11E has the value 32 hexadecimal (50 decimal), the ASCII code for the character *2*. The ASCII code for B is 42 hexadecimal (66 decimal), so change the 2 to a B by typing:

```
-e 11e 42
```

Again, verify the change by dumping the same area of memory you dumped earlier:

```
-d 100 13d
5187:0100  43 68 61 6E 67 65 64 20-62 79 20 44 65 62 75 67   Changed by Debug
5187:0110  2E 54 68 69 73 20 69 73-20 69 74 65 6D 20 42 2E   .This is item B.
5187:0120  0D 0A 41 6E 64 20 74 68-69 73 20 69 73 20 74 68   ..And this is th
5187:0130  65 20 6C 61 73 74 20 69-74 65 6D 2E 0D 0A         e last item...
```

Now the byte at 11e has the value 42 instead of 32 (both hexadecimal).

Storing a File with a Different Name

Although you changed the memory where Debug loaded TEST.DOC, the file itself remains unchanged because you haven't written anything to disk. You can write any area of memory to any file. To keep track of the different versions of the file, you'll save each version under a different name. This requires two steps: changing the file name with the Name command, and writing the area of memory to disk with the Write command.

The Name Command

The Name command changes the name Debug uses the next time you load a file into memory or write an area of memory to a file. It has only one parameter, the file name:

n <filename>

<*filename*> is the file name that Debug uses in the next Load command, which loads a file into memory, or Write command, which writes an area of memory to a file.

For example, type the following to change the name Debug will use the next time you load or write a file to TEST1.DOC:

-n test1.doc

There is no apparent effect; there will be no real effect until you enter a Load or Write command.

The Write Command

The Write command writes an area of memory to the file that was either loaded by the Debug command or most recently named with the Name command. It has one parameter, the starting address of the area of memory it is to write to a disk file:

w <start>

<*start*> is the address of the beginning of the area of memory Debug is to write to disk. If you omit <start>, Debug starts at address 100.

To write from memory to disk starting at address 100, type:

-w

Debug responds by telling you (in hexadecimal, of course) how many bytes it wrote:

Writing 003E bytes

3E in hexadecimal is 62 in decimal (you can ignore the leading zeros). Debug wrote 62 bytes from memory to the file you named TEST1.DOC. Because you didn't tell the Write command where to start, it started writing from address 100. The file should contain the modified version of TEST.DOC you created with the two Enter commands. To check this, return to DOS and display the file with the Type command.

The Quit Command

The Quit command returns to DOS. It doesn't save a file or perform any other processing, so make sure you have saved any work with the Write command before entering it. It has no parameters:

```
q
```

Type the Quit command to return to DOS:

```
-q
A>_
```

Verifying Your Debug Work

To make sure you've got both files—TEST.DOC and TEST1.DOC—type the following Directory command using the * wildcard character:

```
A>dir test*
 Volume in drive C is FORSYTHWOLF
 Directory of  C:\DOS\DEBUG

TEST     DOC      62   2-16-86  12:09p
TEST1    DOC      62   2-16-86   1:31p
         2 File(s)   2678784 bytes free
A>_
```

If TEST1.DOC isn't there, go back to the heading "Using Debug to Examine and Change a File" and start over again, making sure that you change the name with the Name command and save the area of memory with the Write command.

Now to make sure the files are different. Display both versions with two Type commands:

```
A>type test.doc
This is item 1.
This is item 2.
And this is the last item.

A>type test1.doc
Changed by Debug.This is item B.
And this is the last item.

A>_
```

In TEST1.DOC, you changed the first line to read *Changed by Debug*. The first two lines of TEST.DOC are combined in TEST1.DOC because the last two characters you entered with the Enter command (the *g* and the period) replaced the carriage-return and line-feed characters that separated the first and second lines. DOS doesn't find a carriage return and line feed until the end of the former second line (which now reads *This is item B*. because you replaced the 2 with a B).

Adding to a File

The changes to TEST.DOC left its length unchanged. Changing the length of a file requires one additional step, to make sure that Debug writes the correct number of bytes. Start by loading TEST.DOC with Debug again:

```
A>debug test.doc
```

Debug loads TEST.DOC into memory starting at address 100. The file is 62 (3E hexadecimal) bytes long, so it fills memory from 100 through 13D. Dump this memory by typing:

```
-d 100 13d
xxxx:0100  54 68 69 73 20 69 73 20-69 74 65 6D 20 31 2E 0D   This is item 1..
xxxx:0110  0A 54 68 69 73 20 69 73-20 69 74 65 6D 20 32 2E   .This is item 2.
xxxx:0120  0D 0A 41 6E 64 20 74 68-69 73 20 69 73 20 74 68   ..And this is th
xxxx:0130  65 20 6C 61 73 74 20 69-74 65 6D 2E 0D 0A         e last item...
```

To add something to the end of the file, simply use an Enter command to change memory starting at the first byte after the end of the file. The last byte of the file is at 13D, so the starting address for the Enter command would be 13E. To add ✱✱✱ *Postscript* ✱✱✱ at the end of TEST.DOC, type:

```
-e 13e "*** Postscript ***"
```

This adds 18 bytes, making a total of 80 bytes to be written to the file (from 100 through 14F). Dump 50 hexadecimal bytes of memory starting at 100 by typing:

```
-d 100 14F
xxxx:0100  54 68 69 73 20 69 73 20-69 74 65 6D 20 31 2E 0D   This is item 1..
xxxx:0110  0A 54 68 69 73 20 69 73-20 69 74 65 6D 20 32 2E   .This is item 2.
xxxx:0120  0D 0A 41 6E 64 20 74 68-69 73 20 69 73 20 74 68   ..And this is th
xxxx:0130  65 20 6C 61 73 74 20 69-74 65 6D 2E 0D 0A 2A 2A   e last item...**
xxxx:0140  2A 20 50 6F 73 74 73 63-72 69 70 74 20 2A 2A 2A   * Postscript ***
```

That's what you want in the new file. But if you type a Write command now, Debug will write 3E hexadecimal (62 decimal) bytes, just as it did before; it has no way of knowing that now you want to write 50 hexa-decimal (80 decimal) bytes. Yet just as you can tell Debug what file name to use, you can tell it how many bytes to write. This takes you just a bit deeper into the inner workings of the computer's microprocessor.

The Microprocessor's Registers

The microprocessor in your computer has several bytes of its own memory, divided into 14 areas called *registers*. Just as you use a check register to keep track of your checks, the microprocessor uses its registers to keep track of what it's doing. The only reason you need to care about registers—unless you plan to write programs—is that Debug uses one of these registers to control how many bytes it writes whenever you enter a Write command.

The Register Command

The Register command lets you display or change the contents of the registers. To display the registers, type an *r*:

-r

Debug responds by displaying the names and contents of the registers, as shown in Figure 5-3. As usual, numbers that may vary (and don't matter) are shown as *xxxx*.

```
AX=xxxx  BX=xxxx  CX=003E  DX=xxxx  SP=xxxx  BP=xxxx  SI=xxxx   DI=xxxx
DS=xxxx  ES=xxxx  SS=xxxx  CS=xxxx  IP=xxxx   NU UP EI PL NZ NA PO NC
xxxx:0100 xx                 xxxxxx
```

Figure 5-3. Register command display.

A register is two bytes long. The Register command displays the two-character name of each register (AX, BX, and so on through IP), followed by an equal sign, followed by the number stored in the register. Happily, you can ignore most of this.

The highlighted register in Figure 5-3, named CX, is the only one you need care about, because it's the one that Debug uses to control how many bytes it writes when you enter a Write command.

(If you're looking for the fourteenth register, the eight two-character abbreviations at the end of the second row represent the contents of the last register; you can ignore them. You can also ignore the third line of the output, which starts with an address.)

To change the contents of a register, enter the Register command with one parameter:

r <name>

<name> is the name of the register whose value you want to change. Debug prompts you for the new value. If you omit <name>, Debug displays the value of all registers, as in Figure 5-3.

The reason for this longish aside about registers is that you increased the number of bytes to be written to a file from 62 (3F hexadecimal) to 80 (50 hexadecimal). Debug looks at the CX register to see how many bytes to write to a file, so you must put the correct value in CX. And in hexadecimal, of course.

First, type a Register command, naming CX:

```
-r cx
```

Debug responds by repeating the name of the register (in uppercase) and its current value (in hexadecimal), then prompting for a new value with a colon on the next line:

```
-r cx
CX 003E
:_
```

Sure enough, CX contains 3E hexadecimal (62 decimal), which is the length of TEST.DOC. When you load a file into Debug, it reads the length of the file from the directory entry and puts the length into CX. That's how Debug knew how many bytes to write earlier when you changed memory and wrote TEST1.DOC to disk: You didn't change the length and you didn't change CX, so it wrote the same number of bytes that it read.

If you pressed the Enter key now without typing anything, the contents of CX wouldn't change. To change the value in CX, type the new value. You increased the number of bytes to 50 hexadecimal (80 decimal), so type *50*:

```
-r cx
CX 003E
:50
```

Display the registers to verify that CX contains the correct value:

```
-r
AX=xxxx  BX=xxxx  CX=0050  DX=xxxx  SP=xxxx  BP=xxxx  SI=xxxx  DI=xxxx
DS=xxxx  ES=xxxx  SS=xxxx  CS=xxxx  IP=xxxx  NV UP EI PL NZ NA PO NC
xxxx:0100 xx            xxxxxx
```

Now Debug knows how many bytes to write. The next time you enter a Write command, Debug will write 50 hexadecimal (80 decimal) bytes. To keep all these versions separate, change the file name to TEST2.DOC with a Name command before entering the Write command. Type:

```
-n test2.doc
-w
Writing 0050 bytes
```

Leave Debug with the Quit command to return to DOS so you can verify this work:

```
-q
A>_
```

You should have three test files; check with a Directory command:

```
A>dir test?.doc

 Volume in drive C is FORSYTHWOLF
 Directory of  C:\DOS\DEBUG

TEST     DOC      62   2-16-87  12:09p
TEST1    DOC      62   2-16-87   1:31p
TEST2    DOC      80   2-16-87   2:15p
        3 File(s)   2662400 bytes free
A>_
```

The files are there, and the lengths are right. Again, you can make sure by displaying them. This time, however, instead of using three Type commands, use one Copy command:

```
A>copy test?.doc con
TEST.DOC
This is item 1.
This is item 2.
And this is the last item.
TEST1.DOC
Changed by Debug.This is item B.
And this is the last item.
TEST2.DOC
This is item 1.
This is item 2.
And this is the last item.
*** Postscript ***        1 File(s) Copied

A>_
```

The *Files(s) copied* message is on the same line as *** *Postscript* *** because you didn't enter a carriage return and line feed at the end of TEST2.DOC.

Why Use Such an Editor?

The clearest message from these examples is that it would be pretty painful to use Debug as a text editor. But you can create and modify files with Debug and, more to the point, Debug can handle any type of data. You'll use a word processor or text editor to create and change text files, but Debug is an ideal tool for working with files that contain non-text data, such as programs or commands that control the printer or display.

Creating a Small Program

A few small programs that work with DOS to make your computer more useful are described later in this book. You will use Debug to create these programs, even if you don't know how to program. To simplify the process, you won't use the Debug commands directly; you'll use your word processor or text editor to create a text file that contains Debug commands, then start Debug with its input redirected to the text file.

The Debug commands in the text file are explained later in this chapter.

A Debug Script File That Creates a Program

Because a text file containing a series of commands and other data for a program is analogous to a script for a play, such a file is sometimes called a *script file* or simply a *script*. The remainder of this chapter shows you how to make a script file that instructs Debug to create a short program and write the program to a file. After creating the script file, you'll start Debug with its input redirected to the script file, then test the resulting program.

The script file contains Debug commands that:

1. Create a short assembly-language program.

2. Set the file name to FLASH.COM.

3. Set the CX register to the number of bytes in the program.

4. Write the program to a file named FLASH.COM.

5. Quit Debug and return to DOS.

The last step is crucial. If you redirect a program's input to a file, the program *never* looks for input from the keyboard. If you don't put the Quit command in the script file, Debug keeps looking for input after the end of the file; you won't be able to stop Debug because it pays no attention to the keyboard. You'll have to restart DOS to regain control.

Figure 5-4 (on the following page) shows the script file that creates the program. Create it with a text editor (such as Edlin) or your word processor (if it lets you store a file with no formatting codes). You could use the Copy command to copy from the console to the file, but you'd have to type the file without error; you'll feel less pressure if you know that you can go back and correct any typing mistakes.

The line numbers followed by a colon are for reference only; make certain that the file contains exactly what is shown following the colon on each line. Some commands should look familiar, such as the Register command in lines 13 and 14, Name in line 15, Write in line 16, and Quit in line 17.

When you have entered the file, proofread it against Figure 5-4, correct any errors, then store it with the name FLASH.SCR.

```
 1: a 100
 2: mov bh,0
 3: mov cx,7d0
 4: mov ah,2
 5: mov dx,0
 6: int 10
 7: mov ah,8
 8: int 21
 9: mov ah,a
10: int 10
11: jmp 105
12:
13: r cx
14: 16
15: n flash.com
16: w
17: q
```

Figure 5-4. Debug script file with line numbers.

To make sure FLASH.SCR is on the disk, type the following Directory command:

```
A>dir flash.scr

Volume in drive C is FORSYTHWOLF
Directory of  C:\DOS\DEBUG

FLASH    SCR      133   2-15-86   9:34p
        1 File(s)   2936832 bytes free

A>_
```

If DOS responds *File not found,* create the file again and be sure to save it as FLASH.SCR.

FLASH.SCR fits on one screen, so display it with the Type command:

```
A>type flash.scr
```

Figure 5-5 shows the file without line numbers. Proofread this against the output of the Type command. Make certain that the first line is *a 100,* that there is a blank line between *jmp 105* and *r cx* (line 12 in Figure 5-4), and that the last line is *q* (a Quit command). If you omit or misplace either of these lines, Debug won't create FLASH.COM and you'll have to restart DOS.

```
a 100
mov  bh,0
mov  cx,7d0
mov  ah,2
mov  dx,0
int  10
mov  ah,8
int  21
mov  ah,a
int  10
jmp  105

r cx
16
n flash.com
w
q
```

Figure 5-5. Debug script file without line numbers.

Redirecting Debug's Input to a Script File

To redirect the input of Debug to a script file, you use the < character, just as when you redirect the input of the Sort, Find, or More filter commands. To start Debug and tell it to read its commands from FLASH.SCR, type:

A>debug < flash.scr

If all goes well, your screen should display the commands in FLASH.SCR and Debug's responses. Figure 5-6 shows how your system should respond; again, *xxxx* is used to represent numbers that vary from system to system.

```
-a 100
xxxx:0100  mov  bh,0
xxxx:0102  mov  cx,7d0
xxxx:0105  mov  ah,2
xxxx:0107  mov  dx,0
xxxx:010A  int  10
xxxx:010C  mov  ah,8
xxxx:010E  int  21
xxxx:0110  mov  ah,a
xxxx:0112  int  10
xxxx:0114  jmp  105
xxxx:0116
-r cx
CX 0000
:16
-n flash.com
-w
Writing 0016 bytes
-q

A>_
```

Figure 5-6. Debug's response to FLASH.SCR.

Did It Work?

If your system responds for a while and then stops (perhaps displaying what looks like a series of error messages), and you can't get any response from the keyboard, don't worry. You haven't damaged either the machine or any files; there's probably a mistake in FLASH.SCR, and Debug is still looking for input from the file instead of the keyboard. Do the following:

1. Turn the power switch off, wait five seconds or so, and turn the power switch back on. DOS will go through its startup routine.

2. Load FLASH.SCR with your word processor or text editor. Proofread it against Figure 5-5 until you're satisfied that it's identical (making certain that the first line is *a 100,* there's a blank line at the end of the program statements, and the last line is *q,* as described earlier).

3. Enter the Debug command again, redirecting input to FLASH.SCR.

The responses to the Register and Write commands at the end of Figure 5-6 are just like the responses you saw when you used those commands earlier, working with the text files. Debug treats commands in a script file just as if you had typed them.

The Name and Write commands tell Debug to save 16 hexadecimal (22 decimal) bytes in a file named FLASH.COM. Make sure it's there by typing:

```
A>dir flash.com

Volume in drive C is FORSYTHWOLF
Directory of  C:\DOS\DEBUG

FLASH    COM      22  2-15-86   7:54p
         1 File(s)   2961408 bytes free

A>_
```

If FLASH.COM isn't there, or isn't 22 bytes long, go back and proofread FLASH.SCR, correct any errors, and enter the Debug command again.

Testing Your Creation

You've created a program, but you may have no idea what it does. It's fairly simple: FLASH.COM waits for you to type a character, fills the screen with that character and waits for you to type another character, fills the screen with *that* character, and so on until you stop it by pressing Ctrl-Break (or Ctrl-C if you don't have a Break key).

Try it. Because it is a command file (its extension is COM, just like CHKDSK or DEBUG), all you need to type is its name:

`A>flash`

Nothing happens immediately. Now press *f*.

If nothing happens, there's probably a mistake in the program. Press Ctrl-Break (or Ctrl-C). If that doesn't restore the system prompt, try to restart DOS by pressing Ctrl-Alt-Del. If that doesn't work, turn the power switch off for five or ten seconds, then turn it back on. When DOS displays the system prompt, use your text editor or word processor to proofread FLASH.SCR and correct any mistakes. This time, pay special attention to the program statements (lines 2 through 11 in Figure 5-4).

If the screen fills with the character you typed, type another character. You will find that the machine displays a screenful of characters almost as fast as you can type just one. The program you created isn't very big, but it sure is fast. This program demonstrates just how fast a computer is.

To end the program, press Ctrl-Break (or Ctrl-C). This leaves your screen filled with the last character you typed. To make the screen less confusing, you can press the space bar (filling the screen with spaces) before you press Ctrl-Break. If you stopped the program with the screen filled with some other character, just clear the screen by typing *cls*.

Creating a Program with the Assemble Command

You just produced the program named FLASH.COM by creating a file of Debug commands with a word processor or text editor, then starting Debug with its input redirected to that file. You can also create that same program directly in Debug using the Assemble command.

The Assemble Command

The Assemble command translates statements in *assembly language*—a semi-readable language of instructions for the microprocessor—into a more compact form meaningful to the microprocessor but essentially unreadable by humans, often called *machine language*. The Assemble command has only one parameter, the address where you want the translation to begin:

a <address>

<*address*> is the location in memory at which Debug is to begin storing the translated instructions you will enter. If you omit <address> the first time you enter an Assemble command, Debug begins storing translated instructions at address 100. If you omit <address> on subsequent translations, Debug begins storing translated instructions at the first byte following the last batch of statements you translated with an Assemble command.

When you enter an Assemble command, Debug prompts you for the first instruction by displaying the starting address. After you type an instruction and press Enter, Debug stores the translated statement and prompts you for the next statement by displaying the address where it will store the next translated statement.

The Unassemble Command

Like the Assemble command, Unassemble has one parameter, the address where you want the reverse translation to begin:

u <address>

<*address*> is the location at which Debug is to begin translating the contents of memory to assembly-language statements. If you omit <address> the first time you enter an Unassemble command, Debug begins translating memory at address 100. If you omit <address> on subsequent translations, Debug begins translating memory at the first byte following the last area of memory you translated with an Unassemble command.

Chapter Summary

- You can use Debug to create, examine, or change any sort of file by loading the file into memory, using Debug commands to modify the memory where the file was loaded, then writing the modified memory back to the file.

- Debug displays and accepts only hexadecimal numbers.

- Debug provides none of the built-in convenience or protections of a word processor or text editor. If you use Debug to work with a valuable file (text, data, or a program), protect yourself by making a copy of the file and working with the copy

- Although Debug is poorly suited for working with text files, its capabilities make it an excellent tool for working on files that contain a mixture of text and other data, such as files of commands that control a printer or the display.

- If you redirect Debug's input to a script file, be sure the script file includes *all* input, especially the Quit command.

CHAPTER
6

Advanced Batch-File
Techniques

Batch files are your key to making the computer work the way you work. Without batch files, the computer controls how you use it. Batch files put *you* in charge.

This chapter gives some guidelines for designing batch files, describes several techniques for writing batch files, and demonstrates most of the techniques with a short example. The techniques apply to any batch file; the remainder of the book describes several batch files that use these techniques to tailor the appearance and behavior of DOS to your needs.

This chapter also describes the Command command, which loads another copy of the DOS command processor and lets you use batch commands in a batch file just as you would use any other command. As you'll see, this significantly increases the power of your batch files.

Some Guidelines for Designing Batch Files

Whether the subject is machines, books, programs, or batch files, *easy to use* almost always means *harder to make*. A batch file that uses the bare minimum of commands to perform a task isn't always the best solution. It probably gives no clue about the proper way to use it, and you may run the risk of damaging files if you don't enter the batch command exactly right. You can write a batch file so that its use is clear and the possibility of damaging side effects is eliminated by spending some time thinking about how the batch command will be used, what could go wrong, and how you want the screen to look.

The following guidelines can help you design and produce batch files that are easy and safe to use:

- Keep the screen easy to read and attractive while the command is running. The next section describes several techniques you can use.

- Display brief helpful or reassuring messages, especially if the batch command performs several different operations, so that you—or whoever uses the batch command—will be reassured that everything's OK.

- Avoid costly mistakes. If a batch command has several parameters—or if entering it incorrectly could damage a file—have the batch command display brief instructions if it is entered with no parameters. You'll appreciate the help if you only use the batch command once every few months, and it also lets others use the batch command with little or no instruction from you.

- Anticipate errors that someone might make, both when entering the batch command and when responding to prompts or menu selections while the batch command is running. Try to make it impossible for the person using the batch command to make an error (this sought-after quality is sometimes called *bulletproof*). You may have to settle for making it difficult to damage or erase a file, but the effort to make your batch files bulletproof will be time well spent.

- Provide conveniences. If the batch file creates temporary files, for example, erase them after they've served their purpose. If someone might want to print a file after using the batch command, offer that as an option at the end of the batch file.

Make Your Screens Attractive and Readable

Simple, uncluttered screens that give unambiguous instructions let anyone use a batch command quickly and confidently. The techniques for designing good screens are straightforward:

- Keep the screen free of distracting messages. Start the batch file with *echo off*, and redirect Copy command output to NUL (the null output device, where output just disappears).

- Separate groups of related information with blank lines. Use Echo commands in batch files and blank lines in any files that the batch file displays with the Type command.

- Use display attributes such as reverse video, high intensity, or color (if your system uses it) to highlight important information. But don't overdo it: Remember the boy who cried "Wolf!"

- Use the extended graphics characters to frame related groups of information, represent keytops, or simply to make the screen more attractive. You can write batch files whose displays have the same professional appearance as most application programs.

There's one *don't* in writing batch files: Don't beep unless it's absolutely necessary to get the attention of the person using the batch command. If overused, the beep not only loses its attention-getting quality, but it quickly becomes an irritant. Save it for those few really important situations that deserve a shout.

Conventions for Entering Batch Files

You'll notice that the batch files in this book follow a few conventions: Label names are in uppercase, commands are in lowercase; if a batch file includes labels, the commands are indented three spaces; and similar labels are used in different batch files when the circumstances are similar.

Conventions like these aren't for the benefit of the person who *uses* the batch file, but the person who *writes* or *revises* the batch file. They don't affect what the batch command does, they make it easier to see how the batch command works. You don't have to follow these conventions, but you might find that they make writing batch files easier and quicker, and they really help if you decide to go back and change a batch file several months after you wrote it.

Some Hints for Writing Batch Files

Writing batch files involves some risks you usually don't face when you use an application program: You might do something that makes it necessary to restart DOS, and there's a chance you might inadvertently erase a file. Fortunately, you can take a few steps to minimize these risks.

Before You Start

The Break command controls how often DOS checks to see if you have pressed Ctrl-C (or Ctrl-Break). You want DOS to check as often as possible, so make sure BREAK is on when you're working on batch files. There is little penalty for setting BREAK on (some operations are a bit slower), so it's probably safest to put *break = on* in your AUTOEXEC.BAT file and type *break = off* at the system prompt when you don't want it.

If you're using Version 3 of DOS, protect yourself against inadvertently changing or deleting valuable files by making them read-only with the Attribute command (*attrib + R <filename>*). This is a good practice even if you're not working on batch files.

Do your batch-file work in a separate directory, then copy the finished files to the \BATCH directory or wherever you keep your finished batch files. If you use a RAM disk for working on batch files, be sure to copy from the RAM disk to a real disk fairly often; if you have to restart DOS, the contents of the RAM disk are lost. (For information about setting up and using a RAM disk, see Chapter 9.)

If you use floppy disks, remove all disks that contain valuable files from the disk drives when you're working on batch files. If you use a fixed disk, make sure that all your valuable files are backed up before you test a batch file. You should back up as a matter of course, but it's even more important when you're working on batch files.

If a Batch File Doesn't Work Right

As you may know already, batch files don't always work right the first time. The bigger and more elegant the batch file, the more likely it is to behave perversely. Sometimes the problem is obvious, but there are times when finding and fixing the problem takes a combination of insight and patience. DOS gives you a few clues; here's how to interpret them:

- If DOS displays *File not found* while a batch file is running, but the batch file doesn't use files, you may have used one or more of the redirection symbols in a message displayed with an Echo command. You can't use <, >, or | for anything except redirection—not even in a Remark command—because DOS tries to carry out the redirection *before* it carries out the command. (You can, however, include them in a file that is displayed by a batch file.)

  For example, if you include the line *echo Type < to redirect input* inside a batch file, DOS tries to redirect input from a file named TO. If there is no such file, DOS displays *File not found*. If there is a file named TO, the Echo command displays *Type redirect input*. If you put *echo Type > to redirect output* in a batch file, the Echo command doesn't display anything and DOS creates a file named TO that contains *Type redirect input*. This can be a particularly nasty error: If the first word that follows the > character is the name of an existing file, running the batch file replaces the original file with no warning.

- If DOS displays *Bad command or file name* while a batch file is running, check the batch file for a misspelled command name, a CD command to the wrong directory, or a pipe-redirection character (|). If you put *echo Type | to pipe output* in a batch file, DOS displays *Bad command or file name* because there is no command file named TO, and the Echo command doesn't display anything.

- If DOS displays *Intermediate file error during pipe,* make sure that there is a carriage return at the end of the last line of the batch file.

- If DOS displays *Label not found,* make sure there is a colon before each label in the batch file.

- If a batch file that has labels refuses to carry out some commands, endlessly repeats the same series of commands, or seems to be doing nothing, press Ctrl-C and check the batch file for two labels with the same name. DOS always searches for a label from the beginning of the batch file, so it never sees the second label.

If a batch file simply won't do what it's supposed to and gives you no clues about what's wrong, remove the *echo off* command from the beginning and try the batch file again. Now DOS displays each command before it carries out the command. This makes the screen a mess, but lets you follow along command-by-command. If things on the screen scroll by too quickly, use Ctrl-S to stop and start the display. This usually leads you to the general area, if not the exact command, that is causing the problem. After you correct the problem, don't forget to replace the *echo off* command at the beginning of the file.

And never forget that a batch file does exactly what you tell it to do. All you have to do is figure out *exactly* what you told it to do.

Use Separate Files for Large Menus or Displays

If a menu or other screen requires more than a few lines of text, it's usually quicker to put the text into a separate file and use a Type command to display it, rather than use a long series of Echo commands. This method has some other advantages: It's usually easier to revise a text file than it is to change several Echo commands; the same text file can be used by more than one batch file; and you can copy and revise the text file if another batch file requires a similar display.

The disadvantages of displaying text files are that each additional file takes up at least 2K bytes of disk space on a hard disk, and you must keep track of the text files as well as the batch file.

Preparing for the Examples

The rest of this chapter demonstrates some useful techniques for your batch files. The remaining chapters of the book describe several batch files, some of which you may want to keep or adapt for your own use. To keep your batch files together, create a subdirectory named BATCH in the root directory and change to that directory by typing:

```
A>md batch
A>cd batch
```

To use these batch files from any other directory, add \BATCH to your command path: Start by typing a Path command with no parameters to display the current paths. Then type another Path command that repeats the output of the first Path command, adding a semicolon and \batch at the end. For example, if your command paths were A:\ and A:\DOS, the exchange would look like this:

```
A>path
PATH=A:\;A:\DOS
A>path=a:\;a:\dos;a:\batch
A>_
```

You'll also probably want to add \BATCH to the Path command in your AUTOEXEC.BAT file so that your batch files are always available.

Some Useful Batch-File Techniques

You can apply the techniques described in the remainder of this chapter to any batch file, regardless of its purpose. In addition to the examples in this chapter, the techniques are used in batch files throughout the remaining chapters of the book.

Echoing a Blank Line

If you're using Version 2 of DOS, you can echo a blank line with an Echo command followed by two spaces. This doesn't work with Version 3, but you still have two ways to echo a blank line with the Echo command:

- If you're using Edlin or copying the console to create a batch file, follow the Echo command with a space and press F7; this puts character 0 in the command. Edlin echoes character 0 as ∧@ when you enter it, and either ∧@ or @∧ when you display the file with the List or Page command.

- If you're using a program that prevents F7 from producing character 0, follow the Echo command with a space and type Alt-255, which puts character 255 in the command. Character 255 is echoed as a blank.

Both methods also work with Version 2.

Checking Whether a Parameter Was Typed

If you write a batch file that assumes the batch command will be entered with at least one parameter, be sure to consider what the effect would be if someone entered the command without a parameter. If you don't use the batch command frequently, you could forget the parameter, and someone else may not know how to use the batch command. In particular, watch out for how you test the value of the parameters.

For example, if a batch file contains *if not %1= =fred goto END* and the batch command is entered with no parameter, DOS displays *Syntax error* and continues with the next command. The error message is distracting, perhaps even disconcerting. But, depending on what commands follow, further consequences can be much more serious because, even though the first parameter isn't *fred,* the batch command behaves as if it were.

To avoid this, enclose both the replaceable parameter symbol (% followed by a number) and the comparison string in quotation marks: *if not "%1"= ="fred" goto END.* Now DOS handles the absence of the parameter just like any other parameter value; it doesn't display an error message and processes the If command correctly, skipping any commands that follow the If command and going to the label END.

To check specifically for the absence of a parameter, use two quotation marks with nothing between as the comparison string: *if "%1"= = "".*

Using the For Command Outside a Batch File

You can type the DOS commands designed for use in batch files, such as Echo, Goto, and For, at the system prompt. Most of them, such as Echo and Goto, aren't especially useful outside a batch file. The For command, however, can be a quick way to carry out a single command on a series of files. For example, the Type command doesn't allow wildcard characters, but you could display all the files with the extension DOC by typing *for %p in (∗.doc) do type %p* at the system prompt.

If you find yourself typing the same For command more than once or twice at the system prompt, however, you're probably better off writing a short batch file.

Using Batch Commands in Other Batch Files

A batch command returns control to DOS after it carries out the last command in the batch file. This means that if you put a batch command in the middle of a batch file, the commands that follow the batch command are ignored. You can, however, put a batch command at the end of a batch file, because there are no more commands to be carried out in the original batch file. Because you can use this technique to link a series of batch files, it's called *chaining* batch files.

But it would be more useful if a batch file could use a batch command just like it uses any other command, carrying out the batch command and continuing with the next command. This capability of executing a batch file from within another batch file is referred to as *calling*, because you call the command in to do something, and when it finishes you continue with the business at hand.

Even though DOS doesn't permit one batch command to call another, you can achieve the same effect with a seldom-used DOS command.

The Command Command

COMMAND.COM is the DOS *command processor*, the program that checks what you type and passes your instructions along to DOS. It is automatically loaded and executed when you start DOS. Like any other file whose extension is COM, you can run this program by entering its name. Also like other DOS commands, you refer to the program by its name, so it's the Command command.

Typing *command* loads and executes another copy of COMMAND.COM. The first copy—the one that looked at the Command command you entered—isn't gone; it's put into a sort of suspended animation, and springs back to life when you end the new command processor with an Exit command. This all might seem unnecessarily convoluted, so try a couple of quick examples.

Type the following:

```
A>command
```

DOS responds by loading another copy of COMMAND.COM, which displays the startup message you normally see when you first start the system. Enter a Directory command:

```
A>dir
```

DOS reacts to commands as it always does. Now type the Exit command, which ends this copy of COMMAND.COM:

```
A>exit
```

DOS displays the system prompt without appearing to do anything else, but now you're back to the original copy of COMMAND.COM.

Note: Some application programs, such as Microsoft Word, let you enter a single DOS command from within the application. If you enter a Command command, DOS displays the startup message and it looks like you have exited from the application and returned to DOS; you can enter commands, change directories, and in general do whatever you like. But all this is happening with the second copy of COMMAND.COM. The first copy of COMMAND.COM is still in memory, waiting for the second copy to end. To return to your application program, end the second copy of COMMAND.COM with an Exit command. Be careful, however, not to change or delete any files the application program is using, or the program may become confused and you'll have to restart your system.

You can also load another copy of COMMAND.COM to execute a command and automatically return to the previous copy of COMMAND.COM without typing an Exit command. This form of the Command command has two parameters:

```
command /c <command>
```

/c tells DOS to carry out *<command>* and automatically return to the previous copy of COMMAND.COM.

<command> is any command, including a batch command or even another Command command.

This is the form of the Command command that lets you use batch commands in batch files. You enter the batch command—and any parameters it requires—following the /C parameter.

For example, you would type the following to load another copy of COMMAND.COM, display the directory, and automatically return to the current command processor:

```
A>command /c dir /w
```

The directory was displayed by the second copy of COMMAND.COM; the system prompt that follows it was displayed by the first.

There's Still No Free Lunch

As you'll see in the rest of the book, using COMMAND.COM this way lets you write more flexible and powerful batch files. This power doesn't come without some penalty: Loading another copy of COMMAND.COM takes a little more than 3000 bytes of memory, and adds to the time required to carry out a batch command.

But 3000+ bytes is a small price to pay for the additional capability, and COMMAND.COM loads fairly quickly from a fixed disk. It takes longer to load from a floppy disk, of course, but you can minimize the penalty by loading it from a RAM disk. (See Chapter 9 for more information about using a RAM disk.)

Command Examples

The DOS environment, which is described in Chapter 8, controls such characteristics as the command path and system prompt. Each copy of COMMAND.COM starts out with the environment of the previous copy that loaded it. However, if you change the environment of a copy of COMMAND.COM, the changes are lost when it ends and returns to the copy that loaded it. This is easy to demonstrate. Load a new command processor by typing:

```
A>command
```

DOS displays the startup message. Type the following command to change the system prompt:

```
A>prompt DOS here:
DOS here:_
```

DOS displays the new system prompt. Now type an Exit command to end this copy of COMMAND.COM:

```
DOS here:exit
A>_
```

DOS displays the original system prompt, because you have returned to the previous copy of COMMAND.COM.

It is faily simple to check the amount of memory each additional copy of COMMAND.COM requires with the Check Disk (chkdsk) command. First, type the following to see how much memory is available:

A>chkdsk

The last line of the response tells you how much memory is available. Now type a Command command to execute the Check Disk command:

A>command /c chkdsk

The number in the last line of this response should be about 3000 less than the number in the previous example; the actual difference is how much memory COMMAND.COM requires. You can load as many copies of COMMAND.COM as you like; type the following to load two copies, the second of which executes the Check Disk command:

A>command /c command /c chkdsk

This time the difference in memory available should be twice the previous difference, because you loaded COMMAND.COM, then you loaded it again. You're back to the original version because both Command commands included the /C parameter, so both automatically returned to the previous copy.

Using the Command Command in a Batch File

An example using two short batch files shows how you use the Command command to execute a batch command from within another batch file. Make sure you're in the directory \BATCH, and copy from the console, or use Edlin or your word processor, to create the files named FIRST.BAT and SECOND.BAT shown in Figure 6-1.

FIRST.BAT:

```
1: echo off
2: for %%p in (%1) do command /c second %%p
3: echo *** Completed the jobs. ***
```

SECOND.BAT:

```
1: echo off
2: echo Some useful processing to %1.
```

Figure 6-1. Using the Command command to call another batch command.

The For command in line 2 of FIRST.BAT carries out a Command command for each member of %1 (most likely a file name with wildcards). The Command command, in turn, carries out SECOND.BAT, specifying the current value of %%p as a parameter.

To test these files, type:

A>first *.*

DOS responds by displaying two lines for each file in the directory \BATCH: the system prompt followed by *echo off,* and *Some useful processing to* followed by the file name. DOS loads and executes SECOND.BAT once for each file in the root directory; if you're using floppy disks, you can hear DOS load the file each time. When it has carried out SECOND.BAT for each file in the root directory, FIRST.BAT displays *∗∗∗Completed the jobs.∗∗∗* and returns to DOS.

In this example, SECOND.BAT simply echoes a message, but it could carry out a whole series of commands. Without the Command command in line 2 of FIRST.BAT—if it read simply *for %%p in (%1) do second.bat*—DOS would carry out SECOND.BAT once and return to the system prompt.

A Batch File Can Call Itself

As you'll see, the ability to call one batch file from another is most valuable, but it doesn't come without cost. In the previous example, you used two batch files to do one job. Each file requires the minimum disk-storage space, and you have to keep track of both of them. But it isn't necessary to call a different batch file; a little sleight of hand with a parameter allows you to combine them into a single file that calls itself to accomplish the same thing.

Look at the batch file in Figure 6-2. As you can see, lines 1, 3, and 4 are almost identical to FIRST.BAT in the previous example, and line 7 is the heart of SECOND.BAT. But lines 2 and 5 are new, there are a couple of labels that weren't there before, and there's a parameter called *trick* at the end of line 3. What's happening here?

```
1:     echo off
2:     if "%2"=="trick" goto DO_IT
3:     for %%p in (%1) do command /c self %%p trick
4:     echo *** Completed the jobs. ***
5:     goto END
6: :DO_IT
7:     echo Some useful processing to %1.
8: :END
```

Figure 6-2. SELF.BAT: A batch file that calls itself.

Here's what SELF.BAT does when you type *self *.**:

1. The If command in line 2 doesn't find a second parameter at all, let alone *trick,* so the Goto command isn't carried out.

2. The For command in line 3 carries out a Command command for each file in the directory \BATCH (*%1 is *.**). Each Command command, in turn, loads and carries out the SELF batch command with two parameters: The first is the file name and the second is *trick.*

3. The new copy of COMMAND.COM loads and runs SELF.BAT. This time the If command in line 2 finds that %2 is, indeed, *trick,* so it carries out the *goto DO_IT* command.

4. Line 7 echoes the message, and this copy of SELF.BAT ends, returning to COMMAND.COM. This copy of COMMAND.COM ends (the /C parameter says carry out just one command), returning to the previous copy of COMMAND.COM, which is still in line 3 of SELF.BAT with a list of file names. It repeats steps 3 and 4 for each file.

Create and save SELF.BAT, then type *self *.**. The result should be the same as when you typed *first *.** in the previous example. You have accomplished the same task using one file instead of two. This technique is used in a batch file to print a series of files in Chapter 11.

Redirecting the Output of a Batch Command

If you have ever tried to redirect the output of a batch command, you've discovered that you can't. If, in the previous example, you typed *self *.* > self.out,* for example, DOS would create a file named SELF.OUT but wouldn't write anything in it; the file's length would be 0.

You can, however, redirect the output of the Command command. If you entered SELF.BAT, type:

```
A>command /c self *.* > self.out
```

DOS churns away but doesn't display anything, and finally displays the system prompt. Now type:

```
A>type self.out
```

There's the output of the batch command, redirected to SELF.OUT. Erase it by typing *erase self.out.*

Time- and Date-Stamping Files and Other Output

You can use DOS to put the current time and date in a file or on printed output. Because this is like using a rubber stamp to put the time and date on a piece of paper, it's often called *time stamping* or *date stamping*.

The technique involves redirecting the input of a Time or Date command to a file that contains nothing but a carriage return, and redirecting the output to the file or device that is to be stamped. DOS responds to the carriage return by leaving the time or date unchanged.

First, create a file that contains a carriage return by typing:

```
A>copy con cr.dat
<Enter>
<F6><Enter>
        1 File(s) copied

A>_
```

Now type the following Date command to see how the basic technique works:

```
A>date < cr.dat
Current date is Fri 10-16-1987
Enter new date (mm-dd-yy):

A>_
```

But you don't want the second line in a file, of course, so pipe the output of the Date command to a Find command, and redirect the output of the Find command to a file named DATE.TMP:

```
A>date < cr.dat | find "C" > date.tmp
```

If you're using Version 2, DOS displays *Enter new date:*, but only the date stamp is written to the file. Verify this by displaying DATE.TMP:

```
A>type date.tmp
Current date is Fri 10-16-1987
```

To put a date or time stamp at the end of a file, use two > symbols to redirect the output of the Date or Time command and add it to the target file. Create a test file, then put a time stamp at the end by typing:

```
A>copy con file1.doc
This is a test file.
<F6><Enter>
        1 File(s) copied

A>time < cr.dat | find "C" >> file1.doc
```

Remember, if you're using Version 2, DOS displays *Enter new time:* after the Time command.

Putting a time or date stamp at the beginning of a file requires a couple of temporary files: One is the date or time stamp itself, and the other is the combination of the date or time stamp and the original file. You already created DATE.TMP, which contains the date stamp. FILE1.DOC is a test file that has a time stamp at the end; type the following to combine DATE.TMP and FILE1.DOC, putting a time stamp at the beginning, and display the resulting temporary file named DATE.$$$:

```
A>copy date.tmp+file1.doc date.$$$ > nul
```

```
A>type date.$$$
Current date is Fri 10-16-1987
This is a test file.
Current time is 16:44:12.68
```

```
A>_
```

Redirecting the output of the Copy command to NUL means you don't see the messages that acknowledge the names and number of files copied. If you used this technique in a batch file to add a date or time stamp at the beginning of FILE1.DOC, you would erase the original (FILE1.DOC) and rename DATE.$$$ to FILE1.DOC.

To clean up your directory, type the following:

```
A>erase date.$$$
```

```
A>erase date.tmp
```

```
A>erase file1.doc
```

```
A>_
```

Note: You didn't erase CR.DAT, so you can use the Time or Date command this way again. Whenever you redirect the input of either the Time or Date command, make certain that the file to which you redirect the input contains nothing but a carriage return. If it doesn't contain a carriage return, or if it contains an invalid reply to the Time or Date command, DOS will wait for the proper input from the file. But there's nothing more in the file and you won't be able to enter the input from the keyboard, so you'll have to restart DOS.

How Long Did That Take?

Figure 6-3 shows a short batch file that uses time stamps to record how long DOS takes to carry out a command. The technique is simple: It displays the current time, carries out the specified command, and displays the current time again.

```
1: echo off
2: echo *** Starting time
3: time < cr.dat | find "C"
4: %1 %2 %3 %4 %5 %6
5: echo *** Ending time
6: time < cr.dat | find "C"
```

Figure 6-3. TIMER.BAT: A DOS stopwatch.

The only line of note is line 4: It contains nothing but replaceable parameters. This line is the event being timed. Including this many replaceable parameters lets you time almost any command.

Enter *TIMER.BAT*, then test it by typing:

```
A>timer vol

A>echo off
*** Starting time
Current time is 17:09:33.74

 Volume in drive A is FORSYTHWOLF
*** Ending time
Current time is 17:09:35.82

A>_
```

The difference between the starting and ending times in this example is 2.08 seconds. Your system may be faster or slower, depending on what type of computer you have and how you're using it.

TIMER.BAT can show you some interesting things about your system. Typing *timer*, for example, shows you how long TIMER.BAT itself takes to do its work because there's no command for DOS to carry out. Try it. If you have a RAM disk, make it the current drive, copy TIMER.BAT and CR.DAT to it, and type *timer* again to see what difference using a RAM disk makes. Now copy FIND.EXE to the RAM disk and type *timer* again; you should see a substantial difference. This batch file can be a handy tool for measuring the speed of your system.

In addition to the techniques described in this chapter, you can use the extended graphics characters to draw frames around related information or represent keytops and use the ANSI.SYS commands to control display attributes such as reverse video and color.

All these features make your batch files longer, but the added readability and convenience almost always make it worth the effort—especially if you use many batch files or if your batch files are used by others. The batch files in the remainder of the book use these techniques, and more, to make them both powerful and easy to use.

Chapter Summary

- Design your batch files, don't just write them.

- Display instructions if the batch file needs parameters or if using it incorrectly could erase valuable files.

- Make your batch files easy to use by keeping the screen uncluttered and displaying helpful or reassuring messages.

- Don't use redirection symbols (<, >, or |) in a batch file for any purpose other than redirection.

- The Command command lets you use other batch commands just as you use DOS commands.

CHAPTER

7

Designing an Interactive Menu System

A menu system tailored to the programs you use makes your computer a much more productive tool. A properly designed menu system can eliminate most of the time you spend changing directories and starting programs. It isn't necessary to buy a menu program; DOS itself includes everything you need to build a rudimentary menu system, and with the addition of a short program called REPLY.COM—which you'll create in this chapter—you can make a menu system as interactive as you like.

In addition to showing you how to create REPLY.COM, this chapter shows the basic techniques of creating menus, checking responses, and displaying help information. Chapter 14 uses the techniques described in this chapter, and batch programs described in following chapters, to show you how to create a multi-level menu system to handle several application programs.

Making Batch Commands Interactive: REPLY.COM

REPLY.COM is a short program that identifies the key most recently pressed. That doesn't sound like much, but it lets you personalize your batch files as much as you like by carrying out different commands depending on what key is pressed.

DOS stores a number, called *errorlevel,* in its area of memory. You can test the value of *errorlevel* with the If command. REPLY.COM waits for you to press a key, then sets the value of *errorlevel* to the key code of the key that you pressed.

Because the If command checks for an *errorlevel* equal to or greater than the number you specify, you must check for key codes in descending order, starting with the highest and proceeding to the lowest. If the key codes you're looking for aren't in a single sequence, you also must be sure to check for the gaps. The reason for this, and the method, will become clear after a few examples.

The key code of the standard typewriter portion of the keyboard is the ASCII code of the character, as shown in Appendix C. The extended key code of the special keys—the function keys, keypad keys, and combinations with the Alt and Ctrl keys—is two numbers, as shown in Appendix D. Because the first number of an extended key code is always 0, REPLY.COM sets *errorlevel* to the second number.

Some ASCII codes are the same as the second number of the extended key code of other keys. This creates some duplications: The semicolon and function key F1, for example, both set *errorlevel* to 59; Alt–B and 0 (zero) both set *errorlevel* to 48. This shouldn't create a problem, because the duplicated keys are generally unrelated and won't interfere with each other.

Creating REPLY.COM with Debug

Chapter 5 describes how to use Debug to create a program. If you haven't gone through the examples there, you should probably do so before continuing with this section.

Type the following lines to start the Debug program and create REPLY.COM:

```
A>debug
-a 100
xxxx:0100 mov ah,8
xxxx:0102 int 21
xxxx:0104 cmp al,0
xxxx:0106 jnz 10a
xxxx:0108 int 21
xxxx:010A mov ah,4c
xxxx:010C int 21
xxxx:010E <Enter>
-_
```

Type the following Unassemble command to display the program, and proofread the result against Figure 7-1.

```
-u 100 10d
```

Debug responds with:

```
xxxx:0100 B408        MOV     AH,08
xxxx:0102 CD21        INT     21
xxxx:0104 3C00        CMP     AL,00
xxxx:0106 7502        JNZ     010A
xxxx:0108 CD21        INT     21
xxxx:010A B44C        MOV     AH,4C
xxxx:010C CD21        INT     21
-_
```

Figure 7-1. Unassemble command output for REPLY.COM.

If your output doesn't agree with Figure 7-1, go back to the heading "Creating REPLY.COM with Debug" and enter the program, unassemble it, and proofread it again.

If your output agrees with Figure 7-1, type the following commands to store REPLY.COM on disk and quit Debug:

```
-r cx
CX 0000
:e
-n reply.com
-w
Writing 000E bytes
-q
```

You should be back in DOS with the system prompt on the screen.

A Quick Test of REPLY.COM

Remember, REPLY.COM just sets the *errorlevel* equal to the key code of the next key pressed. If you don't check for *errorlevel,* REPLY.COM behaves just like the Pause command—halting processing until a key is pressed—without the *Strike a key when ready . . .* message. The first test of REPLY.COM is easy—just type:

```
A>reply
```

Nothing should happen. In particular, there should be no system prompt. (If there is a system prompt, type *reply* again. If the system prompt appears again, go back to the heading "Creating REPLY.COM with Debug" and enter the program again. If there's a more serious problem with the program, you may have to restart the system by pressing Ctrl-Alt-Del or even turning the power on and off.)

There's no system prompt because REPLY.COM is waiting for you to press a key. So press any key. DOS should display the system prompt. This may seem like a trivial job for a program to do, but even this limited action is useful, because it lets you pause in a batch file without displaying the *Strike a key when ready . . .* message. However, it's hardly the reason REPLY.COM is so valuable.

There's no sign of whether REPLY.COM set *errorlevel* to the code of the key you just pressed, but it's pretty easy to test with a short batch file.

Using REPLY.COM to Accept Any Key

The first demonstration of REPLY.COM is a batch file called MENU-1.BAT that displays a two-item menu and waits for you to reply. If you press F1, it clears the screen. If you press F2, it displays the directory. If you press any other key, it returns to DOS.

Using Edlin or a word processor, enter MENU-1.BAT as shown in Figure 7-2. (You could copy from the console, but the Copy command doesn't let you go back and change a line after you have pressed Enter, and this file is a bit long to type perfectly.)

The labels in MENU-1.BAT don't have to be in uppercase and you don't have to enter the blanks at the beginning of the lines that aren't labels. These are conventions that make it a bit easier to see how the batch file works, but they don't affect what the batch file does. The line numbers are for reference only.

```
 1:    echo off
 2:    cls
 3:    echo F1 - Clear the screen
 4:    echo F2 - Display the directory
 5:    echo Press any other key to quit.
 6:    reply
 7:    if errorlevel 61 goto END
 8:    if errorlevel 60 goto F2
 9:    if errorlevel 59 goto F1
10:    goto END
11: :F1
12:    cls
13:    goto END
14: :F2
15:    dir
16: :END
```

Figure 7-2. MENU-1.BAT: A short menu.

Here's how MENU-1.BAT works:

- Lines 1-6 clear the screen, display the menu, and run REPLY.COM.

- Line 7 checks whether the key code is equal to or greater than 61 (to see if a function key other than F1 or F2 was pressed). Because the If command checks whether *errorlevel* is equal to or greater than the specified number, you must check from the largest value to the smallest. The batch file does something only if F1 or F2 is pressed, so this If command says don't do anything (*goto END*) if the key pressed was F3 or greater.

- Line 8 says if the key code is 60 (function key F2 was pressed), go to the label F2. Line 7 eliminated the possibility that any key whose code is higher than 60 was pressed, so this If command isolates the F2 key.

- Line 9 says if the key code is 59 (function key F1 was pressed), go to the label F1. Lines 7 and 8 eliminated the possibility that any key whose code is higher than 59 was pressed, so this If command isolates the F1 key.

- Line 10 says go, to the label END, exiting the batch file without doing anything. Just as the If command in line 7 ignores all keys higher than F2, this If command ignores all keys lower than F1.

- Lines 11-13 define what happens if F1 was pressed: The screen is cleared and control returns to DOS.

- Lines 14-16 define what happens if F2 was pressed: The directory is displayed.

Save the file, then type *menu-1*. You should see your menu:

```
F1 - Clear the screen
F2 - Display the directory
Press any other key to quit
-
```

Press F1. DOS should clear the screen. Type *menu-1* again, then press F2. DOS should display the directory. Try it a few more times, pressing other keys to make sure that any key other than F1 or F2 simply returns to DOS.

Using REPLY.COM to Accept Only Certain Keys

MENU-1.BAT accepts any key, but acts on only F1 and F2; it returns to DOS if any other key is pressed. This isn't always the best way to handle replies, especially if an incorrect response can do something damaging, such as erase a file. You can modify MENU-1.BAT so it accepts only F1 or F2, and continues to wait for a reply until one of those keys is pressed.

Figure 7-3 shows the revised version of MENU-1.BAT that ignores all keys except F1 and F2. The changes are shown in italics. Make a copy of MENU-1.BAT and use Edlin or your word processor to make the changes, then save the revised file as MENU-2.BAT.

```
 1:    echo off
 2:    cls
 3:    echo F1 - Clear the screen
 4:    echo F2 - Display the directory
 5:    echo Press F1 or F2
 6: :REPLY
 7:    reply
 8:    if errorlevel 61 goto REPLY
 9:    if errorlevel 60 goto F2
10:    if errorlevel 59 goto F1
11:    goto REPLY
12: :F1
13:    cls
14:    goto END
15: :F2
16:    dir
17: :END
```

Figure 7-3. MENU-2.BAT: A short menu that requires a correct response.

The changes are minor:

- In line 5, change *Press any other key to quit* to *Press F1 or F2*.

- Insert a new line 6, the label *:REPLY*.

- In lines 8 and 11 (lines 7 and 10 in Figure 7-2), change *END* to *REPLY*. Now, when you press any key other than F1 or F2, the batch file goes back to run REPLY.COM again instead of returning to DOS. The only way to end the batch file is to press F1 or F2 (or Ctrl-C to cancel it).

Make the changes and save the revised batch file as MENU-2.BAT. Type *menu-2*. You should see your menu, but with a different instruction line:

```
F1 - Clear the screen
F2 - Display the directory
Press F1 or F2
-
```

F1 and F2 should behave as before, but pressing any other key has no effect; the batch file just waits for you to press either F1 or F2.

REPLY.COM can be used in any sort of batch file, not just a menu. For example, if you're preparing to format a floppy disk, you might issue a prompt that says *Press F1 to format the disk; any other key cancels,* reducing the possibility of inadvertently formatting the wrong disk. You'll find batch files in this book that use both approaches to pressing a key that was not specified in the batch file.

Using REPLY.COM to Isolate a Single Key

You can isolate a single key entered in response to REPLY.COM with an If command that includes another If command. Type the following to create a file named MENU-3.BAT:

```
A>copy con menu-3.bat
echo off
echo Press F1 to display the directory; any other key quits.
reply
if errorlevel 59 if not errorlevel 60 dir
<F6><Enter>
        1 File(s) copied

A>_
```

The first If command selects all keys whose code is equal to or greater than 59, and the second If command selects all keys whose code is less than 60. Only key code 59—function key F1—passes both tests. Type *menu-3*; if you press F1, DOS displays the directory. If you press any other key, DOS simply displays the system prompt.

To generalize: The following command carries out *<command>* if the key whose code is *x* was pressed in response to REPLY.COM:

```
if errorlevel x if not errorlevel x + 1 <command>
```

This technique is used to process responses to REPLY.COM in batch files in the remainder of the book.

Displaying Additional Information with a Batch File

Sometimes a menu or other screen might justify additional instructions—especially if you don't see it often or if someone less experienced with DOS will see it—but you'd rather keep the screen as uncluttered as possible.

Why not use the same technique that many application programs use: Display help information only if a particular key is pressed. You can do this by modifying MENU-2.BAT so that pressing Alt-H displays additional instructions.

Figure 7-4 shows a revised version of MENU-2.BAT that carries out several Echo commands that display additional information if Alt-H is pressed; the changes to MENU-2.BAT are in italics. Make a copy of MENU-2.BAT and use Edlin or your word processor to make the changes, then save the revised file as MENU-4.BAT.

Note: {ESC} in Figure 7-4 and the following figures represents the Escape character (ASCII 27). If you're using Edlin, enter the Escape character by typing Ctrl-V[. If you're using Microsoft Word or another word processor that accepts control characters, type Alt-27.

```
 1:     echo off
 2:     cls
 3:     echo F1 - Clear the screen
 4:     echo F2 - Display the directory
 5:     echo Press F1 or F2 (or Alt-H for help)
 6:  :REPLY
 7:     reply
 8:     if errorlevel 61 goto REPLY
 9:     if errorlevel 60 goto F2
10:     if errorlevel 59 goto F1
11:     if errorlevel 35 if not errorlevel 36 goto HELP
12:     goto REPLY
13:  :F1
14:     cls
15:     goto END
16:  :F2
17:     dir
18:     goto END
19:  :HELP
20:     echo {ESC}[18;50HThis information is displayed
21:     echo {ESC}[19;50Honly when Alt-H is pressed.
22:     echo {ESC}[20;50HThere is no other effect on
23:     echo {ESC}[21;50Hthe batch file.
24:     goto REPLY
25:  :END
```

Figure 7-4. MENU-4.BAT: A batch file that displays help information.

Again, there aren't many changes:

● In line 5, add the phrase *(or Alt-H for help)*.

● Insert line 11, which goes to the label *HELP* if Alt-H (key code 35) is pressed.

● Insert lines 18-24. The message displayed by each Echo command begins with an ANSI.SYS command that positions the cursor, starting in row 18, column 50 (the ANSI.SYS commands are described in Chapter 3).

Make the changes and save the revised batch file as MENU-4.BAT. Now type *menu-4*. The instruction line includes an additional option:

```
F1 - Clear the screen
F2 - Display the directory
Press F1 or F2 (or Alt-H for help)
-
```

Function keys F1 and F2 work just as they did in MENU-2.BAT, but press Alt-H. MENU-4.BAT displays the help information at the lower right, then goes back to wait for you to press F1 or F2.

You can elaborate the help information by using display attributes, such as reverse video or color, or by enclosing the information in a box using the extended characters, but this is the basic mechanism for displaying additional information on demand.

Erasing Part of the Display with a Batch File

Once you have displayed additional information, you might want to erase it. You can modify MENU-4.BAT so that the batch file displays the help information, then erases it when any key is pressed.

Figure 7-5 shows the revised version of MENU-4.BAT that displays the help information, then uses REPLY.COM to wait for you to press a key and, regardless of what key is pressed, erases the help information and goes back to wait for you to press F1 or F2. The changes are in italics. Make a copy of MENU-4.BAT and use Edlin or your word processor to make the changes, then save the revised file as MENU-5.BAT.

```
 1:     echo off
 2:     cls
 3:     echo F1 - Clear the screen
 4:     echo F2 - Display the directory
 5:     echo Press F1 or F2 (or Alt-H for help)
 6:  :REPLY
 7:     reply
 8:     if errorlevel 61 goto REPLY
 9:     if errorlevel 60 goto F2
10:     if errorlevel 59 goto F1
11:     if errorlevel 35 if not errorlevel 36 goto HELP
12:     goto REPLY
13:  :F1
14:     cls
15:     goto END
16:  :F2
17:     dir
18:     goto END
19:  :HELP
20:     echo {ESC}[18;50HThis information is displayed
21:     echo {ESC}[19;50Honly when Alt-H is pressed.
22:     echo {ESC}[20;50HThere is no other effect on
23:     echo {ESC}[21;50Hthe batch file.
24:     echo {ESC}[22;50H{ESC}[7mPress any key to continue.{ESC}[m
25:     reply
26:     echo {ESC}[18;50H{ESC}[K
27:     echo {ESC}[19;50H{ESC}[K
28:     echo {ESC}[20;50H{ESC}[K
29:     echo {ESC}[21;50H{ESC}[K
30:     echo {ESC}[22;50H{ESC}[K
31:     goto REPLY
32:  :END
```

Figure 7-5. MENU-5.BAT: A batch file that erases part of the screen.

The changes:

- Insert lines 24-30:
    - Line 24 adds the instruction *Press any key to continue.* The ANSI.SYS command *{ESC}[7m* starts reverse video; *{ESC}[m* turns off all attributes (returns to normal display).
    - Line 25 waits for you to press a key.
    - Lines 26-30 move the cursor to the beginning of each line of the help information and erase to the end of the line.

Make the changes and save the revised batch file as MENU-5.BAT. Now type *menu-5* and press Alt-H. The help information includes an additional line:

```
This information is displayed
only when Alt-H is pressed.
There is no other effect on
the batch file.
Press any key to continue.
```

Press any key. The help information is erased and the batch file waits for you to press F1 or F2 (or display the help information again).

Adding more features like this makes your batch files longer, but the added convenience is worth it, especially if you have many batch files or if others will be using the batch files you write.

Changing Both the Display and Behavior of a Batch File

Because ANSI.SYS commands let you display information anywhere on the screen, you can not only display additional information in a batch file, you can change what is already displayed. For example, you could include more than one set of menu choices in a single batch file and switch back and forth between the alternate sets by pressing a specified key.

Figure 7-6 shows a batch file based on MENU-5.BAT that lets you change the menu choices by pressing the right-arrow key. It's somewhat longer than MENU-5.BAT, because there are two complete sets of commands that display choices, check your response, and carry out the appropriate commands.

Because the differences from MENU-5.BAT are substantial, it's probably easier to enter it from scratch. Create a file named MENU-6.BAT and enter the lines shown in Figure 7-6.

```
 1:    echo off
 2:    cls
 3:    echo F1 -
 4:    echo F2 -
 5:    echo Press F1 or F2 (or right arrow to change the choices)
 6: :OPTION_1
 7:    echo {ESC}[1;6H{ESC}[KClear the screen
 8:    echo {ESC}[2;6H{ESC}[KDisplay the directory
 9: :REPLY
10:    reply
11:    if errorlevel 77 if not errorlevel 78 goto OPTION_2
12:    if errorlevel 61 goto REPLY
13:    if errorlevel 60 goto F2
14:    if errorlevel 59 goto F1
15:    goto REPLY
16: :F1
17:    cls
18:    goto END
19: :F2
20:    dir
21:    goto END
22: :OPTION_2
23:    echo {ESC}[1;6H{ESC}[KDisplay the disk volume label
24:    echo {ESC}[2;6H{ESC}[KDisplay the DOS version
25: :REPLY_2
26:    reply
27:    if errorlevel 77 if not errorlevel 78 goto OPTION_1
28:    if errorlevel 61 goto REPLY_2
29:    if errorlevel 60 goto F2_2
30:    if errorlevel 59 goto F1_2
31:    goto REPLY_2
32: :F1_2
33:    vol
34:    goto END
35: :F2_2
36:    ver
37: :END
```

Figure 7-6. MENU-6.BAT: A batch file that presents two sets of choices.

How MENU-6.BAT works:

- Lines 1-5 clear the screen and display the parts of the menu that don't change. Notice that only the key names (F1 and F2) are permanently displayed; because the choices themselves can be changed, they are shown separately. To keep this example to a reasonable size, the instructions in line 5 include a description of how to change the choices so that no additional help information is needed.

- Lines 6-8 display the first set of menu choices. ANSI.SYS commands are used to position the cursor (*{ESC}[1;6H*) and erase to the end of the line (*{ESC}[K*) before displaying the choices. Erasing to the end of the line allows for alternate menu choices of different lengths.

- Lines 9-15 run REPLY.COM to wait for a key to be pressed, and evaluate the response. These lines differ from MENU-5.BAT in two ways:

  - There's no check for Alt-H because what was previously help information is now a permanent part of the display.

  - Line 11 checks to see whether the right arrow (key code 77) was pressed; if it was, the batch file goes to the label OPTION_2 to display the other set of options.

- Lines 16-21 carry out the first set of menu choices. This is just like MENU-5.BAT.

- Lines 22-37 are near-duplicates of lines 6-21, but related to the second set of menu options:

  - Lines 22-24 display the second set of menu options, just as lines 6-8 display the first set of menu options. The new choices described in lines 23 and 24 are carried out by the Volume and Version commands in lines 33 and 36.

  - Lines 25-31 wait for a key to be pressed and evaluate the response, just as lines 9-15 wait for and evaluate the response to the first set of options.

  - Lines 32-37 carry out the second set of menu options, just as lines 16-21 carry out the first set of menu options.

Enter the file, save it as MENU-6.BAT, and type *menu-6*. The menu now includes the instruction for changing the menu:

```
F1 - Clear the screen
F2 - Display the directory
Press F1 or F2 (or right arrow to change the choices)
```

Press the right-arrow key. Now the display should read:

```
F1 - Display the disk volume label
F2 - Display the DOS version
Press F1 or F2 (or right arrow to change the choices)
```

Press F1. MENU-6.BAT should display the volume label. Type *menu-6* again, and this time press F1 without pressing the right-arrow key. MENU-6.BAT should clear the screen. Both sets of options are available from the same batch file.

This is a great deal of work to offer four choices, especially since they would be handled better by a single four-choice menu. But what if a menu offers 20 options? A batch file described in Chapter 11 does just that: It displays a menu for sending commands to the printer, using this technique to divide the choices into two manageable sets.

The examples in this chapter used a simple two-choice menu to illustrate some of the techniques of designing menus. Chapter 14 combines these techniques with many of the batch files described in following chapters, to set up a system of menus and submenus that you can use for day-to-day operation of your system and all your application programs.

Chapter Summary

- The program REPLY.COM lets you write interactive batch commands that present menus of choices and evaluate the user's response to those choices.

- A batch file can display help information—or any other additional information—at the press of a key.

- A batch file can erase or change part or all of what it displays.

SECTION

II

Customizing
Your System

Controlling
the Environment
and CONFIG.SYS

DOS sets aside a small area of memory to keep track of certain information, such as the names of the directories in the command path and the definition of the system prompt. This area of memory is called the *environment;* you can examine and change it with the Set command.

The term *configuration* refers to the hardware that DOS must control and the way DOS allocates (or *configures*) its memory. A file named CONFIG.SYS in the root directory of the system disk contains *configuration commands* that give DOS instructions about its configuration.

This chapter shows you how to control the environment and CONFIG.SYS to your advantage.

The Environment

The environment contains *environment variables,* each of which has a name and value. The Set command displays, changes, or deletes these environment variables. For example, type a Set command with no parameters to display the name and value of each environment variable:

```
A>set
```

You should see something like this:

```
COMSPEC=A:\COMMAND.COM
PATH=A:\DOS;A:\BATCH;A:\WORD;A:\123;A:\
PROMPT=$p$g
A:\>
```

If you're using a PC/XT or compatible, the drive letter in your display will be *C* rather than *A*. The name of each environment variable is to the left of the equal sign, and the value is to the right:

Name	Value
COMSPEC	A:\COMMAND.COM
PATH	A:\DOS;A:\BATCH;A:\WORD;A:\123;A:\
PROMPT	pg

The COMSPEC (for *command specification*) environment variable tells DOS the drive letter and path name of the program that interprets the commands you type, passes instructions along to DOS, and displays messages. Except in unusual circumstances, this program is COMMAND.COM, as shown in the example above. You needn't concern yourself with the COMSPEC environment variable, except to make sure that you don't erase COMMAND.COM from the specified drive and directory.

The PATH environment variable shows every directory you specified in the most recent Path command. If you haven't specified a command path, there is no PATH environment variable.

The PROMPT environment variable shows the system-prompt definition you specified in the most recent Prompt command. If you haven't defined a system prompt, there is no PROMPT environment variable.

The environment lets DOS keep track of this information regardless of the current drive or directory or what program is running. You can use the Set command to display or change these environment variables, or to create new ones.

Controlling the Environment with the Set Command

A moment ago you typed a Set command with no parameters to display the environment variables. To change an environment variable, you include a parameter that consists of the name of the variable, an equal sign, and the new value. For example, to change the system prompt, you would type *set prompt =* followed by the new prompt definition.

Because you may have a long prompt already defined, you needn't actually type this example, but if you typed *set prompt = [$p]*, the system prompt would be the current drive and directory enclosed in brackets. Displaying the environment variables again with the Set command would show *PROMPT = [$p]*. Typing *set prompt = [$p]* has the same effect as typing *prompt [$p]*; you can change the PATH and PROMPT environment variables with either the Set command or the Path and Prompt commands.

You can delete an environment variable by typing *set* followed by the name of the environment variable and an equal sign. For example, typing *set prompt =* has the same effect as typing *prompt*: It deletes any system-prompt definition and reverts to the standard system prompt (A>, for example).

Using Environment Variables in a Batch File

You can use the name of an environment variable in a batch file to represent the variable's value, much as you use a replaceable parameter. When DOS finds the name of an environment variable enclosed in percent signs (such as *%prompt%*) in a batch file, it replaces the name with the value of the environment variable, just as it replaces *%1* with the first parameter typed with the batch command.

For example, this book suggests several times that you create a batch file to restore your preferred system prompt. Here's a short batch file that uses an environment variable to display the current prompt definition and create a batch file named PROMPTRS.BAT that defines the current prompt. Type the following to create ENV.BAT:

```
A>copy con env.bat
echo off
echo The current prompt definition is %prompt%
echo prompt %prompt% > promptrs.bat
^Z
        1 File(s) copied

A>_
```

Now run ENV.BAT:

```
A>env
```

DOS should display *The current prompt definition is* followed by the definition of the system prompt. The output of the second Echo command—*prompt* followed by the current prompt definition—is redirected to create PROMPTRS.BAT.

Note: If the system prompt is the standard DOS prompt (A>), there is no environment variable named PROMPT; the environment variable *%prompt%* in each Echo command is replaced with nothing (not a space, but no character at all). Nothing, therefore, follows the message *The current prompt definition is* and PROMPTRS.BAT contains just *prompt* (which, of course, defines the standard prompt).

To verify that PROMPTRS.BAT works, type the following to change the system prompt to *COMMAND*:

```
A>prompt COMMAND<Space><Enter>
```

The system prompt changes to COMMAND. If you display the environment variables by typing *set*, they should include *PROMPT = COMMAND*.

Now use the batch command created by ENV.BAT:

```
COMMAND promptrs
```

DOS should echo the word *prompt*, followed by the previous prompt definition, and the system prompt should return to its previous form. You can confirm that the PROMPT environment variable has changed by typing *set* once again.

If you type the ENV.BAT command when your preferred system prompt is defined, you create PROMPTRS.BAT, which restores your preferred system prompt.

Displaying the Directories in the Command Path

If the value of an environment variable consists of more than one part separated by semicolons—such as the value of PATH—DOS treats each part as a separate value. The first time you use the environment variable in a batch file DOS retrieves the first part of the value, the second time you refer to it DOS retrieves the second part, and so on. After DOS has retrieved the last part, it replaces the environment variable with nothing, just as it replaces *%1* with nothing if no parameter was entered with the batch command.

SHOWPATH.BAT is a batch file that displays each directory in the command path by using a For command whose set is *%path%;* the effect is the same as specifying the set as a file name with wildcard characters: DOS retrieves each part of the set in turn.

If your command path includes a lot of directories, SHOWPATH.BAT is a quick way to check which directories it contains and their sequence.

Type the following to create SHOWPATH.BAT:

```
A>copy con showpath.bat
echo off
echo COMMAND PATH DIRECTORIES
for %%p in (%path%) do echo %%p
^Z
        1 File(s) copied

A>_
```

Test it by typing:

```
A>showpath
```

DOS should display something like this:

```
COMMAND PATH DIRECTORIES
A:\DOS
A:\BATCH
A:\WORD
A:\123
A:\

A>_
```

It's much easier to find a directory name in this display than to pick it out of a string of directory names separated by semicolons.

Creating Your Own Environment Variables

You can create your own environment variables with the Set command. For example, type the following two Set commands to create an environment variable named DRIVE and display the result:

```
A>set drive=a:
A>set
```

The display of environment variables includes one that wasn't there before:

```
DRIVE=a:
```

Note that DOS makes the name of an environment variable uppercase, even if you type it in lowercase.

If you ran a batch file now that contained %*drive*% on a line by itself, DOS would replace %*drive*% with *a:*, the command to set the current drive to *A*. By changing the value of the environment variable named *drive* before using this batch command, you could control the current drive it sets. Environment variables give you another way of controlling the behavior of batch commands.

You delete an environment variable that you create just as you delete any other environment variable. Type the following two Set commands to remove DRIVE and display the result:

```
A>set drive=
A>set
```

DRIVE should be gone.

It's also possible to create an environment variable that has multiple values, like PATH. For example, if you typed *set users = matt;mark;luke;john*, then typed *set*, the last environment variable displayed would be *USERS = matt;mark;luke;john*.

An Environmental Concern: The Limits to Growth

Like any other environment, the DOS environment is finite. DOS initially sets aside 160 bytes for it (127 in Version 2), then expands it as you define a command path, define a system prompt, or create environment variables with the Set command. DOS continues to expand the environment up to a theoretical maximum size of 32K bytes, but with catches: The environment cannot be expanded during the execution of a batch file (such as AUTOEXEC.BAT), and as soon as you run a stay-resident program (such as Mode, Print, Sidekick, or ProKey), DOS fixes the environment at its current size.

Because you most likely use either an AUTOEXEC.BAT file or a stay-resident program—or maybe both—the environment is, practically speaking, limited to 160 bytes. DOS displays *Out of environment space* if you try to expand the environment beyond its limit. As you will see, if you haven't already encountered that frustrating message, this can limit the number of directories in your command path or the length of your system-prompt definition.

There isn't much help for this in Version 2, unless you're willing to get rid of your AUTOEXEC.BAT file and type the Path and Prompt commands before you start your stay-resident programs each time you start DOS. There's not much chance of that. But you can probably live with the restriction by settling for a fairly short path and system-prompt definition.

The problem is largely solved in Version 3, because you can expand the environment to nearly 1000 bytes (32768 bytes in DOS 3.2) with a configuration command described later in this chapter under "Increasing the Size of the Environment."

Configuration Commands

The CONFIG.SYS file contains configuration commands that tell DOS how to set up the system. Each time you start or restart the system, DOS reads CONFIG.SYS, carries out the commands it contains, then runs AUTOEXEC.BAT; to change the configuration, therefore, you must change CONFIG.SYS and restart DOS.

The configuration commands tell DOS such things as:

- Which file contains a *device driver*—a program that tells DOS how to control a device such as a RAM disk or a mouse.

- How much memory to set aside for dealing with files.

- How often to check to see if you have pressed Ctrl-C (or Ctrl-Break).

- If you're using Version 3, how large to make the environment.

You'll change CONFIG.SYS to add a new device, to try to improve disk performance, or to increase the size of the environment. Remember, though, changes to CONFIG.SYS don't take effect until you restart DOS.

The Device Configuration Command

Your CONFIG.SYS file might well include some Device commands, including one or more of the following:

- device = c:\dos\ansi.sys

- device = c:\dos\vdisk.sys

- device = mouse.sys

- device = clock.sys

ANSI.SYS and VDISK.SYS are included with DOS. Chapter 3 describes how to use the ANSI.SYS commands to control the display and keyboard, and Chapter 9 describes how to use VDISK.SYS to create a RAM disk. MOUSE.SYS tells DOS how to use a mouse, and CLOCK.SYS most likely tells DOS how to use the clock–calendar on a multifunction accessory card.

If you add a device that requires a device driver, follow the instructions in its documentation to add the Device command to CONFIG.SYS.

A rare, but vexing, situation is possible if you're using Version 2 of DOS. If the last line of CONFIG.SYS is a Device command, make sure that there is a carriage return at the end of the line. If there isn't a carriage return, DOS may reply that it can't find the device driver when you start the system, even though the Device command is correct and the device driver is exactly where it should be.

The Buffers Configuration Command

When a program asks DOS to read some data from a disk, DOS reads from the disk, stores the data in an area of memory called a *buffer*, and then transfers the data to the program. The Buffers configuration command tells DOS how many buffers to create in memory.

The number of buffers can affect the speed of disk operations. Regardless of the amount of data a program requests, DOS reads and stores 512 bytes (one sector) in a buffer. The next time the program asks for data from the disk, DOS first looks in its buffers. If the data is in a buffer, DOS transfers the data to the program without reading from the disk; only if the data isn't in a buffer does DOS read from the disk again. Transferring data from one area of memory (the buffer) to another (the requesting program) is much faster than reading from a disk, so buffers can save time.

If all its buffers are full, DOS reuses the buffer least recently used, so the more buffers DOS uses, the more likely it is that DOS will find the data a program wants in a buffer. Up to a point, increasing the number of buffers speeds up many programs, especially database programs and DOS itself if your directory structure has several levels.

As always, there's a price: Each buffer takes 528 bytes of memory, reducing the memory available to other programs. Assigning too much memory to buffers slows down some programs, and can even prevent a program from running at all. Creating too many buffers can slow the system down even if the program that's running isn't affected, because DOS must search through all buffers for the requested data, which sometimes could take longer than simply reading the data from the disk in the first place.

If you don't specify otherwise, DOS uses two buffers on an IBM PC or PC/XT and computers compatible with those models, or three buffers on an IBM PC/AT and computers compatible with that model.

Tailoring the number of buffers to your system—the type of disk drives, amount of memory, and types of programs you use—can speed disk operations. It may take a bit of tinkering to find the best values. Peter Norton (author of *The Peter Norton Programmer's Guide to the IBM PC*) suggests that you start by putting a Buffers configuration command in CONFIG.SYS that specifies one of the following values:

Computer Model	Buffers =
IBM PC and compatibles	8
IBM PC/XT and compatibles	16
IBM PC/AT and compatibles	32

Add the Buffers command to CONFIG.SYS, restart DOS, and use your system for a while. If you're satisfied with the improvement, you're through; if you're not satisfied, increase the number of buffers by half (substitute 12, 24, and 48 for the preceding numbers), restart DOS, and try your system again. If the increased number of buffers makes the system faster, you should probably be satisfied; more buffers could well just slow things down. If the increased number of buffers makes the system slower, reduce the number of buffers and try again. You can probably find some number of buffers that results in faster system operation than the number that DOS assumes.

The Files and FCBS Configuration Commands

Just as you must open a file folder before you can use the papers it contains, DOS must open a disk file before it can use the data it contains. DOS limits how many files a program can have open at one time; the Files and FCBS configuration commands let you control this limit.

If you don't specify otherwise, DOS assumes a value of 8 for the Files configuration command and 4 for the FCBS command. This should be sufficient for most routine work. Some programs, however, such as a database program or a local area network, may require that you increase one or both of these limits, especially if you also use the Share command that permits file sharing for networks and multitasking programs. The program's manual should tell you what values to specify with the Files and FCBS configuration commands that you put in CONFIG.SYS.

Raising the limit on open files increases the amount of memory that DOS uses by 48 bytes for each additional file.

The Break Configuration Command

The Break configuration command controls how quickly DOS responds when you press Ctrl-C (or Ctrl-Break). DOS normally checks to see if you have pressed Ctrl-C only when it reads from or writes to a disk drive, printer, serial port, or other device. However, if you include *break = on* in CONFIG.SYS, DOS responds to Ctrl-C as soon as you press it.

You can also control Break with the regular DOS Break command. Typing *break on* has the same effect as including *break = on* in CONFIG.SYS, and typing *break off* cancels the effect. Some application programs turn break off and leave it off when they return to DOS. You can check the break status by typing *break*; DOS responds either *BREAK is on* or *BREAK is off.*

If you're working on batch files or programs, or using programs that spend much of their time in computations that don't require a device, setting *break = on* sometimes lets you avoid having to restart DOS.

Increasing the Size of the Environment

The program that communicates with you, displaying prompts and other messages and interpreting the commands that you type, is called a *shell* because it surrounds DOS; you see the shell, not the inner workings of DOS. The shell program that almost all DOS computers use is called COMMAND.COM. The Shell configuration command lets you name the shell program to be used; if you don't specify one, DOS assumes you want to use COMMAND.COM.

Most DOS users don't need to name a shell program, but the Shell command gained an interesting and valuable capability in Version 3.1: If you use it to name COMMAND.COM—a redundant command because DOS almost certainly would use COMMAND.COM anyway—you can use a parameter that increases the size of the environment. This removes a potential restriction on the length of your command path or prompt, and can give you room to define several of your own environment variables.

To increase the size of the environment, put the following Shell configuration command in CONFIG.SYS:

```
shell=command.com /p /e:<size>
```

command.com is the name of the shell program.

/p specifies that the shell program is to be permanent. Be sure to include /P; this ensures that DOS will work just as it always does.

/e:<size> specifies the size of the environment.

- If you're using Version 3.1 of DOS, <size> is in multiples of 16 bytes. If you include a Shell command that names COMMAND.COM but doesn't specify /E, DOS assumes a value of 10 (160 bytes). The maximum you can specify is 62 (992 bytes). Unless memory is scarce, specify at least 32 (512 bytes).

- If you're using Version 3.2 of DOS, <size> is in bytes. You can specify any size from 160 (the value DOS assumes if you don't specify an environment size) through 32768. If you don't specify an environment size, or specify <size> less than 160, DOS sets <size> to 160; if you specify more than 32768, DOS sets <size> to 32768. Unless memory is scarce, specify at least 512 bytes.

Suppose you wanted to set the environment to 800 bytes. If you're using Version 3.1, you would put *shell = command.com /p /e:50* in CONFIG.SYS. If you're using Version 3.2, you would put *shell = command.com /p /e:800* in CONFIG.SYS.

If you're using Version 3, make CONFIG.SYS and AUTOEXEC.BAT read-only with the Attribute command when you're satisfied with their contents. This ensures that neither you nor anyone else who uses your computer can inadvertently change or delete these important files.

Setting Up and Using a RAM Disk

A RAM disk is an area of memory that behaves like another disk drive attached to your computer. You don't need any additional hardware to install a RAM disk, just a program that persuades DOS to treat a portion of memory as a disk drive—a disk drive that happens to be very fast.

Version 3 of DOS includes such a program, called VDISK.SYS (for *virtual disk,* another name for a RAM disk). Most add-on memory cards also include a RAM disk program. Even if you don't have a RAM disk program, you still might want to skim this chapter just to see what you're missing.

It's called a RAM disk because the computer's memory is commonly called RAM, for *Random Access Memory.* This term is a tenacious misnomer: Access to memory, in fact, is quite the opposite of random; if it weren't, finding a program or data in memory would be practically impossible. But there's precedent in everyday language for such misnomers: Some cities named Mount Pleasant, after all, are neither on a mountain nor remarkably pleasant. So *RAM disk* it is, a short, punchy name that's easier to say (and remember) than *electronically simulated rotating memory device.*

You can use a RAM disk just as you would use a real disk drive because, as far as DOS is concerned, a RAM disk is just another disk drive. You can create files and subdirectories on it, copy files to and from it, even run the Check Disk (chkdsk) command on it. And a RAM disk is *really* fast, much faster than a real disk drive, because it has no moving parts. Using a RAM disk not only saves time, it also saves wear and tear on your real disk drives.

So what's the catch? Well, a RAM disk requires memory. Because the memory used by a RAM disk isn't available to DOS or other programs, your system must have enough memory to run DOS and all your application programs without the memory you assign to the RAM disk.

And mark this well: The contents of most RAM disks are lost when power is removed from the system or when you restart DOS. So if there is a power failure, you lose any work you have done using the RAM disk that you didn't copy to a real disk. More to the point, it's all too easy to work for several hours and then, relieved at finally finishing, shut down without copying the changed files to a real disk. It's difficult to describe the emotions that follow when you realize what you have done. Try to avoid learning firsthand.

Defining a RAM Disk

If your system can spare the memory and you're using Version 3 of DOS, you can define a RAM disk by putting a DEVICE = VDISK.SYS configuration command in CONFIG.SYS, then restarting the system. The command parameters specify the capacity, sector size, and maximum number of directory entries of the RAM disk.

The VDISK.SYS program automatically assigns the next available sequential drive letter to the RAM disk. For example, if you have two floppy disk drives (A and B), the RAM disk would be drive C; if you have a fixed disk (C), the RAM disk would be drive D. Other programs may require you to assign a drive letter to your RAM disk.

If you have a different RAM disk program, such as SUPERDRV.COM from AST Research, Inc., the details of the command description here won't necessarily apply to your program. Check the manual that came with your RAM disk program for differences.

The DEVICE = VDISK.SYS command has four parameters:

device = vdisk.sys <size> <sector> <directory> /E

<size> is the capacity of the RAM disk in Kbytes. The minimum is 64, and the maximum is the total available memory on your computer. Be sure to leave enough memory to run DOS and your application programs. If you specify less than 64 or more than the total available memory, DOS sets <size> to 64.

<sector> is the size of each sector in bytes. You can specify 128, 256, or 512. A sector on a real disk, regardless of type, contains 512 bytes. If you specify an incorrect value, DOS sets <sector> to 128.

<directory> specifies the number of directory entries allowed on the RAM disk. You can specify any value from 2 through 512. Each directory entry takes up 32 bytes of the RAM disk; DOS increases the number of directory entries, if necessary, to make the directory occupy an integral number of sectors. If you specify an incorrect value, DOS sets <directory> to 64.

/E tells DOS to use extended memory for the RAM disk. This parameter is valid only if you're using an IBM PC/AT or compatible computer and have installed extended memory. A RAM disk in extended memory doesn't reduce the amount of memory available to DOS or application programs. If you specify /E but aren't using an IBM PC/AT or compatible computer with extended memory, DOS displays an error message and doesn't create the RAM disk.

For example, assume that VDISK.SYS is in the directory \DOS on the floppy disk in drive A. To define a 128K RAM disk with 256-byte sectors and room for 64 directory entries, you would include the following command in CONFIG.SYS:

```
device=a:\dos\vdisk.sys 128 256 64
```

To define a 1000K RAM disk with 512-byte sectors and room for 200 directory entries in extended memory on an IBM PC/AT or compatible computer, you would include the following command in CONFIG.SYS:

```
device=a:\dos\vdisk.sys 1000 512 200 /e
```

You can define more than one RAM disk by including more than one DEVICE = VDISK.SYS command in CONFIG.SYS. Each additional RAM disk will be assigned the next available drive letter.

Using a RAM Disk

To take advantage of the speed of the RAM disk, use the Copy command to copy the data files, batch files, and programs you'll be working with to the RAM disk. Be sure to leave enough unused space on the RAM disk, however, to allow for the increased size of files you edit and any backup files that your application programs may create.

To simplify setting up the RAM disk, write a batch file (or batch files) to copy the files and programs you need to work on a project. If you consistently use the same setup, put the Copy commands in AUTOEXEC.BAT so that the RAM disk will be ready to use when DOS first displays the system prompt.

Note: You may not be able to use a copy-protected program from a RAM disk; check the program's manual for instructions or warnings.

If you use a RAM disk regularly, a couple of cautions are in order:

- Back up your work frequently to a real disk. A power failure—or if you forget you're using a RAM disk and turn off the system—means that all your work is lost.

- Leave room for enough directory entries. Using all the directory entries has the same effect as filling the disk. Remember, most word processors and text editors create backup files, so you'll need up to twice as many directory entries as the number of files you work on. Some application programs create temporary files that they delete before returning to DOS; each temporary file also requires a directory entry. A directory entry requires only 32 bytes, so you can safely specify 64 directory entries; that would take up only 2K bytes of the RAM disk and should avoid the problem of filling the disk. If you'll be working with many small files or using several different application programs, specify at least 128 directory entries.

Creating a RAM Disk with a Batch File

There may be times when you'd like to define another RAM disk, or maybe work without the RAM disk for a while so that another program could use the memory, but it's too much trouble to change CONFIG.SYS and restart DOS. You can avoid most of this trouble with the batch file described here—VDISK.BAT—which automates creating a RAM disk: You tell VDISK.BAT what sort of RAM disk you want, and VDISK.BAT takes care of changing CONFIG.SYS and restarting DOS.

You can use VDISK.BAT to add a RAM disk, delete all RAM disks, or delete all RAM disks currently defined and start over with a different RAM disk. Before it restarts DOS to carry out your instructions, VDISK.BAT gives you a chance to change your mind. If you enter *vdisk* with no parameters, it displays instructions and tells you what RAM disks are currently defined.

The batch file is called VDISK.BAT because it works with VDISK.SYS, which comes with Version 3 of DOS. If you don't have Version 3, you can modify VDISK.BAT to work with any RAM disk program that uses a Device command in CONFIG.SYS to set up the RAM disk.

Restarting DOS with a Program

VDISK.BAT resets the system with the program RESET.COM, which has the same effect as pressing Ctrl-Alt-Del. You don't have to use RESET.COM, but it's a small touch that makes VDISK.BAT more convenient. If you prefer not to use RESET.COM, skip this topic and go to "Entering VDISK.BAT"; the description of VDISK.BAT includes instructions for adding a prompt that tells the user when to press Ctrl-Alt-Del.

You create RESET.COM with Debug, using the procedure described in Chapter 5. If you haven't yet gone through the examples in Chapter 5, you might do so before continuing here.

Using your text editor, word processor, or Edlin, create a file named RESET.SCR and enter the lines shown in Figure 9-1.

```
 1:   a 100
 2:   mov   ax,40
 3:   mov   ds,ax
 4:   mov   ax,1234
 5:   mov   [0072],ax
 6:   jmp   f000:e05b
 7:
 8:   r cx
 9:   10
10:   n reset.com
11:   w
12:   q
```

Figure 9-1. RESET.SCR: Restarting DOS with a program.

Proofread RESET.SCR against Figure 9-1 carefully, making certain that line 7 is blank and the last line is *q;* if there is a mistake in either of these lines, you'll have to restart DOS when you try to create RESET.COM. When you're sure that RESET.SCR is correct, save it and type the following Debug command:

```
A>debug < reset.scr
```

DOS should respond as shown in Figure 9-2.

```
-a 100
xxxx:0100 mov ax,40
xxxx:0103 mov ds,ax
xxxx:0105 mov ax,1234
xxxx:0108 mov [0072],ax
xxxx:010B jmp f000:e05b
xxxx:0110
-r cx
CX 0000
:10
-n reset.com
-w
Writing 0010 bytes
-q
```

Figure 9-2. DOS response to creating RESET.SCR.

If nothing seems to happen and the keyboard refuses to respond, restart DOS. Load RESET.SCR with your text editor or word processor and proofread it carefully against Figure 9-1. Correct any errors and enter the Debug command again.

If DOS displays a series of commands and responses after you enter the Debug command, proofread the display against Figure 9-2. If they don't agree, go back and edit RESET.SCR again; proofread it against Figure 9-1, correct any differences, then save it and enter the Debug command again.

Before you test RESET.COM, make sure your system is ready to shut down. In particular, if you're using a RAM disk, copy any files you have changed to a real disk. Now type *reset.* The system should respond just as if you pressed Ctrl-Alt-Del.

Entering VDISK.BAT

VDISK.BAT is a long batch file; many of its 60 lines are devoted to checking for errors, displaying messages, and creating temporary files that allow you to change your mind at the last minute. Even if you don't think you want to use VDISK.BAT, reading through its commands and the explanations that follow might give you some ideas to use in other batch files.

Figure 9-3 shows the commands in VDISK.BAT.

```
 1:    echo off
 2:    a:
 3:    cd \
 4:    if "%1"=="none" goto NONE
 5:    if "%1"=="new"  goto NEW_OR_ADD
 6:    if "%1"=="add"  goto NEW_OR_ADD
 7:    echo <Alt-255>
 8:    echo {ESC}[1mCommand                        Result{ESC}[m
 9:    echo vdisk add {size} {sec} {dir}  Add this RAM disk
       and restart
10:    echo vdisk new {size} {sec} {dir}  Define just this RAM
       disk and restart
11:    echo vdisk none                    Restart with no RAM
       disk
12:    goto STATUS
13: :NONE
14:    copy config.$$$ config.new > nul
15:    goto RESET
16: :NEW_OR_ADD
17:    if not "%2"=="" if not "%3"=="" if not "%4"=="" goto OK
18:    echo {ESC}[7mYou must specify at least 3 VDISK
       parameters.{ESC}[m
19:    goto END
20: :OK
21:    if %1==new copy config.$$$ config.new > nul
22:    if %1==add copy config.sys config.new > nul
23:    if %1==add if exist vdisk.log copy vdisk.log log.new > nul
24:    echo device=c:\dos\vdisk.sys %2 %3 %4 %5 >> config.new
25:    if "%5"=="" echo %2K disk with %3-byte sectors and %4
       directory entries >> log.new
26:    if "%5"=="/e" echo %2K disk with %3-byte sectors and %4
       directory entries in extended memory >> log.new
27: :RESET
28:    cls
29:    echo                  <ALT-7>{ESC}[7m Warning {ESC}[m
30:    echo If you continue, your system will be reset
31:    echo with the following RAM disks defined:
32:    echo <Alt-255>
33:    if exist log.new type log.new
34:    if not exist log.new echo ** None **
35:    echo <Alt-255>
36:    echo Press F1 to continue; any other
37:    echo response cancels this VDISK command.
38:    reply
39:    if errorlevel 59 if not errorlevel 60 goto DO_IT
40:    echo <Alt-255>
41:    echo ** Canceled **
42:    if exist log.new erase log.new
43:    erase config.new
44:    goto STATUS
45: :DO_IT
46:    attrib -r config.sys
47:    erase config.sys
48:    rename config.new config.sys
49:    attrib +r config.sys
50:    if exist vdisk.log attrib -r vdisk.log
51:    if exist vdisk.log erase vdisk.log
52:    if exist log.new rename log.new vdisk.log
53:    if exist vdisk.log attrib +r vdisk.log
54:    reset
55: :STATUS
56:    echo <Alt-255>
57:    echo {ESC}[7m Active RAM Disks {ESC}[m
58:    if exist vdisk.log type vdisk.log
59:    if not exist vdisk.log echo ** None **
60: :END
```

Figure 9-3. VDISK.BAT: Automatically defining a RAM disk.

How VDISK.BAT Works

VDISK.BAT uses two files to keep track of your RAM disks:

- CONFIG.$$$. Contains all the commands you want in CONFIG.SYS except those that create a RAM disk (such as *device = config.sys*). VDISK.BAT copies CONFIG.$$$ to CONFIG.SYS when you delete all RAM disks. This file should at least have the line *device = ansi.sys* in it.

- VDISK.LOG. Contains a description of each RAM disk currently defined in CONFIG.SYS. The presence or absence of VDISK.LOG tells VDISK.BAT whether CONFIG.SYS contains a command that defines a RAM disk: If VDISK.LOG doesn't exist, VDISK.BAT assumes that no RAM disk is currently defined; if VDISK.LOG does exist, VDISK.BAT assumes that at least one RAM disk is defined.

Both CONFIG.$$$ and VDISK.LOG are in the root directory. You create CONFIG.$$$ before you use VDISK.BAT for the first time. VDISK.BAT creates and deletes the VDISK.LOG file as required.

The following explanations describe the line-by-line operation of VDISK.BAT:

- Lines 2 and 3 change the current drive to drive A and the current directory to the root. If you're using a fixed disk, change line 2 to *c:* (or to the drive from which DOS normally starts, if different).

- Lines 4-6 check the first parameter; if it is *none,* VDISK.BAT goes to delete all RAM disk definitions and restart DOS. If the parameter is *new* or *add,* VDISK.BAT goes to define a RAM disk. If it is none of those, VDISK.BAT continues with line 7.

- Lines 7-12 display instructions for using VDISK.BAT, then go to display the RAM disks currently defined and return to DOS. There are 23 spaces in line 8; line up the words *Add, Define,* and *Restart* in lines 9-11. Although lines 9-11 are shown on two lines, enter each as one line.

- Lines 14 and 15 delete all commands that define a RAM disk from CONFIG.SYS by copying CONFIG.$$$ to CONFIG.SYS, then go to reset the system. This restarts DOS with no RAM disks defined.

- Line 17 goes to define a RAM disk only if three parameters are specified after the first. This test is made because VDISK.BAT carries out this command only if the first parameter is *new* or *add* (checked in lines 5 and 6), and it takes at least three parameters to define a RAM disk.

- Lines 18 and 19 display an error message and return to DOS if you didn't specify three parameters after *new* or *add.* Although line 18 is shown on two lines, enter it as one line.

- Line 21 makes a temporary copy of CONFIG.$$$, which is named CONFIG.NEW, that contains no commands that define a RAM disk if the first parameter is *new*. This deletes any RAM disks currently defined.

- Line 22 makes a temporary copy of CONFIG.SYS called CONFIG.NEW that contains any current RAM disk definitions if the first parameter is *add*. This adds the RAM disk being created to any RAM disks currently defined.

- Line 23 makes a temporary copy of VDISK.LOG (if it exists) called LOG.NEW if the first parameter is *add*. Thus, the RAM disk being created will be added to any existing RAM disk, but will be the only RAM disk if none is currently defined.

- Line 24 adds a VDISK.SYS command that defines the RAM disk being created to the temporary copy of CONFIG.SYS created in line 21 or 22. As you'll see, the temporary file is used so that you can change your mind at the last minute and leave your current CONFIG.SYS file unchanged.

- Lines 25 and 26 write a description of the RAM disk being created in VDISK.LOG. The only difference between these lines is that line 26 adds the words "in extended memory" if you include the /e parameter (%5 in the VDISK.BAT command). There's no check for /E (or any other value for this parameter), so if you enter anything other than /e, VDISK.BAT doesn't put the description in VDISK.LOG but does put the DEVICE = VDISK.SYS command in CONFIG.SYS. This causes a discrepancy between VDISK.LOG and CONFIG.SYS; you can correct it by entering another VDISK.BAT command that specifies either the *none* or *new* option. Although lines 25 and 26 are both shown on two lines, enter each as a single line.

- Lines 28-37 clear the screen, warn you that the system is going to be reset, show you the RAM disks that will be defined if you continue, and prompt you to press F1 to reset the system. Lines 33 and 34 show you the RAM disks that will be defined either by displaying VDISK.NEW (the temporary version of VDISK.LOG) or—if there is no VDISK.NEW—by displaying ** *None* **.

- Lines 38 and 39 wait for you to press a key and go to reset the system if you press F1. (You created REPLY.COM in Chapter 7.)

- Lines 40-44 display a blank line and ** *Canceled* **, erase any temporary files, then go to display the RAM disks currently defined and return to DOS. Because all the changes so far have been limited to temporary files, CONFIG.SYS and VDISK.LOG are unaffected.

- Line 46 removes the read-only attribute from CONFIG.SYS. In order for VDISK.BAT to work properly, CONFIG.SYS and CONFIG.$$$ must be identical except for commands that define RAM disks, and VDISK.LOG must contain an accurate description of the RAM disks defined in CONFIG.SYS; to ensure that the files remain accurate, they are kept read-only except when VDISK.BAT itself changes them.

- Lines 47-49 make the temporary copy of CONFIG.SYS the real thing by erasing CONFIG.SYS and changing the name of CONFIG.NEW to CONFIG.SYS, and make the new copy read-only so that it can't be changed inadvertently.

- Line 50 removes the read-only attribute from VDISK.LOG if it exists. This line and the next three check to see whether VDISK.LOG exists, because there is no VDISK.LOG if no RAM disk is currently defined, and DOS displays an error message if you enter an Attribute command for a file that doesn't exist.

- Line 51 erases VDISK.LOG if it exists.

- Line 52 makes the temporary copy of VDISK.LOG (if there is one) the real thing by changing the name of LOG.NEW to VDISK.LOG.

- Line 53 makes the new copy of VDISK.LOG read-only (if it exists).

- Line 54 resets the system. If you aren't using RESET.COM, replace *reset* with the following two commands:

```
echo Press {Ctrl-Alt-Del} to reset the system
reply
```

Keep in mind that if you make this change, then don't reset the system at this point, VDISK.LOG won't accurately describe the RAM disks defined in CONFIG.SYS and VDISK.BAT won't work properly. Using RESET.COM guarantees that if you reply to the warning prompt with F1, the system will be reset and VDISK.LOG will be accurate.

- Lines 56-59 display the RAM disks currently defined either by displaying VDISK.LOG or—if there is no VDISK.LOG—by displaying ** *None* **.

Testing VDISK.BAT

Before you test VDISK.BAT, do the following to prepare the files it uses:

1. If CONFIG.SYS contains any commands that define a RAM disk, delete them. Don't use Edlin to make this change, because it puts a Ctrl-Z (^Z) character at the end of the file and VDISK.BAT won't work correctly.

2. Copy CONFIG.SYS to CONFIG.$$$.

3. Type *attrib +r config.** to make CONFIG.SYS and CONFIG.$$$ read-only.

4. If there is a file in the root directory named VDISK.LOG, rename or erase it.

After these steps, VDISK.BAT assumes the first time you run it that there is no RAM disk command in CONFIG.SYS (which should be correct) because there is no file named VDISK.LOG in the root directory.

If you created VDISK.BAT on a RAM disk, copy it to a real disk before proceeding. Now you're ready to test VDISK.BAT. Type the command with no parameters:

```
A>vdisk
```

VDISK.BAT should respond by displaying its instructions and any RAM disks currently defined:

```
Command                      Result
vdisk add {size} {sec} {dir} Add this RAM disk and restart
vdisk new {size} {sec} {dir} Define just this RAM disk and restart
vdisk none                   Restart with no RAM disk
 Active RAM Disks 
** None **
```

Type the following to define a 64K RAM disk with 128-byte sectors and room for 32 directory entries:

```
A>vdisk add 64 128 32
```

VDISK.BAT clears the screen, beeps, and warns you that if you continue it will reset the system:

```
 Warning 
If you continue, your system will be reset
with the following RAM disks defined:

64K disk with 128-byte sectors and 32 directory entries

Press F1 to continue; any other
response cancels this VDISK command.
```

Press the spacebar to cancel the command. VDISK.BAT displays:

```
** Canceled **

 Active RAM Disks 
** None **

A>_
```

This time you'll go through with it. Type the following to define a 128K RAM disk with 512-byte sectors and room for 64 directory entries:

`A>vdisk add 128 512 64`

Again, VDISK.BAT warns you that if you continue it will reset the system. This time press F1. The system should restart and, in a few moments, display the system prompt.

To verify that things went as they should, first type *vdisk*; VDISK.BAT should display its instructions, then a description of the RAM disk currently active:

`128K disk with 512-byte sectors and 64 directory entries`

All this really tells you is that the file VDISK.LOG contains this line. Verify the existence of the RAM disk by displaying its directory. If you have two floppy disk drives, type *dir c:*; if you're using a fixed disk, type *dir d:*. You should see the empty root directory of the RAM disk.

Sometimes you might want more than one RAM disk. If your system has at least 256K of memory, type the following to add a 64K RAM disk with 256-byte sectors and room for 32 directory entries:

`A>vdisk add 64 256 32`

After the warning, press F1. After the system resets and DOS displays the system prompt, type *vdisk*. Now you should see two descriptions:

```
128K disk with 512-byte sectors and 64 directory entries
64K disk with 256-byte sectors and 32 directory entries
```

Verify the existence of this new RAM disk by displaying its directory. If you have two floppy disk drives, type *dir d:*; if you're using a fixed disk, type *dir e:*. You should see the empty root directory of the RAM disk.

Now decide what sort of RAM disk you would like to routinely use on your system, and create it with the *new* option of VDISK. For example, to create a 360K RAM disk with 512-byte sectors and room for 128 directory entries, you would type *vdisk new 360 512 128*. To create a 1-megabyte RAM disk in extended memory with 512-byte sectors and room for 200 directory entries, you would type *vdisk new 1024 512 200 /e*. To operate with no RAM disks, you would type *vdisk none*.

If VDISK.BAT Just Won't Work

If VDISK.BAT displays all the correct prompts but doesn't create a RAM disk when you reset the system, chances are that you worked on CONFIG.SYS with a text editor that puts a Ctrl-Z at the end of the file. It's easy to get rid of the offending Ctrl-Z with the Type command.

Because the Type command stops displaying a file the first time it encounters a Ctrl-Z, you can make a copy of a file up to the first Ctrl-Z it contains by redirecting the output of the Type command to another file. The following commands get rid of the offending Ctrl-Z by copying CONFIG.SYS to a file named CONFIG.TMP and then deleting the original CONFIG.SYS and renaming the new copy:

```
A>type config.sys > config.tmp     Get rid of the Ctrl-Z
A>attrib -r config.sys             So you can erase CONFIG.SYS
A>erase config.sys                 Get rid of the original
A>rename config.tmp config.sys     Now you've got a good copy
A>attrib +r config.sys             Protect this version
```

Now try VDISK.BAT again; it should work properly. If you have a text editor or word processor that adds a Ctrl-Z to the end of a file, you'll have to repeat this process each time you change CONFIG.SYS; you might want to put these commands in a batch file to simplify the cleanup.

Some Closing Points about VDISK.BAT

Although VDISK.BAT checks to make sure that you enter at least three parameters, it has no way of knowing that you have entered correct parameters. It accepts *vdisk add mairzie doats and doazie doats* as readily as *vdisk add 128 256 32 /e*. DOS may not be able to execute such a command, so be sure to double-check the final verification that VDISK.BAT displays before you press F1 to reset the system.

Unless you tell it otherwise, DOS only recognizes drive letters *a:* through *e:*. If you think you might need more drives than that, put a Lastdrive configuration command in CONFIG.SYS; *lastdrive = g*, for example, would let you use four RAM disks on a PC/XT or compatible machine, and five RAM disks on a two-floppy disk system.

Remember that the root directory must contain CONFIG.$$$, a duplicate of CONFIG.SYS with no RAM disk commands. So, if you change CONFIG.SYS after you start using VDISK.BAT, be sure that you copy CONFIG.SYS to CONFIG.$$$; if you don't do this, the changes you made to CONFIG.SYS will be lost the first time you use VDISK.BAT with either the *new* or *none* options. Don't use Edlin to work on either CONFIG.SYS or CONFIG.$$$, because it puts a Ctrl-Z (^Z) character at the end of the file.

And it's worth repeating two cautions:

- Be sure to back up your work frequently from a RAM disk to a real disk to protect yourself from your own forgetfulness as well as from power failures.

- If you're going to be working with many files or several application programs, specify at least 128 directory entries on your RAM disk.

You wouldn't want to lavish the sort of effort represented by VDISK.BAT on all your batch files, but it shows just how much you can do with DOS. Taking the extra time to anticipate mistakes, display informative or reassuring messages, and provide graceful escape routes adds touches that even some professional application programs lack.

And after using a batch file that looks good while it saves you time, it feels good to lean back and say, "I did that."

CHAPTER
10

Display It Your Way

You stare at the screen a lot. If you're not already intimately familiar with it, you will be. Except for the occasional beep, DOS can only communicate with you by displaying something. Anything you can do to improve this communication shows up right away.

The basic qualities of your display are fixed: its size, shape, and resolution; whether it can display color or graphics; and its screen color, if it's a monochrome monitor. But you can still make your screen more communicative and easier to read. This chapter shows you how to:

- Make the system prompt attractive and useful.

- Control the appearance of the cursor.

- Blank the screen.

- Change the foreground and background colors if you have a color monitor.

Sprucing Up the System Prompt

The Prompt command lets you define a system prompt as spartan or baroque as you like. But keep a couple of things in mind as you tailor the prompt: You want to find the information at a glance, not hunt for it, so the system prompt should be informative but not too busy; and resist the temptation to make the prompt cute—you'll read it hundreds or even thousands of times, and something terribly clever gets old fast.

For demonstration purposes, this chapter defines a system prompt that tells you three things (each is followed by the special code the Prompt command uses to represent it):

- The current drive and directory (*$p*)

- The time (*$t*)

- The date (*$d*)

As you'll see, the following examples treat the current drive and directory more prominently than the date and time because you'll need that information more often.

Some Sample System Prompts

Before you try the following examples, make sure that CONFIG.SYS contains the line *device = ansi.sys,* and that ANSI.SYS is on your system disk. These examples assume that the current directory is \BATCH on drive A; if you have a directory with that name, you might change to it. Otherwise, substitute your current directory name for \BATCH in the examples.

As a starting point in designing a system prompt, type the following Prompt command to display the time, date, and current drive and directory:

`A>prompt $t$d$p`

DOS displays the following prompt (the time and date will be different):

`10:39:09.54Fri 10-16-1987A:\BATCH_`

That's a pretty rough beginning. Everything runs together, making it hard to pick out the information you want. The time is too detailed—even at a track meet, time is kept only to the nearest tenth of a second if a human being holds the stopwatch. You've lost 36 characters from the command line; the cursor is almost in the middle of the screen. Not only that, the prompt runs right into the command you enter. If you typed *dir ∗.com ¦ sort*, for example, the command line would look like this:

`10:39:34.15Fri 10-16-1987A:\BATCHdir ∗.com ¦ sort`

This obviously isn't the ideal solution. But you can correct several problems pretty easily:

- Make the time easier to read by putting three *$h* (backspace) characters after *$t* to erase the hundredths of a second.

- Break the prompt into three lines with *$_* (carriage return), putting the time, date, and current drive and directory on separate lines.

- Separate your commands from the prompt by typing a space after the last character.

Type *prompt* to change the system prompt to the more manageable *A>*, then type the following Prompt command:

`A>prompt $t$h$h$h$_$d$_$p<space>`

Breaking down the elements of this Prompt commmand:

Prompt	Description
$t	Display the time.
hh$h	Backspace three times, erasing the hundredths of a second.
$_	Move to the next line.
$d	Display the date.
$_	Move to the next line.
$p	Display the current drive and directory name.
<space>	To separate the system prompt from the command you type.

This system prompt is much easier to read:

```
10:41:58
Fri 10-16-1987
A:\BATCH _
```

You can find the information much more quickly, it's more obvious where your command will appear when you type it, and you're only giving up nine characters of the command line. (If you want to get rid of the seconds, too, you could put six backspaces—*hhhhhh*—instead of three in the Prompt command.)

But this system prompt takes three lines; to see how fast it eats up the screen, press the Enter key a few times. You can solve that without giving up any of the information.

You'll need to know the current drive and directory far more often than the time or date, but it's still handy to have the time and date on the screen. Why not display the time and date in a fixed location—the upper right corner of the screen is nicely visible, yet out of the way—and repeat the current drive and directory with each new system·prompt?

The ANSI.SYS commands for saving the cursor position, moving the cursor, and restoring the saved cursor position let you do this. Instead of using *$_* to move to the next line, use two ANSI.SYS Move Cursor commands to display the time and date in the upper right corner of the screen. You can keep track of the position of the command line by saving the cursor position before you display the time and date, and restoring the cursor position before you display the current drive and directory.

Type the following Prompt command; because it's quite long, it's shown broken down into each part of the command rather than on the command line, but enter it as a single command (don't enter the explanations listed at the right):

prompt	
$e[s	Save the current cursor position.
$e[1;67H	Move the cursor to row 1, column 67.
$d	Display the date.
$e[2;67H	Move the cursor to row 2, column 67.
$t	Display the time.
hh$h	Backspace three times, erasing the hundredths of a second.
$e[u	Restore the saved cursor position.
$p	Display the current drive and directory name.
<space>	To separate the system prompt from the command you type.

You're going to re-use this Prompt command in a just a moment, so don't type anything after you have pressed the Enter key; don't even press the Enter key again.

Now DOS displays the system prompt in two different parts of the screen. The time and date are in the upper right corner of the screen, starting at column 67 in rows 1 and 2, and the current drive and directory are displayed on the command line:

```
                                                            Fri 10-16-1987
                                                            10:50:07
```

`A:\BATCH _`

Note: If DOS displays only part of the prompt and responds *Out of environment space,* there isn't room in the environment for a system-prompt definition this long (44 bytes). As Chapter 8 explained, there's a limit to the size of the environment, where DOS stores the system-prompt definition. If you're using Version 3 of DOS and haven't put a Shell command in CONFIG.SYS to expand the environment, take the time now to read "Increasing the Size of the Environment" in Chapter 8, then come back and finish this chapter. If you're using Version 2, you'll either have to make room by shortening your command path, or settle for a shorter system-prompt definition (try *prompt $e[7m $p $e[m<space>* — yes, there's a space before and after *$p*).

This two-part system prompt meets the requirements discussed earlier, but there's one last change: If you display the current drive and directory in reverse video, they'll stand out even better. This requires adding a couple of ANSI.SYS commands to the Prompt command. Because the changes occur close to the end of the command, however, you don't have to retype the whole thing; press F3 and DOS should redisplay the last Prompt command you entered:

```
                                                            Fri 10-16-1987
                                                            10:55:03
```

`A:\BATCH prompt $e[s$e[1;67H$d$e[2;67H$t$h$h$h$e[u$p _`

If you haven't used the editing keys before to reuse the last command, the technique is described in Chapter 12.

Press the Backspace key three times; this should erase the space and *$p*:

```
                                                            Fri 10-16-1987
                                                            10:55:03
```

`A:\BATCH prompt $e[s$e[1;67H$d$e[2;67H$t$h$h$h$e[u_`

You're going to finish the command with an ANSI.SYS Set Attribute command to start reverse video, *$p* to display the current drive and directory, another ANSI.SYS Set Attribute command to turn off all display attributes, and a space (don't enter the explanations at the right):

`$e[7m`	Start reverse video.
`$p`	Display the current drive and directory name.
`$e[m`	Restore normal display attributes.
`<space>`	To separate the system prompt from the command you type.

Type the new characters at the end of the previous command:

Fri 10-16-1987
10:56:57

```
A:\BATCH prompt $e[s$e[1;67H$d$e[2;67H$t$h$h$h$e[u$e[7m$p$e[m<space>
```

Now the current drive and directory really stand out:

Fri 10-16-1987
10:56:58

A:\BATCH _

This satisfies the most important goals of a system prompt: It's informative, direct, and easy to read. It doesn't use up the screen too quickly,
because only the current drive and directory are displayed on the command line. If you like this system prompt, take a few moments to put it in
a batch file now while it's still fresh in your mind. Later, you can copy it
to AUTOEXEC.BAT, to the batch file that restores your system prompt
(call it PROMPTRS.BAT), or wherever else you might want it.

Spicing Up the System Prompt with a Bit of Color

Color can be overused to disadvantage, and you might be bumping up
against the size limit of the environment, but if you're using a color display you can add a couple of ANSI.SYS commands to polish your system
prompt. The form of the prompt is unchanged, but the date and time are
displayed in cyan, and the current drive and directory are displayed in
high-intensity yellow on a red background.

Again, the Prompt command is shown broken down into its elements;
enter it as a single command (don't enter the explanations listed at
the right):

prompt	
$e[s	Save the current cursor position.
$e[1;67H	Move the cursor to row 1, column 67.
$e[36m	Set the foreground color to cyan.
$d	Display the date.
$e[2;67H	Move the cursor to row 2, column 67.
$t	Display the time.
hh$h	Backspace three times, erasing the hundredths of a second.
$e[u	Restore the saved cursor position.
$e[1;33;41m	Set the foreground to high-intensity yellow and the background to red.
$p	Display the current drive and directory name.
$e[m	Restore normal display attributes.
<space>	To separate the prompt from the command you type.

This system prompt has the same form as the previous one, but it's displayed in color.

The relative boldness of the colors suits the prominence of what they display. Other colors might suit you better; try some different combinations by changing the ANSI.SYS commands. When you find an effect you like, save the Prompt command in a batch file.

Enough of the Prompt command. In addition to the system prompt, what else is always on the screen? The cursor, of course.

Don't Curse the Cursor

The standard cursor is a blinking underline, but this standard is set in software, not hardware. You may use application programs whose cursor fills the entire character space or half the character space or gets rid of the cursor altogether; some programs use several different types of cursors. The three short programs described here give you the same sort of control over the cursor. They work with all models of the IBM PC and other compatible machines.

The following programs don't affect the blinking, by the way; that *is* fixed in the hardware.

Creating the Programs

You create these programs with Debug, using the procedure described in Chapter 5. If you haven't yet gone through the examples in Chapter 5, you might do so before continuing here.

The description of each program includes two figures. The first shows the contents of the Debug script file you create, and the second shows how DOS should respond when you redirect the input of the Debug command to the script file. Proofread the script files carefully, paying particular attention to the blank line that follows the program statements and making sure that the last line is *q*; if there is a mistake in either of these lines, you'll have to restart DOS when you try to create the COM file.

If nothing seems to happen and the keyboard refuses to respond when you enter the Debug command, restart DOS. Load the script file into your text editor or word processor and proofread it carefully against the figure that shows its contents. After correcting any errors you might have found, enter the Debug command again.

If DOS displays a series of commands and responses after you enter the Debug command, proofread the display carefully against the figure that shows the DOS response to creating the program. If they don't agree, go back and edit the script file again; proofread it carefully against the figure that shows the contents of the script file, then save it and enter the Debug command again.

Would You Prefer a Block Cursor?

Some computers use the type of cursor that fills the entire character space. BIGCURS.COM is a program that changes the cursor to such a solid block. You can change back to the normal cursor with NORMCURS.COM, described next.

Using your text editor, word processor, or Edlin, create a file named BIGCURS.SCR and enter the lines shown in Figure 10-1 (the line numbers are for reference only).

```
 1:  a 100
 2:  mov  ah,1
 3:  mov  cx,10C
 4:  int  10
 5:  int  20
 6:
 7:  r cx
 8:  9
 9:  n bigcurs.com
10:  w
11:  q
```

Figure 10-1. BIGCURS.SCR: Making the cursor a block.

Make certain that line 6 of BIGCURS.SCR is blank and that the last line is a q. When you're sure the file is correct, save it and type the following Debug command:

A>debug < bigcurs.scr

DOS should respond as shown in Figure 10-2.

```
-a 100
xxxx:0100 mov ah,1
xxxx:0102 mov cx,10C
xxxx:0105 int 10
xxxx:0107 int 20
xxxx:0109
-r cx
CX 0000
:9
-n bigcurs.com
-w
Writing 0009 bytes
-q
```

Figure 10-2. DOS response to creating BIGCURS.COM.

If your screen doesn't agree with Figure 10-2, see "Creating the Programs" above for instructions. If your screen agrees with Figure 10-2, type *bigcurs*; the cursor should change to a flashing block.

Restoring the Normal Cursor

Sometimes when an application program changes the shape of the cursor, the cursor stays a hyphen or solid block when the application returns to DOS. You can usually clear the screen and restore the normal cursor with a Mode command; just type *mode mono* or *mode co80*, depending on what sort of monitor you're using. NORMCURS.COM is a short program that also restores the normal cursor, but does it more quickly and doesn't clear the screen.

Using your text editor, word processor, or Edlin, create a file named NORMCURS.SCR and enter the lines shown in Figure 10-3.

```
 1:  a 100
 2:  mov  ah,0f
 3:  int  10
 4:  cmp  al,7
 5:  jz   10d
 6:  mov  cx,607
 7:  jmp  110
 8:  mov  cx,0b0c
 9:  mov  ah,1
10:  int  10
11:  int  20
12:
13:  r cx
14:  16
15:  n normcurs.com
16:  w
17:  q
```

Figure 10-3. NORMCURS.SCR: Restoring the normal cursor.

Make certain that line 12 of NORMCURS.SCR is blank and that the last line is a *q*. When you're sure the file is correct, save it and type the following Debug command:

```
A>debug < normcurs.scr
```

DOS should respond as shown in Figure 10-4.

```
-a 100
xxxx:0100 mov ah,0f
xxxx:0102 int 10
xxxx:0104 cmp al,7
xxxx:0106 jz  10d
xxxx:0108 mov cx,607
xxxx:010B jmp 110
xxxx:010D mov cx,0b0c
xxxx:0110 mov ah,1
xxxx:0112 int 10
xxxx:0114 int 20
xxxx:0116
-r cx
CX 0000
:16
-n normcurs.com
-w
Writing 0016 bytes
-q
```

Figure 10-4. DOS response to creating NORMCURS.COM.

If your screen doesn't agree with Figure 10-4, see "Creating the Programs" for instructions. If your screen agrees with Figure 10-4, type *normcurs*. The block cursor should revert to an underline (the normal cursor).

Making the Cursor Invisible

For those times when you just don't want a cursor at all, NOCURS.COM makes it go away. Only temporarily, of course; NORMCURS.COM or BIGCURS.COM will bring it back.

The next topic, for example, describes a batch file that blanks the screen of your display; the batch file uses NOCURS.COM to make the cursor go away and NORMCURS.COM to restore it. Another time you might not want a cursor (strictly for aesthetic reasons) is when a menu is displayed.

Using your text editor, word processor, or Edlin, create a file named NOCURS.SCR and enter the lines shown in Figure 10-5.

```
 1:  a 100
 2:  mov  ah,1
 3:  mov  ch,20
 4:  int  10
 5:  int  20
 6:
 7:  r cx
 8:  8
 9:  n nocurs.com
10:  w
11:  q
```

Figure 10-5. NOCURS.SCR: Making the cursor invisible.

Make certain that line 6 of NOCURS.SCR is blank and that the last line is a
q. When you're sure the file is correct, save it and type the following Debug
command:

```
A>debug < nocurs.scr
```

DOS should respond as shown in Figure 10-6.

```
-a 100
xxxx:0100 mov ah,1
xxxx:0102 mov ch,20
xxxx:0104 int 10
xxxx:0106 int 20
xxxx:0108
-r cx
CX 0000
:8
-n nocurs.com
-w
Writing 0008 bytes
-q
```

Figure 10-6. DOS response to creating NOCURS.COM.

If your screen doesn't agree with Figure 10-6, see "Creating the Programs"
for instructions. If your screen agrees with Figure 10-6, type *nocurs*; the
cursor should disappear. Now type *bigcurs* to display the block cursor. Finally, type *normcurs* to restore the normal cursor.

The next topic describes a batch file that gives you your first chance to use
these programs.

Make the World Go Away

When you're going to leave the computer for a few hours but don't want to
turn it off, you should make the screen blank. You could turn down the
intensity on your monitor, or even turn the monitor off, but it's simpler to
use a batch file, especially if it's a menu selection.

BLANK.BAT blanks the screen, then restores the display at the touch of a key. It requires three programs you have created: NOCURS.COM and NORMCURS.COM, described earlier in this chapter, and REPLY.COM, which is described in Chapter 7.

Figure 10-7 shows the commands in BLANK.BAT.

```
1:  echo off
2:  cls
3:  nocurs
4:  reply
5:  normcurs
```

Figure 10-7. BLANK.BAT: Making the screen blank.

BLANK.BAT is straightforward:

- Line 2 clears the screen.

- Line 3 turns the cursor off.

- Line 4 waits for you to press a key.

- Line 5 restores the cursor no matter what key you press.

To test BLANK.BAT, type *blank*. The screen should dutifully go blank. Pressing any key should restore the display.

If you assign the BLANK.BAT command to a function key — for example, *{ESC}[0;48;"blank";13p* assigns it to Alt-B — you can blank your screen by pressing Alt-B at the DOS command level. See "The Define Key Command" in Chapter 3 for a description of how to assign a command to a key.

If there's a chance that someone might see the blank screen and, thinking that you forgot, turn your system off, you might put a note on the keyboard warning colleagues against that sort of help.

Discouraging Casual Use with BLANK.BAT

You can add a limited form of security to BLANK.BAT by requiring that a specific key be pressed before the display is restored. It's certainly not very secure — Ctrl-C ends the batch file and returns to DOS — but it can discourage casual use or snooping.

Figure 10-8 shows a revised version of the batch file BLANK.BAT called BLANKSEC.BAT that requires Ctrl-Home (key code 0;119) to restore the screen. To substitute another key, replace *120* in line 6 with the key code of the special key plus 1, and *119* in line 7 with the key code of the special key.

```
1:      echo off
2:      cls
3:      nocurs
4:  :GET_REPLY
5:      reply
6:      if errorlevel 120 goto GET_REPLY
7:      if not errorlevel 119 goto GET_REPLY
8:      normcurs
```

Figure 10-8. BLANKSEC.BAT: Requiring a specific key to restore the screen.

BLANKSEC.BAT is much the same as BLANK.BAT:

● Line 2 clears the screen.

● Line 3 turns the cursor off.

● Line 5 waits for you to press a key.

● Line 6 goes back to wait for another key if the key code of the key pressed is greater than the special key code.

● Line 7 goes back to wait for another key if the key code of the key pressed is less than the special key code.

● Line 8 restores the cursor. Because of the tests in lines 6 and 7, the batch file gets to line 8 only if you press the special key.

To test BLANKSEC.BAT, type *blanksec*. The screen should go blank, but pressing any key other than the special key has no effect (other than loading REPLY.COM from disk if the current directory isn't a RAM disk).

Changing the Screen Colors

The remainder of this chapter deals with changing the foreground and background colors. If you aren't using a color display, you can go on to Chapter 11.

A color display normally displays white characters on a dark screen; in the parlance of ANSI.SYS, this is a white *foreground* on a black *background*. As shown in Chapter 3, you can change these colors with the ANSI.SYS Set Attribute command. Appendix A summarizes all the ANSI.SYS commands; Figure A-3 includes a table of all the foreground and background color codes used by the Set Attribute command.

Just as in Chapter 3, the examples here use the Prompt command to change the displayed colors.

Changing the Foreground Color

The most common colors used by monochrome monitors to display their wares are green, amber, or a pale blue that's almost white. All three have their adherents who make conflicting claims about the efficiency or restfulness of various colors; you can make your color display emulate any of these simply by changing the foreground color.

For example, the most common color used by monochrome displays is green. You can have a green display with one command:

```
A>prompt $e[32m
```

To see the effect of this and the remaining commands in this section, clear the screen and display the directory after changing the color.

Amber is highly touted as more restful than other colors. You can approximate amber with yellow; change the *32* (green foreground) in the preceding command to *33* (yellow foreground):

```
A>prompt $e[33m
```

The appearance of yellow on different color displays varies more than any other color. Adjusting the brightness and contrast controls may help. If the characters look more red than yellow (or amber), you may have to specify high-intensity yellow with the following command:

```
A>prompt $e[1;33m
```

If you specified high-intensity yellow, type the following Prompt command to turn off the high-intensity attribute:

```
A>prompt $e[m
```

Finally, the cyan foreground color comes pretty close to the pale blue used by a few displays:

```
A>prompt $e[36m
```

Again, high-intensity cyan may come closer to the color you want; the command is *prompt $e[1;36m* for high-intensity cyan.

There are three more colors you can try, if you wish: red (31), blue (34), and magenta (35).

Changing the Background Color

You aren't limited to a black background. You can make the background any of the eight (counting black and white) colors. For example, type the following command to change the background to blue:

```
A>prompt $e[1;44m
```

Nothing seems to have changed; there isn't even a system prompt to show the new color because the system prompt consists solely of the command to change the background color. You have to clear the screen to see the new background color:

```
A>cls
```

There's your blue background. Keep in mind this need to clear the screen if you decide to change the standard operating colors of your system.

Changing Both Foreground and Background Colors

Not all combinations of foreground and background colors are useful. Green characters are invisible on a green background, of course, and nearly invisible on a cyan background. Other color combinations, such as high-intensity red foreground on a blue background, are quite distinct but you wouldn't want to look at the screen very long.

The best way to get a feeling for what you like is to try several combinations. You can check them out pretty quickly by using a Prompt command to set the colors, then clearing the screen and displaying the directory to fill the screen. Figure 10-9 shows some combinations with sufficient contrast to read. Appendix A lists all the available colors and their numbers.

Command	Foreground	Background
prompt $e[37;41m	White	Red
prompt $e[37;44m	White	Blue
prompt $e[1;33;41m	High-intensity yellow	Red
prompt $e[1;33;44m	High-intensity yellow	Blue
prompt $e[1;36;44m	High-intensity cyan	Blue
prompt $e[1;37;44m	High-intensity white	Blue
prompt $e[1;37;46m	High-intensity white	Cyan

Figure 10-9. Foreground-background color combinations.

Other combinations are possible, of course. Because color preference is highly subjective, experiment for a while. The high-intensity foreground colors provide better contrast, but you might like normal intensity better. Try several combinations.

If you prefer a dark foreground on a light background, try the combinations shown in Figure 10-10, plus any others that you think you might like.

Command	Foreground	Background
prompt $e[30;47m	Black	White
prompt $e[31;47m	Red	White
prompt $e[34;47m	Blue	White
prompt $e[30;46m	Black	Cyan
prompt $e[31;46m	Red	Cyan
prompt $e[34;46m	Blue	Cyan

Figure 10-10. Color combinations with a light background.

Defining Your Own Standard Colors

You can define your own standard colors by putting an Echo command in AUTOEXEC.BAT that sends the appropriate ANSI.SYS command to the console. For example, if you wanted to set your standard display colors as a high-intensity yellow foreground on a blue background, you would put *echo {ESC}[1;33;44m* in AUTOEXEC.BAT. But there's a bit more to it than that, unfortunately. If you don't plan to define your own standard colors, you can skip these final complications and go on to Chapter 11.

Changing Colors Can Complicate Your Life a Bit

If, in AUTOEXEC.BAT, you define a standard set of colors *and* you define a system prompt that sets display attributes, you'll never see your standard colors unless the prompt definition happens to end by setting the standard colors; DOS displays the system prompt as soon as AUTOEXEC.BAT finishes, and the last display attributes set in the prompt definition are the ones that DOS uses.

For example, a Prompt command example earlier in this chapter displays the current drive and directory in reverse video and ends with *$e[m*, which turns off all display attributes. Each time DOS displayed that particular system prompt, the screen would be set to white foreground on a black background, even if you had defined a different set of colors in AUTOEXEC.BAT.

So your Prompt command must not only define the system prompt, its last act must be to set your standard colors. If you wanted your screen to be blue characters on a cyan background, for example, your Prompt command would have to end with *$e[34;47m*.

Furthermore, if you use BLANK.BAT, it must start by changing the background color to black (insert *echo {ESC}[m* after the first line) because all the Clear Screen command does is erase foreground characters. Only if the background color is black will the screen be blank; if the background is any other color, the screen will be filled with that color. If BLANK.BAT changes the background color to black, it, too, must restore your standard background colors before returning to DOS.

Watch Out for Those Batch Files

In fact, *any* batch file that sets display attributes with an ANSI.SYS command must restore your standard colors before it returns to DOS. You may use several batch files that set a display attribute; this book is full of them. All it takes is one *{ESC}[7m* to turn your display into black characters on a white background or *{ESC}[m* to set what DOS considers normal (white characters on a black background). You'll also find that some of these batch files look fine when the normal attribute is set, but need some revision if different foreground or background colors are set.

Keeping track of all the places where you must restore your standard colors can be a chore. And should you decide to change your standard foreground and background colors, you'll have to change every one of the batch files that restore the standard colors. Yet computers are supposed to relieve drudgery, not create it.

The solution is to create a batch file that includes a Prompt command that restores the system prompt and ends by setting the standard colors, followed by an Echo command that sets the standard colors, and a Clear Screen command. Call this batch file PROMPTRS.BAT, and use it as the last command in any batch file that changes either the prompt or display attributes. (It was suggested earlier that you create a batch file named PROMPTRS.BAT to restore your system prompt; if you did, modify it to match this description.)

For example, suppose you defined your standard colors as black foreground on a cyan background, and your system prompt consisted of the current drive and date displayed in reverse video. Figure 10-11 shows the commands PROMPTRS.BAT would contain.

```
1:   echo off
2:   prompt $e[7m$p[30;46m
3:   echo {ESC}[0;30;46m
4:   cls
```

Figure 10-11. PROMPTRS.BAT: Restoring the prompt and standard colors.

The attributes *30;46* in line 2 cause DOS to set the standard colors each time it displays the system prompt. In line 3, the 0 attribute turns off any attributes that may be set—such as different colors, reverse video, or high intensity—and the attributes *30;46* (again!) set the standard colors immediately (remember, the system prompt isn't displayed until the batch file returns to DOS, so line 2 has a delayed effect). The *cls* command in line 4 fills the screen immediately with the background color.

Make *promptrs* the last command in any batch file that sets a display attribute or changes the system prompt, including AUTOEXEC.BAT. If you get tired of black on cyan as standard colors, just change the attributes in lines 2 and 3 of PROMPTRS.BAT.

Application Programs Get into the Act

Some application programs define their own foreground and background colors. They restore any colors you have defined when they return to DOS, but the screen remains black until you fill it. This is only an aesthetic blemish but, if it bothers you, you can avoid it by running the application program with a two-line batch file: the command that starts the application program followed by *cls*.

It's worth the effort to define your own standard colors if you discover a combination that you prefer. Just take the time to create PROMPTRS.BAT, and you can manage the situation with a minimum of fuss.

CHAPTER
11

Print It Your Way

The printer is a key part of your computer system. Whatever types of application programs you use—word processing, spreadsheets, database, graphics, or something more specialized—the printer makes the documents that record the planning, progress, and completion of your work. Your printer may even remind you how much you use the computer when you run out of paper and discover that that box of 3000 pages is gone.

The first dot-matrix printers offered by IBM were manufactured by Epson. IBM now makes its own printers, but they still use the same commands as those early Epson machines with IBM labels. Because of the size of the Epson-compatible market, most printer manufacturers make dot-matrix printers that use the same commands and character set.

There are exceptions, of course. Laser printers and daisy-wheel printers use different commands, and some dot-matrix printers don't follow the IBM-Epson conventions. If you're buying a new printer, make sure it's compatible, and ask for a demonstration if there's some question. If you have a printer, check the manual; the Introduction may tell you whether the printer follows the industry standard, and there should be a chart or charts that show you whether the printer can print the IBM extended character set.

Competition in the printer market has lowered the cost of dot-matrix printers while increasing the quality. Figure 11-1 illustrates some of the capabilities of today's dot-matrix printers. Chapter 4 showed you how to tap some of the capabilities of your printer; this chapter goes a bit farther, showing you how to apply the printer to some real-life situations.

```
South deals:

          ♠ AK84
          ♥ AKQ2
          ♦ Q10
          ♣ 753

♠ J965              ♠ 7
♥ 10                ♥ 9753
♦ AJ9532            ♦ K
♣ K10               ♣ AQJ8642

          ♠ Q1032
          ♥ J864
          ♦ 8764
          ♣ 9
```

This is Expanded.
This is Compressed.
This is Elite.
This is Proportional.
This is Bold.
This is Italic.
This is Underlined.
This is NLQ (Near Letter Quality).

This is Elite Italic.
This is Compressed Italic.
This is Bold Italic.
This is Proportional Italic.
This is NLQ Expanded Italic.

This is Expanded Compressed.
This is Proportional Underlined.
This is Compressed Underlined.
This is Elite Italic Bold.

Figure 11-1. Sample of dot-matrix printer output.

Printer Commands

As shown in Chapter 4, most printer commands are one, two, or three bytes long. Although most parameters are fixed (such as Alt-15 or the letter *D*), some commands require a parameter whose value can vary, such as the commands that set the page depth or left margin.

You can send commands to the printer by redirecting the output of an Echo command, copying a file of commands to the printer, including printer commands in a file that is to be printed, or with a program that sends commands to the printer.

The examples in Chapter 4 used several printer commands, and this chapter uses several more. Appendix B is a quick reference to the more common printer commands, but the manual that came with your printer is the complete reference. (The manual may use abbreviations such as SO or DC1 to refer to characters whose code is less than 31; Figure C-4 in Appendix C explains these abbreviations and shows which character each represents.)

This is a long chapter. It discusses operating and caring for your printer, explains some of the performance features added to the Print command in Version 3 of DOS, then shows several batch files and programs that let you use some of the capabilities of your printer. It concludes with a batch file that creates a Printer Setup Menu you can use to control the type of print and some of the formatting capabilities built into your printer; this batch file becomes part of the menu system described in Chapter 14.

Operating Your Printer

In addition to turning your printer on and off, adding paper, and changing the ribbon, you should clean it once in a while. Dust and small bits of paper gather inside and can cause problems if left to accumulate. It helps just to open or remove any covers and blow the material out. One of those miniature vacuum cleaners does an even better job; just be sure not to disturb any of the belts, wires, or other exposed parts.

Your printer probably has some special features that you can use by holding down one or more front-panel buttons while you turn the printer on. Most printers can run a *self test,* which prints a test pattern of the standard ASCII characters across the full width of the paper, shifting the pattern one character each line. The self test—a few lines are shown in Figure 11-2—continues for 15 minutes or so, then automatically stops; you can stop it sooner by turning the printer off.

```
 !"#$%&'()*+,-./0123456789:;<=>?@ABCDEFGHIJKLMNOPQRSTUVWXYZ[\]``abcdefghijklmno
 !"#$%&'()*+,-./0123456789:;<=>?@ABCDEFGHIJKLMNOPQRSTUVWXYZ[\]``abcdefghijklmnop
 "#$%&'()*+,-./0123456789:;<=>?@ABCDEFGHIJKLMNOPQRSTUVWXYZ[\]``abcdefghijklmnopq
 #$%&'()*+,-./0123456789:;<=>?@ABCDEFGHIJKLMNOPQRSTUVWXYZ[\]``abcdefghijklmnopqr
 $%&'()*+,-./0123456789:;<=>?@ABCDEFGHIJKLMNOPQRSTUVWXYZ[\]``abcdefghijklmnopqrs
 %&'()*+,-./0123456789:;<=>?@ABCDEFGHIJKLMNOPQRSTUVWXYZ[\]``abcdefghijklmnopqrst
 &'()*+,-./0123456789:;<=>?@ABCDEFGHIJKLMNOPQRSTUVWXYZ[\]``abcdefghijklmnopqrstu
```

Figure 11-2. Printer self test.

You can run the self test even if the computer is turned off or the printer isn't attached to a computer; it's a good way to make sure that you installed a new ribbon correctly or just to make sure the printer is working. To run the self test on an Epson or on most IBM printers, hold down the Form Feed button while you turn the printer on. Check the table of contents in your printer's manual to find the instructions for running its self test.

Another feature of many printers causes the printer to print the two–digit hexadecimal number that represents each character it receives, rather than printing the character itself. For reasons described under "Displaying a File with the Dump Command" in Chapter 5, you're apt to see this feature referred to as *hex dump mode*.

This feature is usually used to test a program or batch file that isn't behaving properly, but you can also use it to see exactly what an application program, such as your word processor or graphics program, sends to the printer. Figure 11-3 shows three lines as they would be printed and the corresponding lines of hexadecimal data the printer would produce.

```
0123456789
0123456789
0 1 2 3 4 5 6 7 8 9

0F  30  20  31  20  32  20  33  20  34  20  35  20  36  20  37  20  38  20  39
0D  0A  1B  34  30  20  31  20  32  20  33  20  34  20  35  20  36  20  37  20
38  20  39  1B  35  12  0D  0A  1B  45  30  20  31  20  32  20  33  20  34  20
```

Figure 11-3. Printer output in ASCII and hexadecimal.

In the hexadecimal portion of Figure 11-3, *30* through *39* are the ASCII codes for the characters 0 through 9, *20* is a space, *0D* is a carriage return, and *0A* is a line feed. The remaining characters are commands. The *0F* in the first byte of the first row is character 15, or the Start Compressed Print command. *1B* is the Escape character, so *1B 34* starting in the third byte of the second row is {ESC}4 (the Start Italics command). Starting with the fourth byte of the third row, *1B 35* is {ESC}5 (the Stop Italics command), *12* (character 18) is the Stop Compressed Print command, *0D 0A* are the carriage return and line feed for the second line, and *1B 45* is {ESC}E (the Start Bold Print command).

To use this feature on an Epson or on most IBM printers, hold down both the Line Feed and Form Feed buttons when you turn the printer on. If you have a different make of printer, check the manual to see whether it offers this feature and, if so, how to start it.

Fine-tuning the Print Command

This topic doesn't describe how to use the Print command, but rather suggests how you might optimize the performance of the Print program. Use of the Print command is covered in the DOS manual and *Running MS-DOS*. If you don't use the Print command very often or if you're satisfied with how it works, you can safely skip this topic and go on to "Printing a File in Pages," which describes the first batch file of this chapter.

The computer can only do one thing at a time, so the Print program doesn't really print a file simultaneously—it takes turns with whatever else the computer is doing. But the IBM PC's clock ticks every 55 milliseconds (55 thousandths of a second), and every time it ticks DOS can switch jobs, so DOS has a chance to switch jobs 18.18 times each second. Things can change so quickly that it seems like two things are happening at the same time.

The 55-millisecond interval between clock ticks, called a *tick,* is the measure of work time that DOS uses. Beginning with Version 3 of DOS, the Print command lets you control how many ticks DOS works before giving Print a chance, and how many ticks Print works before giving control back to DOS. You can also control how much memory the Print program uses to store what it's going to print; this area of memory is called the *print buffer.*

Note: The printer has some memory of its own that it uses to store the data sent to it; this memory is usually called the *printer buffer,* raising the distinct possibility for confusion. Remember, you can control the size of the *print* buffer, but the *printer* buffer is part of the printer's hardware.

The DOS Version 3 Print command includes parameters that let you specify the number of ticks during which DOS has control, the number of ticks during which the Print program has control, and the size of the print buffer. Here, then, are the factors that interact to affect Print program performance:

- The size of the print buffer. You can control this with the /B parameter of the Print command. If you don't specify otherwise, DOS assigns 512 bytes to the print buffer. Increasing /B means that the Print program uses the disk less often, increasing its speed, but also decreases the amount of memory available to other programs.

- The number of ticks that DOS runs and keeps the Print program from working. You can control this with the /S parameter of the Print command. If you don't specify otherwise, DOS assigns eight timer ticks to /S. Increasing /S gives more time to DOS and less time to the Print program.

- The number of ticks that the Print program runs and keeps DOS from working. You can control this with the /M parameter of the Print command. If you don't specify otherwise, DOS assigns two timer ticks to /M. Increasing /M gives more time to the Print program and less time to DOS.

- The number of ticks that the Print program waits before trying again if it tries to send data to the printer when the printer is busy. You can control this with the /U parameter of the Print command. If you don't specify otherwise, DOS assigns one timer tick to /U. Increasing /U also gives more time to the Print program and less time to DOS.

- The size of printer buffer. Because this is part of the printer (hardware, not software), the only control you have is over which printer you buy (some printer buffers are larger than others) or whether you add a larger printer buffer (some printers offer this as an option).

No matter how fast your printer or computer, nor how accurately you specify the Print command parameters, the printer probably won't print at top speed while you're using the computer to do something else. If it did, DOS would seem frozen most of the time, defeating the main purpose of the Print program. On the other hand, if your computer appeared to run at top speed while you were printing a file, the printer might print one line every 20 or 30 seconds; that, too, would be unacceptable.

The object is to allocate enough memory to the print buffer so that the Print program doesn't have to use the disks too often, and to find values for the /S, /M, and /U parameters of the Print command that split up the ticks between DOS and the Print program so that both system performance and printing speed are acceptable. Because so many factors affect performance, you may have to experiment by entering the Print command with some values, then print some files and do something else (such as edit a file or work with a spreadsheet) to see how the system performs. You can specify these parameters only the first time you enter the Print command, so if either DOS or the printer are unacceptably slow, you'll have to restart DOS and enter the Print command with a different set of values.

Figure 11-4 suggests some values for the /B parameter (size of the print buffer). If you choose one of these values, enter the exact number shown; they're all multiples of 512 (the size of a disk sector), which lets DOS use the memory as efficiently as possible.

	Files Printed at One Time		
Typical File Size	*Fewer Than 5*	*5 to 10*	*More Than 10*
Fewer than 4000 bytes	2048	4096	8192
4000 to 8000 bytes	4096	8192	12288
More than 8000 bytes	8192	12288	16384

Figure 11-4. Suggested values of the /B parameter of the Print command.

If you're going to experiment, choose a value for /B from Figure 11-4 and use the following starting values for /S, /M, and /U:

/S:25 /M:5 /U:2

If your printer's buffer is larger than 2K (this is hardware, remember; the printer manual should tell you), start with a larger value for /M to give the Print program time enough to fill the buffer. The ratio of /S to /M determines how DOS and the Print program split the available time, so increase /S to keep the same starting proportions:

/S:35 /M:7 /U:2

In both of these sets of suggested starting values, the Print program gets 20 percent of the available time. To speed up DOS, increase /S, or decrease /M or /U. To speed up the printer, decrease /S, or increase /M or /U. Some changes in the parameters won't seem to have much effect, and the printer may pause at odd moments almost independently of the settings, so it probably isn't worth spending a lot of time trying to find the exact settings that give the best performance. But you can probably improve the performance over the values that DOS assumes with just a few tries.

Printing a File in Pages

Sending a long file to the printer with the Copy command prints continuously, right over the perforations between pages. This is pretty ugly, so word processors and other application programs skip the perforations (so does the Print command). If you'd rather not fire up your word processor or use the Print program to print a short file, you can set up a batch file that skips the perforation.

Most printers recognize commands that specify the length of the page and how many lines to skip at the bottom to avoid the perforation. PRNT.BAT is a batch file that prints a file in pages by sending these commands to the printer, then copying the file to the printer. It also prints the name of the file and the current time and date at the top of the first page, and accepts wildcard characters. It's an easy way to handle quick print jobs such as rough drafts of letters or a bunch of batch files.

Figure 11-5 explains the printer commands used in PRNT.BAT.

Printer Commands

Form Feed	\<character 12\> Advances the paper to the top of the next page.
Set Left Margin	{ESC}l\<col\> Sets the left margin to the specified column.
Set Page Depth	{ESC}C\<0\>\<inches\> Sets the page length to the specified number of inches.
Skip Perforation	{ESC}N\<lines\> Skips the specified number of lines at the bottom of each page. If you adjust the paper in the printer to the top of a page, the perforation skip leaves top and bottom margins equal to half the perforation skip. The perforation skip is always calculated in lines, regardless of the line spacing, so the perforation skip gets pretty small if you specify a perforation skip of a few lines and small line spacing.
Set Tab Positions	{ESC}D\<tab1\>\<tab2\>\< . . . \>\<character 0\> Sets the tabs to the columns specified by \<tab1\>, \<tab2\>, and so on up to 32 tabs in a line. Specify each tab position with the character whose code corresponds to the column number: column 1 would be Alt-1, for example, and column 10 would be Alt-10. End the list of tab positions with character 0.
Set Repeating Tab Positions	{ESC}e\<character 0\>\<cols\> Sets a tab position every specified number of columns across the line. {ESC}e\<character 0\>\<character 5\>, for example, sets a tab at columns 5, 10, 15, and so on. Most printers accept Alt-128 as well as character 0. Some printers call this command Set Tab Unit.

Figure 11-5. Printer commands used to print in pages.

Most printers also accept Alt-128 where *\<character 0\>* is shown in Figure 11-5. Because Alt-128 can be entered using the Alt-key technique, it is used in place of character 0 in this book. If your printer doesn't accept Alt-128, substitute character 0.

Remember, these commands are for Epson-compatible printers. If your printer uses different commands, these won't have the intended effect. Your printer should have corresponding commands, however; check the manual and substitute the command it recognizes.

Figure 11-6 shows the commands in PRNT.BAT.

```
 1:    echo off
 2:    if not "%1"=="" goto OK
 3:    echo {ESC}[7mYou must specify a file name.{ESC}[m
 4:    echo Please re-enter the command.
 5:    goto END
 6: :OK
 7:    if "%2"=="print" goto PRINT_IT
 8:    date < c:\batch\cr.dat | find "C" > stamp.$$$
 9:    time < c:\batch\cr.dat | find "C" >> stamp.$$$
10:    for %%p in (%1) do command /c prnt %%p print
11:    erase stamp.$$$
12:    goto END
13: :PRINT_IT
14:    if exist %1 goto GOT_FILE
15:    echo {ESC}[7mI can't find a file named %1{ESC}[m.
16:    goto END
17: :GOT_FILE
18:    echo {ESC}C<Alt-128><Alt-11>{ESC}N<Alt-6>{ESC}l<Alt-1>
       {ESC}D<Alt-23><Alt-128>> prn
19:    copy stamp.$$$ prn > nul
20:    echo                              > prn
21:    echo  FILE: %1 <tab> ‖      > prn
22:    echo                           > prn
23:    echo {ESC}l<Alt-5>{ESC}e<Alt-128><Alt-8>> prn
24:    copy %1 prn > nul
25:    echo <Alt-12>> prn
26:    echo ** File {ESC}[7m%1{ESC}[m printed
27: :END
```

Figure 11-6. PRNT.BAT: Print files with title and date stamp.

PRNT.BAT uses the technique described under "A Batch File Can Call Itself" in Chapter 6 to carry out several commands for each of a series of files. It does this by using the Command command to call itself for each file, specifying the file name as the first parameter and *print* as the second parameter.

Create PRNT.BAT with your text editor or word processor and enter the commands shown in Figure 11-6. The following explanations describe how PRNT.BAT works:

• Line 2 skips the following error message if you specify the name of a file.

• Lines 3 through 5 warn you that you must specify the name of a file, then return to DOS.

- Line 7 skips directly to the commands that print the file if the second parameter is *print*. The commands in lines 8–12 are carried out only the first time PRNT.BAT runs; they're skipped each time PRNT.BAT calls itself to print a file.

- Lines 8 and 9 create a temporary file named STAMP.$$$ that contains a date and time stamp.

- Line 10 uses the Command command to call PRNT.BAT once for each file specified by %1. Each time PRNT.BAT calls itself, it specifies *print* as the second parameter so that the If command in line 7 will skip the commands in lines 8–12 and just print the file.

- Line 11 erases the temporary file that contains the date and time stamps.

- Line 12 returns to DOS after all the files have been printed. This is the actual end of the batch file.

- Line 14 skips the following error message if the file you specified exists.

- Lines 15 and 16 warn you that the file you specified doesn't exist, then return to DOS.

- Line 18 sends four commands to the printer:

Command	Description
{ESC}C<Alt-128><Alt-11>	Sets the page length to 11 inches.
{ESC}N<Alt-6>	Sets the perforation skip to six lines.
{ESC}l<Alt-1>	Sets the left margin to column 1.
{ESC}D<Alt-23><Alt-128>	Sets one tab at column 23.

Although line 18 is shown on two lines, enter it as a single line.

- Line 19 prints the date and time stamps.

- Lines 20–22 print a title block at the top of the page that contains the name of the file. The block uses the following box-drawing characters:

╔ Alt-201 ═ Alt-205 ╗ Alt-187
╚ Alt-200 ║ Alt-186 ╝ Alt-188

Press the Tab key once between %1 and *Alt-186* in line 21. Line 18 sets one tab at column 23 so that the right edge of the title block is in the correct position regardless of the length of the file name.

- Line 23 sends two commands to the printer:

Command	Description
{ESC}l<Alt-5>	Sets the left margin to column 5.
{ESC}e<Alt-128><Alt-8>	Sets a tab every eight columns across the line.

- Line 24 copies the file to the printer.

- Line 25 sends a Form Feed command to the printer, advancing the paper to the top of the next page. When you enter Alt-12, your word processor will probably break the line and display a new page mark. This looks like trouble, but don't worry: The correct characters are in the file.

- Line 26 displays the name of the file that was printed.

- Line 27 ends the copy of PRNT.BAT that was called to print a file. It returns to the Command command in line 10. If there is another file to be printed, another Command command is carried out, which calls PRNT.BAT again; when there are no more files to be printed, the Goto command in line 12 ends PRNT.BAT.

Testing PRNT.BAT

Test PRNT.BAT with a short text file; if there isn't one in the current directory, create it by copying the console. The examples assume you have a file named TEST.DOC.

First, make sure the printer is turned on and the paper is adjusted to the top of a page, then type the PRNT.BAT command with no parameter:

`A>prnt`

It should warn you to specify a file and return to DOS. Now type the command again, specifying TEST.DOC:

`A>prnt test.doc`

After some disk activity, the printer should print the current date and time, the title block with the name of the file, and then the file itself.

Finally, type the command and specify a file that doesn't exist:

`A>prnt 123.456`

PRNT.BAT should tell you that it can't find that file and return to DOS.

You can use PRNT.BAT to print a series of files by using a wildcard character in the file name. To print all the files with the extension DOC, for example, you would type *prnt *.doc*.

If you prefer a particular combination of typeface, line spacing, or other formatting features, put the commands in line 23 of PRNT.BAT. You could even create separate versions for printing with different combinations of commands.

You can incorporate the Printer Setup Menu, described later in this chapter, into PRNT.BAT by adding a few commands. This menu lets you control the type of print, line spacing, and other printer features each time you print a file. See "Combining the Printer Setup Menu and PRNT.BAT" at the end of the chapter.

Printing Really Small

When the occasion demands, your printer can print quite small, yet remarkably readable, characters packed closely together. Figure 11-7 shows an example of this output.

STANDARD SCREW THREADS

The Unified and American Screw Threads included in Table 87 are taken from the publication of the American Standards Association, ASA B1.1--1949. The coarse-thread series is the former United States Standard Series. It is recommended for general use in engineering work where conditions do not require the use of a fine thread. The fine-thread series is the former "Regular Screw Thread Series" established by the Society of Automotive Engineers. The fine-thread series is recommended for general use in automotive and aircraft work, and where special conditions require a fine thread. The extra-fine-thread series is the same as the former SAE fine series and the present SAE extra-fine series. It is used particularly in aircraft and aeronautical equipment where (1) thin-walled material is to be threaded; (2) thread depth of nuts clearing ferrules, coupling flanges, etc., must be held to a minimum; and (3) a maximum practicable number of threads is required within a given thread length.

TABLE 87. STANDARD SCREW THREADS

Sizes	Basic Major Diameter D	Thds per Inch N	Basic Pitch Diameter * E	Minor Diameter Ext Thds K_s	Minor Diameter Int Thds K_n	Section at Minor Diameter at D - $2h_b$	Stress Area §
	Inches		Inches	Inches	Inches	Sq In.	Sq In.
Coarse-thread Series--UNC and NC (Basic Dimensions)							
1(.073)	0.0730	64	0.0629	0.0538	0.0561	0.0022	0.0026
2(.086)	0.0860	56	0.0744	0.0641	0.0667	0.0031	0.0036
3(.099)	0.0990	48	0.0855	0.0734	0.0764	0.0041	0.0048
4(.112)	0.1120	40	0.0958	0.0813	0.0849	0.0050	0.0060
5(.125)	0.1250	40	0.1088	0.0943	0.0979	0.0067	0.0079
6(.138)	0.1380	32	0.1177	0.0997	0.1042	0.0075	0.0090
8(.164)	0.1640	32	0.1437	0.1257	0.1302	0.0120	0.0139
10(.190)	0.1900	24	0.1629	0.1389	0.1449	0.0145	0.0174
12(.216)	0.2160	24	0.1889	0.1649	0.1709	0.0206	0.0240

* British: Effective Diameter
§ The stress area is the assumed area of an externally threaded part which is used for the purpose of computing the tensile strength.

Figure 11-7. How small is small?

Printing this small requires changing both the type of print and the line spacing. Two new printer commands are used:

Printer Commands

Set Line Spacing in ½₁₆″	{ESC}3 <units> Sets the line spacing to the specified number of ½₁₆ths of an inch.
Start Superscript	{ESC}SO Starts printing superscript print, a smaller version of the typeface currently in effect, printed higher on the line than normal. If you change the typeface without stopping superscript, the printer prints the superscript form of the new typeface.

Figure 11-7 is printed in compressed superscript. The characters are the same width as compressed print (17 per inch) but not as high, so the line spacing can be reduced. Standard line spacing is six per inch, or $^{36}\!/_{216}''$; the line spacing in Figure 11-7 is $^{15}\!/_{216}''$. This combination yields a maximum of 133 characters in a line and 14.4 lines per inch, or 144 lines on an 11–inch page with ½″ top and bottom margins.

Only three printer commands are required to print this small:

Command	Description
<Alt-15>	Start compressed print.
{ESC}S0	Start superscript print.
{ESC}3<Alt-15>	Set line spacing to $^{15}\!/_{216}''$.

It takes only a moment to try this with your printer. First, create a batch file named TINY.BAT and enter the two lines shown in Figure 11-8.

```
1: echo off
2: echo <Alt-15>{ESC}S0{ESC}3<Alt-15> > prn
```

Figure 11-8. TINY.BAT: Printing really small.

If you don't have a short text file in the current directory, copy from the console to create one named SHORT.DOC:

```
A>copy con short.doc
This is a file to see
just how small the printer
can print.  How small is it?
^Z
        1 File(s) copied

A>_
```

Now type the TINY.BAT command and copy the test file to the printer (if you're using a file of your own, substitute its name for SHORT.DOC):

```
A>tiny

A>echo off

A>copy short.doc prn
        1 File(s) copied

A>_
```

The printer should print the file. You may have to look closely.

Note: Some word processors let you specify the font (type of print) and line spacing. Figure 11-7, for example, was printed using Microsoft Word, specifying a font of six-point Pica Superscript and a line spacing of five points (one point equals $\frac{1}{72}''$ or $\frac{3}{216}''$, so five points is $\frac{15}{216}''$).

You probably wouldn't use such small printing every day, but it might be just the thing to print that huge spreadsheet or make a permanent record of some data you don't refer to very often, or print your New Year's resolutions.

Sending Commands to the Printer with a Program

In addition to redirecting the output of the Echo command and copying a file to the printer, you can use a program to send commands to the printer. Such programs can be quite small, often less than 20 bytes, and have the advantage of not sending a line feed as the Echo command does.

But a program is stored in a file, and any file, no matter how small, takes up the minimum amount of space required by the type of disk on which it's stored. A 1-byte file, for example, takes up 4096 (4K) bytes on a 10-megabyte fixed disk.

So even if you limited yourself to 25 of the most common printer commands and combinations, the printer command files would take up 25K bytes on a 360K floppy disk, 50K bytes on a 20-megabyte fixed disk, and 100K bytes on a 10-megabyte fixed disk. That's a lot of disk space to give up just to avoid adjusting the paper in the printer to the top of a page.

That's why, with one exception, this book doesn't use programs to send commands to the printer. The exception is due to an idiosyncrasy of the IBM Graphics Printer (originally Epson MX-80): Unlike almost all other Epson and Epson-compatible printers, you can't reset it with {ESC}@.

A Program to Reset the IBM Graphics Printer

PRNTREST.COM is a small program that resets all Epson–compatible printers, including the IBM Graphics Printer. If your printer resets when you send it {ESC}@, you can skip this topic and go on to "The Printer Setup Menu."

You create PRNTREST.COM using Debug. The procedure is described in Chapter 5. If you haven't yet gone through the examples in Chapter 5, you might do so before continuing here.

Using your text editor, word processor, or Edlin, create a file named PRNTREST.SCR and enter the lines shown in Figure 11-9.

```
 1:  a 100
 2:  mov  ah,1
 3:  sub  dx,dx
 4:  int  17
 5:  int  20
 6:
 7:  n prntrest.com
 8:  r cx
 9:  8
10:  w
11:  q
```

Figure 11-9. PRNTREST.SCR: Resetting the IBM Graphics Printer.

Proofread PRNTREST.SCR against Figure 11-9. Make certain that line 6 is blank and that the last line is a *q*; if there is an error in either of those lines, you'll have to restart DOS when you try to create PRNTREST.COM. When you're sure there are no differences, save PRNTREST.SCR.

To create PRNTREST.COM, type the following Debug command:

A>debug < prntrest.scr

If nothing seems to happen and pressing a key has no effect, restart DOS, proofread PRNTREST.SCR against Figure 11-9, correct any differences, and re-enter the Debug command.

DOS should respond as shown in Figure 11-10. To check this, proofread the display against Figure 11-10. If you find any differences, proofread PRNTREST.SCR against Figure 11-9, correct any differences, and re-enter the Debug command.

```
-a 100
xxxx:0100 mov ah,1
xxxx:0102 sub dx,dx
xxxx:0104 int 17
xxxx:0106 int 20
xxxx:0108
-n prntrest.com
-r cx
CX 0000
:8
-w
Writing 0008 bytes
-q
```

Figure 11-10. DOS response when creating PRNTREST.COM.

If the screen agrees with Figure 11-10, try PRNTREST.COM. Make sure
the printer is on, and type the PRNTREST command:

A>prntrest

If the print head isn't at the left margin, it should return and you should
hear the sound the printer makes when you turn the system on or
restart DOS.

The Printer Setup Menu

The remainder of this chapter describes the most ambitious batch file yet
in the book — one that makes your printer more useful by letting you send
commands to it with a single keystroke. It's also a good demonstration of
batch-file techniques and gives you a major part of the menu system
described in Chapter 14.

The Printer Setup Menu is actually two menus in one. It lets you switch
between two sets of options: a set of commands that selects the typeface,
and another set that controls formatting characteristics such as line spacing
and page length. A separate window gives instructions for using the menu.

Figures 11-11 and 11-12 show the Typeface commands and Page Format commands as displayed by the Printer Setup Menu.

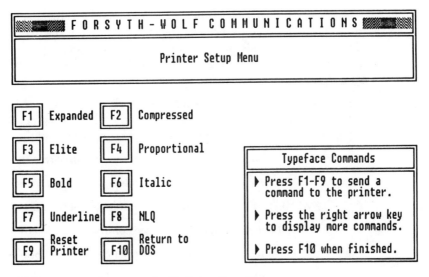

Figure 11-11. Typeface commands of the Printer Setup Menu.

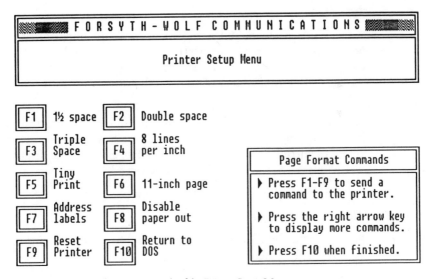

Figure 11-12. Page format commands of the Printer Setup Menu.

As Figures 11-11 and 11-12 show, the basic form of the menu remains unchanged; only the choices for function keys F1 through F8 and the title in the instruction window change.

The Printer Setup Menu is simple to operate: You press the function keys to send commands to the printer, press the right-arrow key to display the other set of commands, and press F10 when you're ready to print. All that remains is to position the paper at the top of the page and copy the file to the printer.

You can simplify this even further by calling the Printer Setup Menu from PRNT.BAT; see "Printing a File in Pages" earlier in this chapter and "Combining the Printer Setup Menu and PRNT.BAT" at the end of this chapter.

The Printer Setup Menu requires one batch file and three text files:

- PRNTMENU.BAT contains the commands that operate the menu.
- PRNTMENU.DOC contains the unchanging part of the menu.
- PRNTOPT1.DOC contains the Typeface commands options.
- PRNTOPT2.DOC contains the Page Format commands options.

It also requires REPLY.COM. If you haven't yet created this program, see "Making Batch Commands Interactive: REPLY.COM" in Chapter 7.

Entering the Files

Although the batch file and text files may look forbidding at first, they're not difficult to enter. The description for each file includes the Alt-key codes for the box-drawing characters, and suggests ways that you can use the cut-and-paste capability of your word processor or text editor to simplify the job.

After you enter each text file, you can make sure it's correct by displaying it with the Type command. If, partway through, you're not sure you have entered something correctly, just save the file, exit to DOS, display the file, and compare it to the figure that illustrates it.

It will go much more quickly than you think.

Entering PRNTMENU.DOC

Figure 11-13 shows the contents of PRNTMENU.DOC. The line numbers, as usual, are for reference only.

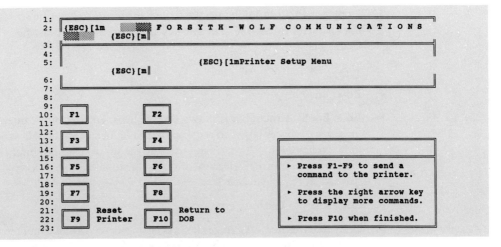

Figure 11-13. PRNTMENU.DOC: The Printer Setup Menu without options.

Use the cut-and-paste capability of your word processor to make the job easier:

1. Enter line 1, using the following Alt-key codes for the box-drawing characters:

╔ Alt-201   ═ Alt-205   ╗ Alt-187

Alt-205 is used 72 times in this line. If your word processor lets you copy characters within a line, type Alt-205 six times and copy it 11 times.

2. Enter line 2, using the following Alt-key codes for the box-drawing and shading characters:

║ Alt-186   ░ Alt-176   ▒ Alt-177   ▓ Alt-178

Although it is shown on two lines, enter it as one line; there is one space between the *S* at the end of *COMMUNICATIONS* and the first shading character. You should change the title, of course, to herald your own enterprise. The ANSI.SYS commands display the title in high intensity, then return to normal. Because of them, the final Alt-186 is seven spaces past the end of line 1.

3. Copy line 1 to line 3. Change the first character to Alt-204 and the last character to Alt-185. The Alt-key codes for the box-drawing characters:

╠ Alt-204   ╣ Alt-185

4. Enter line 4.

5. Enter line 5. Although it is shown on two lines, enter it as one line; there are 29 spaces between the *u* at the end of *Menu* and the following *{ESC}*. The ANSI.SYS commands display the subtitle in high intensity, then return to normal. Because of them, the final Alt-186 is seven spaces past the end of line 3.

6. Copy line 4 to line 6.

7. Copy line 1 to line 7. Change the first character to Alt-200 and the last character to Alt-188. The Alt-key codes for the box-drawing characters:

╚ Alt-200   ╝ Alt-188

8. Line 8 is blank.

9. Enter lines 9–11. The Alt-key codes for the box-drawing characters are shown in steps 1 and 7.

10. Copy lines 9–11 four times. Now you have all ten function keys.

11. Correct the numbers inside the function-key boxes in lines 13, 16, 19, and 22.

12. Add the first line of the instruction window to line 13. There are 20 spaces between the edge of the F4 box and the upper left corner of the instruction window, and 30 Alt-205 characters across the top of the instruction window. Line up the rest of the window frame with this top border.

13. Add the second line of the instruction window to line 14. Copy from the lower right corner of the F4 symbol through the end of the line to the end of lines 15 through 22, then use overstrike to change the lines to match Figure 11-13. The Alt-key codes for the box-drawing characters are shown in steps 1, 2, and 3. The ► character is Alt-16.

14. Copy line 13 from the edge of the F4 symbol through the end of the line to the end of line 23. Change the lower left corner character to Alt-200 and the lower right corner character to Alt-188.

15. Add the choices for F9 and F10 in lines 22 and 23.

Save PRNTMENU.DOC, exit to DOS, display the file with the Type command, and compare the display to Figure 11-11 (ignore the menu choices and instruction-window title). Correct any differences, and go on to enter the option files.

Entering PRNTOPT1.DOC and PRNTOPT2.DOC

PRNTOPT1.DOC and PRNTOPT2.DOC display the choices for F1 through F8. They include ANSI.SYS commands to position the choices. Figure 11-14 shows the contents of PRNTOPT1.DOC and PRNTOPT2DOC.

```
PRNTOPT1.DOC

1:   {ESC}[14;45H{ESC}[1m      Typeface Commands    {ESC}[m
2:   {ESC}[9;8H          {ESC}[9;24H
3:   {ESC}[10;8HExpanded {ESC}[10;24HCompressed
4:   {ESC}[12;8H          {ESC}[12;24H
5:   {ESC}[13;8HElite    {ESC}[13;24HProportional
6:   {ESC}[15;8H          {ESC}[15;24H
7:   {ESC}[16;8HBold     {ESC}[16;24HItalic
8:   {ESC}[18;8H          {ESC}[18;24H
9:   {ESC}[19;8HUnderline{ESC}[19;24HNLQ


PRNTOPT2.DOC

1:   {ESC}[14;45H{ESC}[1m      Page Format Commands{ESC}[m
2:   {ESC}[9;8H          {ESC}[9;24H
3:   {ESC}[10;8H1½ space {ESC}[10;24HDouble space
4:   {ESC}[12;8HTriple   {ESC}[12;24H8 lines
5:   {ESC}[13;8HSpace    {ESC}[13;24HPer inch
6:   {ESC}[15;8HTiny     {ESC}[15;24H
7:   {ESC}[16;8HPrint    {ESC}[16;24H11-inch page
8:   {ESC}[18;8HAddress  {ESC}[18;24HDisable
9:   {ESC}[19;8Hlabels   {ESC}[19;24Hpaper out
```

Figure 11-14. PRNTMENU option files (PRNTOPT1.DOC and PRNTOPT2.DOC).

As you can see, these two files consist primarily of ANSI.SYS commands and spaces. The spaces are necessary because the choices for corresponding function keys in the two different command sets aren't the same length; if the spaces weren't included, the extra characters in the longer choices would remain on the screen when the shorter choice was displayed.

Because the two files are so similar, it's pretty easy to enter them. Start by creating PRNTOPT1.DOC:

1. Enter line 1. The ANSI.SYS command displays the instruction-window title in high intensity. There are four spaces between the *s* of *Commands* and the following *{ESC}*.

2. Enter line 2. There are nine spaces between the *H* at the end of *{ESC}[6;8H* and the following *{ESC}*. Although they aren't shown, there are 15 spaces at the end of the line; be sure to enter them.

3. Copy line 2 seven times.

4. Using overstrike, change lines 3 through 9 to match PRNTOPT1.DOC in Figure 11-14. Be sure not to change the number of spaces in the middle or at the end of any line.

5. Save PRNTOPT1.DOC, exit to DOS, and display it with the Type command. You should see two columns of choices and *Typeface Commands* to the right of the choice *Bold*.

6. Copy PRNTOPT1.DOC to create PRNTOPT2.DOC.

7. Edit PRNTOPT2.DOC and, using overstrike, change it to match PRNTOPT2.DOC in Figure 11-14. Only the wording of the choices and the instruction-window title change; the ANSI.SYS commands are the same. Again, be sure not to change the number of spaces in the middle or at the end of any line.

8. Save PRNTOPT2.DOC, exit to DOS, and display it with the Type command. You should see two rows of choices and *Page Format Commands* to the right of the word *Print*.

Now to enter the batch file.

The Printer Setup Menu Batch File

PRNTMENU.BAT displays the Printer Setup Menu, sends commands to the printer when you press a function key, changes the menu options if you press the right-arrow key, and returns to DOS when you press F10. Except for the number of choices, it's basically an extension of the batch file MENU-6.BAT described in Chapter 7 and shown in Figure 7-6.

Instead of using Echo commands, PRNTMENU.BAT uses Type commands to display the menu (PRNTMENU.DOC) and the options (PRNTOPT1.DOC and PRNTOPT2.DOC). Not only is this faster, it holds down the size of PRNTMENU.BAT. In general, the larger the batch file, the harder it is to remember just how it works or where everything happens.

There's a penalty in disk space for not using Echo commands, but it isn't severe: Combining all four files into PRNTMENU.BAT would save you 2K bytes if you use floppy disks, 4K bytes if you use a 20-megabyte fixed disk, or 12K bytes if you use a 10-megabyte fixed disk. The saving in disk space, however, probably isn't worth the increased size of the batch file. If, after entering and using the Printer Setup Menu, you would like to merge all four files, see "Combining the DOC Files with PRNTMENU.BAT" later in this chapter.

Figure 11-15 shows the commands in PRNTMENU.BAT.

```
 1:     echo off
 2:     cls
 3:     type prntmenu.doc
 4: :CHOICE_1
 5:     type prntopt1.doc
 6: :REPLY_1
 7:     reply
 8:     if errorlevel 77 if not errorlevel 78 goto CHOICE_2
 9:     if errorlevel 69 goto REPLY_1
10:     if errorlevel 68 goto END
11:     if errorlevel 67 echo {ESC}@> prn
12:     if errorlevel 66 if not errorlevel 67 echo {ESC}n> prn
13:     if errorlevel 65 if not errorlevel 66 echo {ESC}-1> prn
14:     if errorlevel 64 if not errorlevel 65 echo {ESC}4> prn
15:     if errorlevel 63 if not errorlevel 64 echo {ESC}E> prn
16:     if errorlevel 62 if not errorlevel 63 echo {ESC}p1> prn
17:     if errorlevel 61 if not errorlevel 62 echo {ESC}M> prn
18:     if errorlevel 60 if not errorlevel 61 echo <Alt-15>> prn
19:     if errorlevel 59 if not errorlevel 60 echo {ESC}W1> prn
20:     goto REPLY_1
21: :CHOICE_2
22:     type prntopt2.doc
23: :REPLY_2
24:     reply
25:     if errorlevel 77 if not errorlevel 78 goto CHOICE_1
26:     if errorlevel 69 goto REPLY_2
27:     if errorlevel 68 goto END
28:     if errorlevel 67 echo {ESC}@> prn
29:     if errorlevel 66 if not errorlevel 67 echo {ESC}8> prn
30:     if errorlevel 65 if not errorlevel 66 echo {ESC}C<Alt-9>> prn
31:     if errorlevel 64 if not errorlevel 65 echo {ESC}C<Alt-128><Alt-11>
        {ESC}N<Alt-6>> prn
32:     if errorlevel 63 if not errorlevel 64 echo <Alt-15>{ESC}S0{ESC}3
        <Alt-15>> prn
33:     if errorlevel 62 if not errorlevel 63 echo {ESC}0> prn
34:     if errorlevel 61 if not errorlevel 62 echo {ESC}31> prn
35:     if errorlevel 60 if not errorlevel 61 echo {ESC}3H> prn
36:     if errorlevel 59 if not errorlevel 60 echo {ESC}36> prn
37:     goto REPLY_2
38: :END
39: cls
```

Figure 11-15. PRNTMENU.BAT: The Printer Setup Menu batch file.

Entering PRNTMENU.BAT

All but a few lines of PRNTMENU.BAT is made up of two nearly identical parts, so just as you used the cut-and-paste capability of your word processor to simplify entering the DOC files, you can simplify entering PRNTMENU.BAT. (*Note:* Although some lines are shown on two lines, enter them as one line.)

1. Enter lines 1 through 8.

2. Copy line 8 eleven times.

3. Change lines 9 through 19 to match Figure 11-15.

4. Enter line 20.

5. Copy lines 4 through 20.

6. Change lines 21 through 37 to match Figure 11-15. Only the labels and printer commands change.

7. Enter lines 38 and 39.

Save PRNTMENU.BAT.

How PRNTMENU.BAT Works

As the line-by-line descriptions show, lines 4–20 and lines 21–37 of PRNTMENU.BAT are the same except for the labels and printer commands:

- Line 3 displays the unchanging part of the menu.

- Line 4 is the first line of the Typeface Commands part of the batch file.

- Line 5 displays the options and instruction window title of the Typeface commands.

- Line 7 waits for you to press a key.

- Line 8 goes to display the Page Format commands if you press the right-arrow key (the key code for the right-arrow key is 77).

- Line 9 goes back to wait for you to press a key if the code of the key you press is from 69 through 77. This is necessary because of the gap in key codes between the check for key code 77 (right arrow) in line 8 and the check for key code 68 (F10) in line 10.

- Line 10 returns to DOS if you press F10.

- Lines 11 through 19 send a command to the printer depending on which function key you press:

Line	Key Code	Function Key	Printer Command
11	67	F9	Reset.
12	66	F8	Start Near Letter Quality.
13	65	F7	Start Underline.
14	64	F6	Start Italic.
15	63	F5	Start Bold.
16	62	F4	Start Proportional.
17	61	F3	Start Elite.
18	60	F2	Start Compressed.
19	59	F1	Start Expanded.

- Line 20 goes back to wait for you to press a key if you pressed any key other than F1 through F10. This is the last command of the Typeface Commands part of the batch file.

- Line 21 is the first line of the Page Format Commands part of the batch file.

- Line 22 displays the options and instruction-window title of the Typeface commands.

- Line 24 waits for you to press a key.

- Line 25 goes to display the Typeface commands if you press the right-arrow key (the key code for the right-arrow key is 77).

- Line 26 goes back to wait for you to press a key if the code of the key you press is from 69 through 77. This is necessary because of the gap in key codes between the check for key code 77 (right arrow) in line 25 and the check for key code 68 (F10) in line 27.

- Line 27 returns to DOS if you press F10.

- Lines 28 through 36 send a command to the printer depending on which function key you press:

Line	Key Code	Function Key	Printer Command
28	67	F9	Reset.
29	66	F8	Disable paper-out detector.
30	65	F7	Set page depth to nine lines.
31	64	F6	Set page depth to 11 inches, and set perforation skip to six lines.
32	63	F5	Start compressed print, and start superscript, and set line spacing to $15/216''$.
33	62	F4	Set line spacing to eight lines per inch.
34	61	F3	Set line spacing to $108/216''$ (character 108 is *l*).
35	60	F2	Set line spacing to $72/216''$ (character 72 is *H*).
36	59	F1	Set line spacing to $54/216''$ (character 54 is *6*).

- Line 37 goes back to wait for you to press a key if you pressed any key other than F1 through F10.

If you print PRNTMENU.BAT in order to proofread it (or just to have a copy of it), be advised: The file contains lots of printer commands, and the printer will carry out each one of them. The printed copy will be, well, interesting, but still readable.

Using the Printer Setup Menu

Before you test the Printer Setup Menu for the first time, do the following:

- If you created the files on a RAM disk, copy all four to a real disk. Be sure to take the time to do this; you don't want to lose the time you spent entering them.

- Make sure all four files are in the current directory.

- Make sure REPLY.COM is either in the current directory or a directory in the command path.

Now start the Printer Setup Menu by typing:

`A>prntmenu`

DOS should display the Printer Setup Menu with the Typeface commands as shown in Figure 11-11. Press the right-arrow key; PRNTMENU.BAT should display the Page Format commands, as shown in Figure 11-12.

Press F9 to reset the printer. The printer should make the same sound it makes when you turn the computer on or restart DOS.

Try some of the other commands. For example, select the Typeface commands (press right arrow if necessary), press F3 for Elite type, press the right arrow key to select the Page Format commands, press F1 for double-spaced printing, then press F10 to leave the Printer Setup Menu. Make sure the printer is turned on and the paper is adjusted to the top of a page, and print a short file by copying it to the printer or, if you entered it, with PRNT.BAT. The file should be printed double-spaced in the Elite typeface.

If this test worked, you're ready to test all the options. The next two topics describe the options of both the Typeface commands and the Page Format commands of the Printer Setup Menu.

The Typeface Commands

When the the Typeface commands are displayed, as shown in Figure 11-11, F1 through F8 select different typefaces such as Expanded, Compressed, and Elite. As Figure 11-1 at the beginning of the chapter shows, you can combine most of the Typeface commands. To avoid overheating the print head, however, most printers won't print Compressed and Bold at the same time; they cancel Compressed and print Bold normal type. So if you select both F2 (Compressed) and F5 (Bold), then print a file, the file is printed in Bold normal-sized type.

F9 resets the printer. Use this when you start, or if you change your mind after selecting some options and decide to start over.

F10 returns to DOS without resetting the printer, so any choices you make are in effect the next time you print a file. Many application programs, including word processors and spreadsheets, reset the printer each time you print something, so printer options you select with the Printer Setup Menu may have no effect.

The Page Format Commands

Figure 11-12 shows the Page Format commands. The choices include:

- F1 through F4 set the line spacing. The normal line spacing is six lines per inch, the same as a standard typewriter. (In the units of measure that most printers use, six lines per inch is a line spacing of $^{12}/_{72}$" or $^{36}/_{216}$"). The Page Format commands offer four options; the first three are more widely spaced than normal, the last is more closely spaced):

Command	Description
F1	Space-and-a-half ($^{18}/_{72}$" or $^{54}/_{216}$").
F2	Double space ($^{24}/_{72}$" or $^{72}/_{216}$").
F3	Triple space ($^{36}/_{72}$" or $^{108}/_{216}$").
F4	Eight lines per inch ($^{9}/_{72}$" or $^{27}/_{216}$").

- F5 (tiny print) prints very small type with very narrow line spacing. For an example and description of the printer commands involved, see the section on "Printing Really Small" earlier in this chapter.

- F6 (11-inch page) sets the printer page depth to 11 inches and the perforation skip to six lines. If you select F6, return to DOS, and copy a file to the printer, the printer won't print over the perforations in continuous-form paper. (If you copy several files to the printer, however, it won't separate the files.) For a description of the printer commands involved and some cautions about printing files this way, see "Printing a File in Pages" and Figure 11-7 earlier in this chapter.

- F7 (Address labels) sets the page depth to nine lines. This prints a file of names and addresses on address labels whose top edges are 1½" apart if there is a Form Feed command (or your word processor's New Page command) between each entry in the file. Because address labels come in various sizes, you may have to change the Page Depth command in PRNTMENU.BAT. Measure how far it is from the top of one address label to the top of the next, convert the distance to sixths of an inch, and replace the *Alt-9* in line 30 of Figure 11-15 with the result. If the distance is one inch, for example, replace the *Alt-9* with *Alt-6*.

- F8 (Disable paper out) tells the printer not to stop printing when it's close to the bottom of the page. Use this option if your printer stops printing before the end of page when you print on single sheets, such as letterhead. A word of caution: If you select this option and then print a file longer than one page with a single sheet in the printer, the printer will continue printing beyond the end of the paper and print on the platen.

- F9 (Reset printer) and F10 (Return to DOS) are the same as F9 and F10 when the Typeface commands are displayed.

Changing the Printer Setup Menu

You may want to change some of the options of the Printer Setup Menu. You could change F9 and F10 so that they don't have the same effect in both sets of commands, for example, or you might want to replace some of the commands with printer options you use more often.

Changing a Menu Item

To change a menu item, you must change both the title displayed in PRNTOPT1.DOC (for the Typeface commands) or PRNTOPT2.DOC (for the Page Format commands), and the command that is carried out in the appropriate *if errorlevel* command in PRNTMENU.BAT.

For example, suppose that you wanted to call F3 in the Page Format commands *Left Margin 6* instead of *Triple Space,* and wanted it to set the left margin to column 6 instead of setting the line spacing to triple space. The printer command to set the left margin to column 6 is *{ESC}l<Alt-6>*. Make the following three changes:

- Change *Triple* in line 4 of PRNTOPT2.DOC (Figure 11-14) to *Left,* followed by two spaces.

- Change *Space* and the three spaces that follow in line 5 of PRNTOPT2.DOC to *Margin 6.*

- Change *echo {ESC}3l> prn* at the end of line 34 of PRNTMENU.BAT (Figure 11-15) to *echo {ESC}l<Alt-6> prn.*

PRNTMENU.BAT carries out only one command per menu choice. You could change it so that a menu selection carried out several commands by substituting a Goto command for the Echo command after the appropriate *if errorlevel* command, then carrying out the required commands at the label named in the Goto command, and going back to REPLY_1 or REPLY_2.

For example, suppose that you wanted F8 in the Typeface commands to copy all files with the extensions DOC and TXT from the directory C:\WP to your RAM disk (drive D). You would make the following changes:

1. Change *NLQ* in line 9 of PRNTOPT1.DOC (Figure 11-14) to *Fill D:*.

2. Change *{ESC}n* in line 12 of PRNTMENU.BAT to *goto COPY*.

3. Insert the following commands after line 20 of PRNTMENU.BAT (Figure 11-15):

```
:COPY
    copy c:\wp\*.doc d:
    copy c:\wp\*.txt d:
    goto REPLY_1
```

If you change one of the Page Format commands this way, the last command would be *goto REPLY_2* instead of *goto REPLY_1*.

Using Programs Instead of Redirecting the Echo Command

If you prefer to use programs rather than redirecting Echo commands to send commands to the printer, make sure the COM or EXE files are in the current directory or a directory that is in the command path, then replace the Echo command following the appropriate *if errorlevel* command with the name of the command file.

For example, to use PRNTREST.COM instead of *echo {ESC}@> prn* to reset the printer, change *echo {ESC}@> prn* to *resetprt* in lines 11 and 28 of PRNTMENU.BAT (Figure 11-15).

Combining the DOC Files with PRNTMENU.BAT

To incorporate PRNTMENU.DOC into PRNTMENU.BAT, insert *echo* followed by a space at the beginning of each line of PRNTMENU.DOC, then replace line 3 of PRNTMENU.BAT (*type prntmenu.doc*) with the revised version of PRNTMENU.DOC. To be on the safe side, don't erase PRNTMENU.DOC until you have successfully tested the new version of PRNTMENU.BAT.

To incorporate PRNTOPT1.DOC and PRNTOPT2.DOC into PRNTMENU.BAT, insert *echo* followed by a space at the beginning of each line of both files, then replace line 5 of PRNTMENU.BAT (*type prntopt1.doc*) with the revised version of PRNTOPT1.DOC and replace line 22 (*type prntopt2.doc*) with the revised version of PRNTOPT2.BAT. Again, play it safe and don't erase PRNTOPT1.DOC or PRNTOPT2.DOC until you have successfully tested the new version of PRNTMENU.BAT.

The Printer Setup Menu demonstrates just how much you can do with DOS. It's no little effort to write a batch file like this, but the effort pays off each time PRNTMENU.BAT saves you a bit of time or encourages you to use your printer in a way you might not otherwise try. When you incorporate PRNTMENU.BAT into the menu system described in Chapter 14, you'll have a menu system that manages most of the routine uses of your computer, letting you move from application to application with the press of a key rather than changing directories and typing commands.

Combining the Printer Setup Menu and PRNT.BAT

If you have entered both PRNT.BAT and the Printer Setup Menu, you have two batch files that send commands to the printer and print files in pages. It seems only natural to combine them, so that you could use one batch file to print a series of files using the printer commands you want. It's fairly simple; Figure 11-16 shows the commands you insert in PRNT.BAT to incorporate the Printer Setup Menu.

```
1:    command /c prntmenu prnt
2:    echo <Alt-7>Ready to print {ESC}[1m%1{ESC}[m. Position paper at
      top of page.
3:    echo {ESC}[7mPress F1 to print, any other key to cancel.{ESC}[m
4:    reply
5:    if errorlevel 59 if not errorlevel 60 goto CONTINUE
6:    echo ** Print canceled.
7:    goto END
8: :CONTINUE
```

Figure 11-16. Additions to PRNT.BAT to incorporate the Printer Setup Menu.

Insert the commands shown in Figure 11-16 after line 7 of PRNT.BAT (Figure 11-6).

- Line 1 uses the Command command to call PRNTMENU.BAT. It specifies *prnt* as a parameter so that PRNTMENU.BAT can determine whether it was run by itself or called by another batch file. As you'll see in a moment, this lets you add a command to PRNTMENU.BAT that changes the wording of the F10 choice.

- Lines 2 and 3 beep and display a message that reminds you to position the paper at the top of a page. The beep is used because if you don't position the paper, the files may not be printed in proper pages. If the beep is too irritating, remove the *Alt-7*.

- Line 4 waits for you to press a key.

- Line 5 proceeds to print the files if you press F1.

- Lines 6 and 7 note that you canceled printing and return to DOS.

Save the revised version of PRNT.BAT and test it by typing *prnt* followed by the name of a file. You should see the Printer Setup Menu, and it should work just as it did when you tested it earlier. Select the printer options you want, then press F10. PRNT.BAT should remind you to position the paper at the top of a page; press F1 to print the file. It's a pretty slick way to print files the way you want them.

One last thing. The option for F10 in the Printer Setup Menu reads *Return to DOS*. That isn't true now; when you finish choosing your printer options, PRNTMENU.BAT returns to PRNT.BAT which prints your file. You can fix that by adding just one command to PRNTMENU.BAT.

The word *Return* is displayed on row 21 of the display and *to DOS* is displayed on row 22, so all you have to change is what's displayed on row 22. Because PRNT.BAT calls PRNTMENU.BAT with the parameter *prnt*, you can use an If command to check for a parameter and, if it's *prnt*, change what's displayed on row 22 with an Echo command.

Insert the following command after line 5 of PRNTMENU.BAT:

```
if "%1"=="prnt" echo {ESC}[22;24HPrint File
```

Now the F10 choice is accurate, and the chapter is ended. Save the revised version of PRNTMENU.BAT and turn your printer off. It's earned a rest.

CHAPTER
12

Increasing Your
Keyboard's IQ

You spend most of your time at the computer with your hands on the keyboard—the primary tool for communicating with DOS and application programs. Any changes that make the keyboard better suited to your needs can pay big dividends. This chapter describes a few such changes; it shows you how to:

- Use the editing keys to correct or re-use the last command.

- Redefine the keyboard to let you type the box–drawing characters, carry out a DOS command by pressing a single key, or carry out a whole series of commands by pressing a single key.

- Speed up the repeat action of an IBM PC/AT or compatible computer.

Using the Editing Keys to Edit DOS Commands

DOS doesn't just throw away a command after you press the Enter key, it keeps the command in memory until you press Enter again. The editing keys, shown in Figure 12-1, behave just as they do in Edlin; you can use them to display that last command and enter it again, either unchanged or with changes.

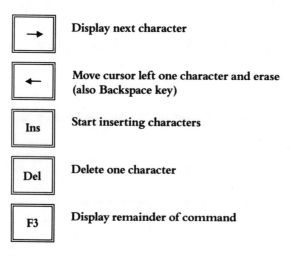

→   **Display next character**

←   **Move cursor left one character and erase (also Backspace key)**

Ins   **Start inserting characters**

Del   **Delete one character**

F3   **Display remainder of command**

Figure 12-1. DOS command-line editing keys.

It takes only a couple of quick examples to show you how the editing keys work. To start, change the directory to \DOS (or wherever you keep your DOS files):

```
A>cd \dos
```

Start with a too-common occurrence: making a mistake while typing a long command. Type the following Directory command, error and all; DOS, of course, chides you for the error:

```
A>dor *.com | sort
Bad command or file name
```

Oops. You meant *dir*. But don't retype the command, just press the right-arrow key. DOS displays the first character of that last command:

```
A>d
```

The whole command is there, waiting for you to use it again. First, correct the error by typing *i*:

```
A>di
```

Now press F3; DOS displays the entire command without the error. Press Enter; DOS carries out the command, just as if you had typed it properly in the first place.

You have used two of the DOS editing keys, the right arrow and F3:

- The right-arrow key displays the next character of the previous command ; each time you press it, it displays another character until you reach the end of the command.

- Pressing F3 is like holding down the right-arrow key until the entire command is displayed: It displays the rest of the command to the end of the line.

You have also used another of the editing features: Whatever you type before displaying the entire command replaces the corresponding characters in the command. The *i* you typed replaced the *o* in the bad command.

Now suppose you meant to display the EXE files, not the COM files, and you'd like to sort the directory entries on column 16 (the file size). No problem. Hold down the right-arrow key and let it repeat until the command is displayed up to the period:

```
A>dir *.
```

If you overshoot, just use the left-arrow key or the Backspace key to back up (if you're cautious, you could press the right-arrow key six times instead of holding it down).

Now type *exe* to replace *com*:

```
A>dir *.exe
```

Finally, press F3 to display the remainder of the command, press the space-bar and type / + 16, and press Enter:

```
A>dir *.exe | sort /+16
```

DOS displays the EXE files sorted by size.

What if you'd rather sort the files in reverse order? Now you'll have to insert some characters, not replace them. That's why there's a key labeled *Ins*. Press F3, then the left-arrow key three times:

```
A>dir *.exe | sort /
```

Press the Ins key, then type *r*, a space, and a /:

```
A>dir *.exe | sort /r /
```

You have used two more of the editing keys, left arrow and Ins:

- The left-arrow key (or the Backspace key; they're equivalent) moves the cursor left one column and erases the character there. It doesn't, however, erase the character from memory—you can display the character again by pressing the right-arrow key.

- The Ins key tells DOS to insert the characters you type next, adding them to the command instead of replacing characters in the command.

Press F3 and Enter to complete and carry out the command. Now DOS displays the directory entries with largest file first.

Finally, what if you decide you'd like to see *all* the files? You'll have to delete *.exe* from the command. That's what the key marked Del is for; it's the last editing key. Each time you press Del before displaying the entire command, DOS deletes one character from the command.

Press the right-arrow key four times:

```
A>dir
```

Now press Del six times. You have to take this operation on faith for a moment because nothing seems to happen, but press F3 to display the rest of the command:

```
A>dir | sort /r /+16
```

You deleted *.exe*. Be careful not to press Enter until you've got the command just the way you want it. Whatever is displayed on the command line when you press Enter becomes the new last command.

The editing keys can save you a lot of keystrokes. After using them for a while, you may never again bang the keyboard in frustration after making a typo in a long command.

Redefining the Keyboard

The application programs you use probably assign special meaning to some or all of the function keys, the keypad keys, perhaps some combinations with the Alt and Ctrl keys, and sometimes even some of the regular character keys. DOS itself gives special meaning to some keys, such as the editing keys described in the previous topic; F6 to mark the end of a file and F7 to produce ASCII character 0; and combinations with the Ctrl key such as Ctrl-C to cancel a command and Ctrl-S to stop the display.

The ANSI.SYS Define Key command, described in Chapter 3, gives you the same sort of control over the keyboard. You can not only change the character a key produces, you can assign a string of characters to a single key. As you'll see in a moment, this presents some real possibilities.

As in Chapter 3, the Prompt command is used to demonstrate this ANSI.SYS command. If you haven't yet gone through the examples in Chapter 3, you might do so before continuing here.

Assigning a Command to a Key

If you frequently use a particular command, especially a long one, it would be much more convenient to enter it with a single keystroke. It's an obvious advantage to press just one key to run *dir *.doc* | *sort /r / + 25* | *more*. You could, of course, write a batch command and give the batch file a single-character name. But you can save both the space the batch file would take on the disk and the time required to load it by assigning the command to a key you normally don't use.

It's easy to demonstrate this with the Prompt command. Type the following to assign *erase *.bak* to Alt-B:

```
A>prompt $e[0;48;"erase *.bak";13p
```

Now when you press Alt-B, DOS displays *erase *.bak* as if you had typed it, and erases all files in the current directory with the extension BAK. This is a quick way to clean up directories with a lot of BAK files.

If you would like this definition—or any other—to be in effect permanently, put the ANSI.SYS command in your AUTOEXEC.BAT file. You can use a Prompt command, as shown here, or an Echo command, as shown in Chapter 3. If you use a Prompt command, be sure to define your system prompt in AUTOEXEC.BAT after redefining the key.

You can assign only one command to a key. As soon as DOS sees a carriage return (character 13) in the string of characters produced by a key, it reacts as if you had pressed the Enter key: It checks to see if what has been entered is a valid command, and ignores any characters that follow.

You can carry out more than one command with a single keystroke by writing a batch file that contains the commands, then assigning the batch command to a key.

For example, suppose that you use a system of menus to select application programs. If the name of the batch file that starts the menu system is MAINMENU.BAT and it's in a directory in the command path, you could assign the batch command to a key combination—Alt-F10, say—and start your menu system from any directory.

Changing the Keyboard Layout

You can redefine the keyboard any way you choose, but chances are you'll most often redefine the function keys or combinations with the Alt and Ctrl keys. There are times, however, when it could be helpful to redefine other keys. The two batch files described here, for example, redefine the keypad keys that normally move the cursor:

- BOX.BAT assigns a set of box-drawing characters to the keypad, letting you type these characters in the extended character set directly from the keyboard.

- UNBOX.BAT reverses BOX.BAT, restoring the normal definition of the keypad keys.

The box-drawing characters are assigned to positions in the keypad that generally correspond to their location in a box. Figure 12-2 shows the layout for the IBM PC, IBM PC/XT, and compatibles. Figure 12-3 shows the layout for the IBM PC/AT and AT-compatible computers.

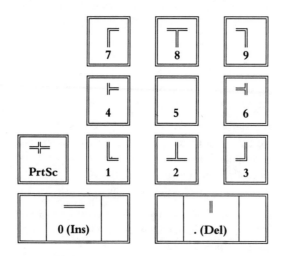

Figure 12-2. Box-drawing characters on an IBM PC and an IBM PC/XT keypad.

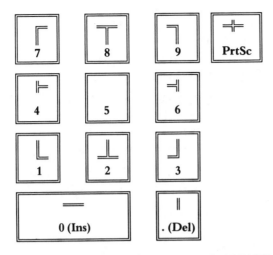

Figure 12-3. Box-drawing characters on an IBM PC/AT keypad.

As mentioned in Chapter 3, you can't use ANSI.SYS to redefine the keys marked with a dash in Appendix D. Of particular interest here, you can't redefine three keys on the keypad: the 5 (the key in the center of the arrow keys), the keypad plus, and the keypad minus. That's why BOX.BAT uses the Ins, Del, and PrtSc keys.

Because UNBOX.BAT restores the original definitions, you'll enter both batch files, then test them together.

Figure 12-4 shows the commands in BOX.BAT.

```
 1:  echo off
 2:  echo {ESC}[0;71;201p
 3:  echo {ESC}[0;72;203p
 4:  echo {ESC}[0;73;187p
 5:  echo {ESC}[0;75;204p
 6:  echo {ESC}[0;77;185p
 7:  echo {ESC}[0;79;200p
 8:  echo {ESC}[0;80;202p
 9:  echo {ESC}[0;81;188p
10:  echo {ESC}[0;82;205p
11:  echo {ESC}[0;83;186p
12:  echo {ESC}[42;206p
13:  cls
```

Figure 12-4. BOX.BAT: Redefining the keypad keys to draw boxes.

BOX.BAT is straightforward, if not especially easy to read. Each Echo command following *echo off* sends an ANSI.SYS Define Key command to the console. The first two numbers in all but the last Echo command identify the key to be redefined (in the first command, for example, *0;71* is the Home key); the last Echo command redefines the asterisk (*), whose key code is 42, because the PrtSc key has the same key code. Appendix D contains the complete list of key codes.

The Define Key command lets you define more than one key, so you could use just one Echo command for all 11 definitions:

```
echo {ESC}[0;71;201;0;72;203;0;73;187;0;75;204;0;77;185;0;79;
     200;0;80;202;0;81;188;0;82;205;0;83;186;42;206p
```

But this would make BOX.BAT even harder to read, and make changing it almost more trouble than it's worth. The minimum disk space required by a file is much larger than BOX.BAT, so there's no advantage in combining all the Define Key commands into one Echo command.

UNBOX.BAT is quite similar to BOX.BAT; it restores each of the 11 keypad keys redefined by BOX.BAT to their original meaning. Figure 12-5 shows the commands in UNBOX.BAT.

```
 1: echo off
 2: echo {ESC}[0;71;0;71p
 3: echo {ESC}[0;72;0;72p
 4: echo {ESC}[0;73;0;73p
 5: echo {ESC}[0;75;0;75p
 6: echo {ESC}[0;77;0;77p
 7: echo {ESC}[0;79;0;79p
 8: echo {ESC}[0;80;0;80p
 9: echo {ESC}[0;81;0;81p
10: echo {ESC}[0;82;0;82p
11: echo {ESC}[0;83;0;83p
12: echo {ESC}[42;42p
13: cls
```

Figure 12-5. UNBOX.BAT: Restoring the keypad keys' definitions.

Using BOX.BAT and UNBOX.BAT

Create BOX.BAT and UNBOX.BAT with your text editor or word processor and enter the commands shown in Figures 12-4 and 12-5. To put the box-drawing characters on the keypad, type the BOX.BAT command:

```
A>box
```

BOX.BAT echoes 11 blank lines, one for each Echo command that follows *echo off*, then clears the screen.

Now try the keypad keys. DOS should display the box-drawing characters. If you press Enter, of course, DOS responds *Bad command or file name*. Notice that the Ins key doesn't repeat. This has nothing to do with BOX.BAT; the Ins key normally never repeats.

To restore the original definitions for the keypad keys, type:

`A>unbox`

UNBOX.BAT, too, echoes 11 blank lines and clears the screen. The keypad keys should have their original meaning.

You could write other batch files that use this technique to put other characters from the extended character set, such as the mathematics symbols or foreign-language characters, temporarily on the keyboard.

To create a file using the box-drawing characters, copy from the console or use one of the batch commands for creating a text file (described in Chapter 13). You can't use your text editor or word processor with the keypad keys redefined. Even if the program doesn't define its own meanings for the keypad characters, you wouldn't be able to move the cursor.

The IBM extended character set includes four sets of box-drawing characters using different combinations of single and double lines. Table C-3 shows all four sets. You could expand BOX.BAT to add the other three sets in different parts of the keyboard, or write four different versions (perhaps called BOX1.BAT through BOX4.BAT) to put any set on the numeric keypad. If you used four different batch files to redefine the keypad keys this way, UNBOX.BAT would restore the numeric keypad after you used any of them.

Speeding Up the IBM PC/AT Keyboard

When you hold down a key, the keyboard waits a moment, then repeats the character until you release the key (or the keyboard buffer is filled). Both the length of the delay and the speed of the repeat action can be changed on the IBM PC/AT and most compatible computers.

The program FAST.COM reduces the delay time and increases the speed of the repeat action; the effect is to make the keyboard much quicker. The program is specific to the IBM PC/AT and compatible computers. You cannot use it with the IBM PC, IBM PC/XT, or computers compatible with those models.

You create FAST.COM using Debug. The procedure is described in Chapter 5. If you haven't yet gone through the examples in Chapter 5, you might do so before continuing here.

Using your text editor, word processor, or Edlin, create a file named FAST.SCR and enter the lines shown in Figure 12-6 (on the next page).

```
 1: a 100
 2: mov    al,f3
 3: out    60,al
 4: mov    cx,2000
 5: loop   107
 6: xor    al,al
 7: out    60,al
 8: int    20
 9:
10: r cx
11: f
12: n fast.com
13: w
14: q
```

Figure 12-6. Debug script for FAST.COM.

Proofread FAST.SCR against Figure 12-6. Make certain that line 9 is blank and that the last line is a *q*. If there is an error in either of these lines, you'll have to restart DOS when you try to create FAST.COM. When you're sure there are no differences, save FAST.SCR.

To create FAST.COM, type the following Debug command:

```
A>debug < fast.scr
```

If nothing seems to happen and pressing a key has no effect, restart DOS, proofread FAST.SCR against Figure 12-6, correct any differences, and re-enter the Debug command.

DOS should respond as shown in Figure 12-7. Proofread the display against Figure 12-7. If there are any differences, proofread FAST.SCR against Figure 12-6, correct any differences, and re-enter the Debug command.

```
-a 100
xxxx:0100 mov  al,f3
xxxx:0102 out  60,al
xxxx:0104 mov  cx,2000
xxxx:0107 loop 107
xxxx:0109 xor  al,al
xxxx:010B out  60,al
xxxx:010D int  20
xxxx:010F
-r cx
CX 0000
:0f
-n fast.com
-w
Writing 000F bytes
-q
```

Figure 12-7. DOS response to creating FAST.SCR.

If your screen agrees with Figure 12-7, you're ready to try FAST.COM. But before you enter the command, hold down any key and notice how quickly the key repeats. Now type the Fast command:

A>fast

Hold down a key again; you should notice a significant difference. If you don't, go back and check everything again.

This increased speed should remain in effect even when you use an application program. FAST.COM can do a lot to reduce your impatience level when you must scroll all the way across a line or use the Backspace key to erase more than a few characters. Although the actual time saved may be small, comfort and satisfaction often depend as much on perceptions as on objective reality. It may take a while to get used to the increased speed, but it's not an unpleasant adaptation.

CHAPTER
13

Playing It Smart
with Files and Disks

M ost of your computer work involves creating, changing, printing, and otherwise dealing with files. The most common use of batch commands is working with files, which are stored on disks. This chapter suggests some ways of working with files and disks that can make your job a bit easier, and describes several batch commands designed specifically to let you manage your files and disks more quickly, easily, and safely.

Naming Your Files

Consistency in naming your files lets you manage them more easily. For example, if you always use an extension with file names but never with directory names, you can display just the subdirectories by typing *dir ∗*. If you use the extension LET for all files that contain letters, you can display the names of all files that contain letters by typing *dir ∗.let*.

Suppose you followed this convention for naming files that contain letters:

● The first three characters identify the recipient.

● The next two characters identify the month (01 through 12).

● The next two characters identify the day (01 through 31).

Now you could display the names of all files that contain letters by typing *dir ∗.let*, display the names of all letters written to HST by typing *dir hst∗*, or display the names of all letters written in July by typing *dir ???07∗*.

In general, the more closely your file names and extensions describe the contents and the more consistent you are in assigning names, the more easily you can keep track of your files.

Setting Up Your Directories

Besides holding your application programs and data files for different management or project responsibilities, your directory system should provide a framework to support the ways you use your computer. Its structure should feel natural, and you should be able to find a particular file without searching through several similar-sounding directories.

Some batch files in this book suggest a few files to be kept in the root directory but, in general, keep it as free of files as possible. Reserve it for subdirectories, COMMAND.COM, AUTOEXEC.BAT, CONFIG.SYS, and a minimum of other files.

Figure 13-1 shows four first-level subdirectories (in the root) that you could use to contain your most frequently used programs and batch files. You may prefer different directory names, but these are the sorts of files you want readily available, yet easily distinguished. In addition to these, of course, you'll want your major application directories such as word processing and spreadsheets. All these directories should be in your command path.

Directory	Description
\DOS	For all DOS files (and nothing but DOS files). This makes it easy to find a DOS file or change to a new DOS version.
\BATCH	For batch files you use frequently, plus other files they require (for example, files for redirecting input such as CR.DAT, described in Chapter 6 and later in this chapter).
\PGM	For utility programs, programs used by your batch files, and application programs that don't require a separate directory.
\MENU	For all files required by your menu system (if you use one), including programs or batch files that you also use independently or that are used by other batch files. This makes it easy to keep track of your menu system or make a copy to transfer to another computer.

Figure 13-1. Suggested subdirectories for programs and batch files.

Prevent Accidental Changes and Deletions

If you're using Version 3 of DOS, you can make a file read-only with the Attribute command; once you have done this, the file can't be changed or deleted until you remove the read-only protection. One inadvertent change or deletion could make you wish you had done it.

It doesn't take long to protect the files that you don't change, or that you change infrequently, or those that simply mustn't be changed accidentally. If all the DOS files are in a directory named \DOS, for example, you can make them all read-only by typing *attrib +r \dos*.**.

Moving Around Through Directories

The .. entry in a directory listing represents the directory immediately above the current one. You can use it to move quickly around a directory structure. For example, if you're in the directory \123\BUDGETS\MKT:

- Type *cd ..* to change to \123\BUDGETS.
- Type *cd ..\..* to change to \123.
- Type *cd ..\mfg* to change to \123\BUDGETS\MFG.

The Batch Files

The remainder of this chapter describes several batch files that make working with files and disks easier and, in some cases, safer.

The batch files are described in independent topics that don't rely on each other. Each topic includes a description of what the batch file does, a figure that shows the commands in the batch file, an explanation of how it works, suggestions for testing it after you have entered it, and, in some cases, suggestions about how you might better tailor it to your use.

Stop Typing Those Long Directory Names

GO.BAT changes to the directory that matches the alias you specify as the first parameter. If you type a file name (including wildcard characters) as the second parameter, GO.BAT changes the directory, clears the screen, and displays the directory entries that match the file name.

You can define as many aliases as you like in the batch file. Using short aliases can make it much faster to change directories, especially if you have a directory structure several levels deep.

Figure 13-2 shows the commands in GO.BAT.

```
 1:    echo off
 2:    if not "%1"=="" goto OK
 3:    cls
 4:    echo {ESC}[1mCommand                   Result{ESC}[m
 5:    echo go {alias}                        Change to directory defined for {alias}
 6:    echo go {alias} {filename}             Change directory and display
 7:    echo                                   entries for {filename}.
 8:    echo <Alt-255>
 9:    echo {ESC}[1mAlias                     Directory{ESC}[m
10:    echo   r                               root
11:    goto END
12:  :OK
13:      if %1==r cd \
14:      if "%2"=="" goto END
15:      cls
16:      dir %2
17:  :END
```

Figure 13-2. GO.BAT: Changing directories quickly.

- Line 2 skips the instructions if you specified at least one parameter.

- Lines 4–8 display instructions for entering the Go batch command followed by a blank line.

- Lines 9–11 display the list of aliases and directories you have defined, then return to DOS. Line 10 defines *r* as the alias for the root directory; this isn't an especially useful alias, but the Echo command is included here as a model for the Echo commands you will add that describe your aliases, which should start here.

- Line 13 starts the list of If commands that check *%1* against the aliases you have defined. Again, the check for *r* as an alias is included here only as a model for the If commands that check for your aliases, which should start here. If *%1* matches an alias, GO.BAT changes to that directory.

- Line 14 returns to DOS if you didn't enter a second parameter.

- Lines 15 and 16 clear the screen and display the directory entries that match the file name you specified as the second parameter.

Testing GO.BAT

GO.BAT requires no other files. First, type the command with no parameters:

```
A>go
```

GO.BAT should display its instructions, followed by the list of aliases and directories you have defined:

```
Command                   Result
go {alias}                Change to directory defined for {alias}
go {alias} {filename}     Change directory and display
                          entries for {filename}

Alias                     Directory
 r                        root
```

Remember, the alias defined here for the root is to give you a model for the Echo and If commands you will add to GO.BAT to define your aliases and directories. To make sure GO.BAT is working, change to the root directory by typing:

```
A>go r
```

If your prompt doesn't show you the current directory, you can type a Change Directory (cd) or Directory command to verify that you have changed directories.

If you're in the root directory, you know that the Change Directory (cd) command in GO.BAT is working correctly. Test the last feature by typing the command again, this time adding a file name as the second parameter:

```
A>go r *.bat
```

GO.BAT should respond by displaying the directory entries for all the batch files in the root directory.

It's hard to appreciate the convenience of GO.BAT when the only alias is for the root directory, which already has an alias. To tailor it to your directories, you insert an Echo command for each alias in place of line 10 in Figure 13-2, and an If command for each alias in place of line 13. Suppose you wanted to define the following aliases for the associated directories:

Alias	Directory
mem	\word\corresp
bgt	\123\budgets
p	\telecomm\xtalk\portflio

You would enter the following Echo commands in place of line 10 in Figure 13-2 (line up the aliases and their directories under the Alias and Directory headings, as shown in Figure 13-2):

```
echo    mem            \word\corresp
echo    bgt            \123\budgets
echo    p              \telecomm\xtalk\portflio
```

You would enter the following If commands in place of line 13 in Figure 13-2:

```
if %1==mem cd \word\corresp
if %1==bgt cd \123\budgets
if %1==p   cd \telecomm\xtalk\portflio
```

Pick the directories and aliases you want to use with GO.BAT, modify the batch file, and stop typing those long directory names and backslashes.

Creating Text Files

The next four batch files let you create text files quickly without using a text editor or word processor. All four use the technique of copying from the console, but each is tailored to a specific use. Because you can't edit what you have entered, these batch files are best suited to short files, although you can use some of them to add to an existing text file.

Creating a Text File Quickly

FILE.BAT clears the screen and displays a ruler that marks the columns. It's a quick way to create a short text file for any use, such as small batch files.

Figure 13-3 shows the commands in FILE.BAT.

```
 1:    echo off
 2:    if not "%1"=="" goto OK
 3:    echo {ESC}[7mYou must specify a file name or prn.{ESC}[m
 4:    echo Please re-enter the command.
 5:    goto END
 6: :OK
 7:    if %1==prn goto START
 8:    if not exist %1 goto START
 9:    echo <Alt-7>{ESC}[7m%1 exists.{ESC}[m
10:    echo Press F1 to replace it, any other key to quit.
11:    reply
12:    if errorlevel 59 if not errorlevel 60 goto START
13:    goto END
14: :START
15:    cls
16:    echo {ESC}[7mPress {F6}-{ENTER} after the last line.{ESC}[m
17:    echo       5    10    15    20    25    30    35    40    45    50    55    60
       65    70    75
18:    echo ┌─────┬────┬────┬────┬────┬────┬────┬────┬────┬────┬────┬────┐
                  ╧                                                      ╛
19:    echo <Alt-255>
20:    copy con %1 > nul
21:    if %1==prn goto END
22:    echo <Alt-255>
23:    echo {ESC}[7m%1 created.{ESC}[m
24:    echo Press F1 to print it, any other key to quit.
25:    reply
26:    if errorlevel 59 if not errorlevel 60 copy %1 prn > nul
27: :END
```

Figure 13-3. FILE.BAT: Creating a text file quickly.

The following explanations describe how FILE.BAT works:

- Line 2 skips the following error message if you specify the name of a file.

- Lines 3–5 warn you that you must specify the name of a file as a parameter and return to DOS.

- Lines 7 and 8 skip the following warning if you specify the printer (PRN) or a file that doesn't exist.

- Lines 9–13 warn you that the file you specified exists, and gives you the opportunity to quit; if you press F1, the existing file is replaced by the file you create. If you press another key, FILE.BAT returns you to DOS.

- Lines 14–16 clear the screen and display instructions.

- Lines 17 and 18 display a ruler that marks columns, followed by a blank line. Although lines 17 and 18 are shown on two lines, enter each as a single line. The Alt-key codes for the graphics characters:

  ┌ Alt-213   = Alt-205   ╤ Alt-209   ╕ Alt-184

- Line 20 copies from the console to the file you specified until you press F6 and Enter.

- Lines 22–27 give you the option of printing the file. Line 21 skips this option if you specify the printer because the file has already been printed.

Testing FILE.BAT

FILE.BAT requires no other files. First, type the command with no parameters:

`A>file`

FILE.BAT warns you that you must specify either a file name or *prn* (for the printer) and returns to DOS:

`You must specify a file name or prn.`
`Please re-enter the command.`

`A>_`

Enter the command again, this time specifying FILETEST.DOC:

`A>file filetest.doc`

FILE.BAT responds by clearing the screen and displaying the instructions and ruler:

`Press {F6}-{ENTER} after the last line.`

```
      5   10   15   20   25   30   35   40   45   50   55   60   65   70   75
```

Now you can type the file. Type:

`WORDS TO LIVE BY`

`When all else fails`
`Use bloody great nails.`
`^Z`

Now FILE.BAT gives you the option of printing the file:

`filetest.doc created.`
`Press F1 to print it, any other key to quit.`

Make sure your printer is turned on, and press F1. FILE.BAT prints the file and returns to DOS.

Now see what happens if you use FILE.BAT to create a file that already exists by typing:

`A>file filetest.doc`

FILE.BAT beeps, warns you that the file exists, and gives you the option of replacing the file or quitting:

```
filetest.doc exists.
Press F1 to replace it, any other key to quit.
```

Press the spacebar or any other key to quit.

The batch file BOX.BAT, described in Chapter 12, redefines the numeric-keypad characters to produce the box-drawing characters from the extended character set. If you enter and execute BOX.BAT before FILE.BAT, you can use the numeric keypad to easily create a text file that contains simple graphic figures such as an organization chart.

Adding to the Beginning or End of a File

ADD.BAT lets you add lines to the beginning or end of a text file. It requires two parameters: the name of the file to be changed, and *beg* or *end* to specify where to add the lines.

Figure 13-4 shows the commands in ADD.BAT.

```
 1:      echo off
 2:      if not "%1"=="" goto ONE_PARM
 3: :INSTRUCT
 4:      echo <Alt-255>
 5:      echo {ESC}[1mCommand                    Result{ESC}[m
 6:      echo add {file name} beg   Add to the beginning of {file}.
 7:      echo add {file name} end   Add to the end of {file}.
 8:      goto END
 9: :ONE_PARM
10:      if "%2"=="" goto INSTRUCT
11:      if %2==beg goto TWO_PRMS
12:      if %2==end goto TWO_PRMS
13:      goto INSTRUCT
14: :TWO_PRMS
15:      if exist %1 goto OK
16:      echo {ESC}[7mI can't find a file named %1.{ESC}[m
17:      goto INSTRUCT
18: :OK
19:      echo <Alt-255>
20:      echo Type the line or lines to be added.
21:      echo {ESC}[7mAfter the last line, press {F6} and {ENTER}.{ESC}[m
22:      echo <Alt-255>
23:      if %2==beg copy con+%1 add.$$$ > nul
24:      if %2==end copy %1+con add.$$$ > nul
25:      erase %1
26:      rename add.$$$ %1
27:      echo <Alt-255>
28:      echo {ESC}[7mNew contents of %1:{ESC}[m
29:      echo <Alt-255>
30:      more < %1
31: :END
```

Figure 13-4. ADD.BAT: Adding to the beginning or end of a file.

The following explanations describe how ADD.BAT works:

- Line 2 skips displaying the instructions if you specify at least one parameter.

- Lines 3-8 display instructions for entering the Add batch command, then return to DOS.

- Line 10 displays the instructions and returns to DOS if you specified only one parameter.

- Lines 11–13 display the instructions and return to DOS if you didn't specify *beg* or *end* as the second parameter.

- Line 15 skips the following error message if the file you specified exists.

- Lines 16 and 17 display an error message and command instructions, then return to DOS if the file you specified doesn't exist.

- Lines 19–22 display a blank line, instructions for how to proceed, and another blank line.

- Line 23 copies the console, then the file you named, to a temporary file named ADD.$$$ if you specified *beg*.

- Line 24 copies the file you named, then the console, to a temporary file named ADD.$$$ if you specified *end*.

- Lines 25 and 26 erase the file you named and change the name of the temporary file from ADD.$$$ to the file you named.

- Lines 27–30 display a blank line, a title line, another blank line, and the new contents of the file.

Testing ADD.BAT

ADD.BAT requires no other files. First, type the command with no parameters:

```
A>add
```

ADD.BAT should display the following instructions and return to DOS:

```
Command              Result
add {file name} beg  Add to the beginning of {file}.
add {file name} end  Add to the end of {file}.
```

Enter the command again, this time specifying the file ADDTEST.DOC and *beg* to add lines to the beginning of the file:

```
A>add addtest.doc beg
```

ADD.BAT warns you that it can't find the file, displays the instructions again, and returns to DOS.

`I can't find a file named addtest.doc.`

Command   **Result**
`add {file name} beg` `Add to the beginning of {file}.`
`add {file name} end` `Add to the end of {file}.`

`A>_`

Type the following to create the test file:

```
A>copy con addtest.doc
"Too much of a good thing
^Z
        1 File(s) copied
```

`A>_`

Now type the command naming ADDTEST.DOC again; this time, ADD.BAT prompts you to enter the lines to be added:

`A>add addtest.doc beg`

```
Type the line or lines to be added.
After the last line, press {F6} and {ENTER}.
```

Type the following to add a couple of lines:

```
Someone once said
(it must have been Mae West)
^Z
```

ADD.BAT shows you the result of adding the lines and returns to DOS:

`New contents of addtest.doc:`

```
Someone once said
(it must have been Mae West)
"Too much of a good thing
A>_
```

Adding to the end of a file works the same way; type the following:

`A>add addtest.doc end`

```
Type the line or lines to be added.
After the last line, press {F6} and {ENTER}.
```

```
is wonderful."
^Z
```

`New contents of addtest.doc:`

```
Someone once said
(it must have been Mae West)
"Too much of a good thing
is wonderful."
```

`A>_`

Creating or Adding to a Note File

NOTE.BAT creates a new file or adds to an existing file, time- and date-stamping each entry. It's a convenient way to keep a collection of dated notes.

Figure 13-5 shows the commands in NOTE.BAT.

```
 1:    echo off
 2:    if not "%1"=="" goto OK
 3:    echo <Alt-255>
 4:    echo You must enter the name of a file as a parameter.
 5:    echo If it doesn't exist, it is created.
 6:    echo {ESC}[7mPlease re-enter the command.{ESC}[m
 7:    goto END
 8: :OK
 9:    if exist %1 goto SHOW_IT
10:    echo -------------------- NOTE FILE %1 > %1
11: :SHOW_IT
12:    cls
13:    more < %1
14:    echo <Alt-255>
15:    echo Type the line or lines to be added to %1.
16:    echo {ESC}[7mAfter the last line, press {F6} and {ENTER}.{ESC}[m
17:    echo <Alt-255> >> %1
18:    date < cr.dat | find "C" >> %1
19:    time < cr.dat | find "C" >> %1
20:    echo -------------------------------- >> %1
21:    copy %1+con note.$$$/b > nul
22:    erase %1
23:    rename note.$$$ %1
24: :END
```

Figure 13-5. NOTE.BAT: Creating or adding to a note file.

The following explanations describe how NOTE.BAT works:

- Line 2 skips the following error message if you specify the name of a file.

- Lines 3–7 warn you that you must specify the name of a file as a parameter, then return to DOS.

- Lines 9 and 10 create the file if it doesn't exist (there are 20 dashes in the title line).

- Lines 11–13 clear the screen and display the file (if the file is new, it contains just the title line).

- Lines 14–17 display a blank line, instructions, and another blank line.

- Lines 18–20 write the current date, current time, and a separator line to the file (there are 30 dashes).

- Line 21 copies the existing file and any lines added from the console to a temporary file named NOTE.$$$.

- Lines 22 and 23 erase the existing file and change the name of the temporary file from NOTE.$$$ to the file name you specified.

Testing NOTE.BAT

NOTE.BAT requires the file CR.DAT, described in Chapter 6. If you haven't yet created CR.DAT, do so now, and place it in the same directory with NOTE.BAT. To test NOTE.BAT, first type the command with no parameters:

```
A>note
```

NOTE.BAT displays the following warning and returns to DOS:

```
You must enter the name of a file as a parameter.
If it doesn't exist, it is created.
Please re-enter the command.

A>_
```

Enter the command again, specifying NOTETEST.DOC; NOTE.BAT prompts you to enter the lines to be added:

```
A>note notetest.doc

-------------------- NOTE FILE notetest.doc

Type the line or lines to be added to notetest.doc.
After the last line, press {F6} and {ENTER}.

This could be the start
of something big.
^Z
A>_
```

NOTE.BAT saves the file and returns to DOS.

Type the following to add to NOTETEST.DOC; NOTE.DOC displays the contents of the file and prompts you to enter more lines:

```
A>note notetest.doc


------------------- NOTE FILE notetest.doc

Current date is Fri 10-16-1987
Current time is 15:45:55.72
-----------------------------

This could be the start
of something big.

Type the line or lines to be added to notetest.doc.
After the last line, press {F6} and {ENTER}.

This is the next entry.
^Z

A>_
```

If you display the file with the Type command, you'll see the second entry with its time and date stamps.

Creating a Fixed-Format File

MEMO.BAT creates a file in fixed format—a simple memo with TO, FROM, and SUBJ lines. It includes an option for printing the file.

Figure 13-6 shows the commands in MEMO.BAT.

```
 1:    echo off
 2:    if "%1"=="" goto NO_FILE
 3:    if not exist %1 goto ENTER
 4:    echo {ESC}[7mThat file exists. If you continue, you'll
       replace it.{ESC}[m
 5:    goto QUIT
 6: :NO_FILE
 7:    echo You didn't specify a file name.
 8:    echo You'll only be able to print the memo.
 9: :QUIT
10:    echo {ESC}[7mPress F1 to continue; any other key quits.{ESC}[m
11:    reply
12:    if errorlevel 59 if not errorlevel 60 goto ENTER
13:    goto END
14: :ENTER
15:    cls
16:    echo {ESC}[7mPress {Enter}{F6}{Enter} after TO.{ESC}[m
17:    type \batch\memoto.dat
18:    copy \batch\memoto.dat+con memo.$$$ > nul
19:    echo {ESC}[7mPress {Enter}{F6}{Enter} after FROM.{ESC}[m
20:    type \batch\memofrom.dat
21:    copy memo.$$$+\batch\memofrom.dat+con > nul
22:    echo {ESC}[7mPress {Enter}{F6}{Enter} after SUBJ.{ESC}[m
```

Figure 13-6. MEMO.BAT: Creating a fixed-form text file.

(continued)

```
23:     type \batch\memosubj.dat
24:     copy memo.$$$+\batch\memosubj.dat+con > nul
25:     echo {ESC}[7mType the memo. Press {F6} and {Enter} at the
        end.{ESC}[m
26:     copy memo.$$$+con > nul
27:     if not "%1"=="" copy memo.$$$ %1 > nul
28:     cls
29:     type memo.$$$
30:     echo <Alt-255>
31:     echo {ESC}[7mPress F1 to print the memo, any other key to
        quit.{ESC}[m
32:     reply
33:     if errorlevel 59 if not errorlevel 60 copy memo.$$$ prn > nul
34:     erase memo.$$$
35: :END
```

Figure 13-6 continued.

The following explanations describe how MEMO.BAT works:

- Line 2 goes to display a warning message if you didn't specify a file name.

- Line 3 skips the following warning message if you didn't specify an existing file.

- Lines 4 and 5 display a message that warns you that there is a file with the name you specified, and go to give you the option of continuing or quitting.

- Lines 7 and 8 display a message that warns you that you didn't specify a file name.

- Lines 9–13 display a message telling you that you can press F1 to continue, wait for you to press a key, then return to DOS if you press any key other than F1.

- Lines 15–17 clear the screen, display instructions for entering the recipient's name, and type MEMOTO.DAT (which contains *TO:*).

- Line 18 copies MEMOTO.DAT plus any lines from the console to the temporary file MEMO.$$$ (which now contains the name of the recipient).

- Lines 19–21 display instructions for entering the sender's name, type MEMOFROM.DAT (which contains the line *FROM:*), then copy MEMO.$$$ plus MEMOFROM.DAT plus any lines from the console to MEMO.$$$ (adding the sender's name).

- Lines 22–24 display instructions for entering the subject, type MEMOSUBJ.DAT (which contains the line *SUBJ:*), then copy MEMO.$$$ plus MEMOSUBJ.DAT plus the console to MEMO.$$$ (adding the subject).

- Lines 25 and 26 display instructions for entering the body of the memo, then copy MEMO.$$$ plus any lines from the console to MEMO.$$$ (adding the body of the memo). Although line 25 is shown on two lines, enter it as a single line.

- Line 27 copies the memo to the file you specified if you specified a file name.

- Lines 28–30 clear the screen and then display the memo followed by a blank line.

- Lines 31–33 tell you that you can print the memo by pressing F1, wait for you to press a key, and print the memo if you press F1.

- Line 34 erases the temporary file MEMO.$$$.

Testing MEMO.BAT

MEMO.BAT requires three temporary files that contain the fixed parts of the file in the directory \BATCH. Type the following to create the files. Note that as you create each file you do *not* press Enter until after you press F6, and that there is a space after the colon and before the F6:

```
A>copy con \batch\memoto.dat
TO: ^Z
        1 File(s) copied

A>copy con \batch\memofrom.dat
FROM: ^Z
        1 File(s) copied

A>copy con \batch\memosubj.dat
SUBJ: ^Z
        1 File(s) copied

A>_
```

Now test MEMO.BAT by typing the command with no parameters:

```
A>memo
```

MEMO.BAT displays a warning and gives you the option of returning to DOS:

```
You didn't specify a file name.
You'll only be able to print the memo.
Press F1 to continue; any other key quits.
```

Press F1. The following dialogue shows how MEMO.BAT prompts you to enter the parts of the memo and your responses to write a short memo; because the use of the Enter key is important to the spacing of the memo, this example shows each time you should press Enter:

```
Press {Enter}{F6}{Enter} after TO.
TO: Thomas Watson<Enter>
<F6><Enter>
Press {Enter}{F6}{Enter} after FROM.
FROM: Alexander Graham Bell<Enter>
<F6><Enter>
Press {Enter}{Enter}{F6}{Enter} after SUBJ.
SUBJ: Message<Enter>
<Enter>
<F6><Enter>
Type the memo. Press {F6} and {Enter} at the end.
I must speak with you about<Enter>
your use of the WATS line.<Enter>
<Enter>
Al<Enter>
<F6><Enter>
```

MEMO.BAT clears the screen, displays the memo, and gives you the option of printing it:

```
TO: Thomas Watson
FROM: Alexander Graham Bell
SUBJ: Message

I must speak with you about
your use of the WATS line.

Al
```

```
Press F1 to print the memo, any other key to quit.
```

Make sure the printer is on and press F1. The file should be printed.

Because you didn't specify a file name, this memo isn't saved. MEMO.BAT also warns you if you specify the name of an existing file, giving you the option of replacing it or returning to DOS.

You could use this same approach—perhaps even modify MEMO.BAT— to create any sort of fixed-format file that you use, such as electronic-mail messages, status reports, or data-entry files.

Adding the Date and Time to a File

STAMP.BAT adds two lines that contain the current date and current time at the beginning of any existing file.

Figure 13-7 shows the commands in STAMP.BAT.

```
 1:     echo off
 2:     if not "%1"=="" goto OK
 3:     echo {ESC}[7mYou must specify a file name.{ESC}[m
 4:     echo Please re-enter the command.
 5:     goto END
 6: :OK
 7:     date < cr.dat | find "C" > stamp.$$$
 8:     time < cr.dat | find "C" >> stamp.$$$
 9:     echo ----------------------------- >> stamp.$$$
10:     copy stamp.$$$+%1 temp.$$$ > nul
11:     erase stamp.$$$
12:     erase %1
13:     rename temp.$$$ %1
14: :END
```

Figure 13-7. STAMP.BAT: Adding date and time stamps to a file.

The following explanations describe how STAMP.BAT works:

- Line 2 skips the following error message if you specify the name of a file.

- Lines 3–5 warn you that you must specify the name of a file as a parameter and return to DOS.

- Lines 7–9 write a date stamp, time stamp, and dividing line to a temporary file named STAMP.$$$.

- Line 10 copies the temporary file, then the file you named, to a second temporary file named TEMP.$$$.

- Line 11 erases the temporary file named STAMP.$$$.

- Lines 12 and 13 erase the file you named and change the name of the temporary file named TEMP.$$$ to the file name you specified.

Testing STAMP.BAT

STAMP.BAT requires the file CR.DAT, which was described in Chapter 6. If you have not already created CR.DAT, do so now and place it in the same directory as STAMP.BAT. First, type the command with no parameters:

A>stamp

STAMP.BAT displays the following warning and returns to DOS:

You must specify a file name.
Please re-enter the command.

A>_

Type the following to create a test file:

```
A>copy con stamptst.doc
This file should be dated.
^Z
        1 File(s) copied

A>_
```

Now type the STAMP.BAT command naming STAMPTST.DOC:

```
A>stamp stamptst.doc
```

There's some disk activity, then DOS displays the system prompt. Type the following to see the result:

```
A>type stamptst.doc

Current date is Fri 10-18-1987
Current time is 16:37:23.35
-------------------------------
This file should be dated.

A>_
```

You can use STAMP.BAT to stamp the date and time on any file.

Finding a File on a Fixed Disk

It isn't hard to forget where you stored a file, especially if your fixed disk contains hundreds of files in a couple of dozen directories. FINDFILE.BAT simplifies the task of finding a file at the expense of a bit of disk space, and usually finds the file in a few seconds.

FINDFILE.BAT takes advantage of the /V option of the Check Disk (chkdsk) command that displays the name of each file. Instead of displaying this list of files, however, FINDFILE.BAT redirects it to a file named ALLFILES.DAT in the root directory, then searches this file with the Find command for all file names that contain the string you specify. Because ALLFILES.DAT is in the root directory, you can use FINDFILE.BAT with any disk.

ALLFILES.DAT isn't an especially large file: It depends on how many files are on the disk and how long the path names are, but each directory entry averages between 30 and 40 bytes. Estimating generously, then, on a floppy disk with about 100 files ALLFILES.DAT might be 4000 bytes long; on a 10-megabyte fixed disk with 750 files, it might be 30,000 bytes long. This isn't a bad price for the convenience.

Because the Check Disk (chkdsk) command can take as long as a minute or more, FINDFILE.BAT doesn't run chkdsk unless you specify *new* as the second parameter or unless ALLFILES.DAT isn't in the root directory. Except when you're doing work that requires changing many files, you won't have to tell FINDFILE.BAT to run chkdsk very often, so the search usually takes no more time than it takes DOS to search ALLFILES.DAT.

Figure 13-8 shows the commands in FINDFILE.BAT.

```
 1:     echo off
 2:     if not "%1"=="" goto OK
 3: :INSTRUCT
 4:     echo <Alt-255>
 5:     echo {ESC}[1mCommand              Result{ESC}[m
 6:     echo findfile STRING      Searches for file names that contain
        STRING.
 7:     echo                      STRING must be entered in uppercase.
 8:     echo findfile STRING new  Forces a Chkdsk command.
 9:     goto END
10: :OK
11:     if "%2"=="new" goto CHKDSK
12:     if not "%2"=="" goto INSTRUCT
13:     if exist \allfiles.dat goto FIND_IT
14: :CHKDSK
15:     echo {ESC}[7mExecuting Check Disk command.{ESC}[m
16:     chkdsk /v > \allfiles.dat
17: :FIND_IT
18:     find "%1" \allfiles.dat
19: :END
```

Figure 13-8. FINDFILE.BAT: Finding a file on a fixed disk.

Note: If you're using Version 2 of DOS, be sure to read "Changes to FINDFILE.BAT for Version 2 Users" (the next section) before testing it.

The following explanations describe how FINDFILE.BAT works:

- Line 2 skips the instructions if you specified at least one parameter.

- Lines 4–9 display instructions for entering the Findfile batch command and return to DOS.

- Line 11 goes to carry out a Check Disk command if you entered *new* as the second parameter.

- Line 12 goes to display the instructions and return to DOS if you entered anything other than *new* as the second parameter.

- Line 13 goes directly to the search of ALLFILES.DAT if that file exists in the root directory.

- Line 15 displays a message notifying you that a Check Disk command is to be carried out.

- Line 16 carries out a Check Disk command, redirecting the output to ALLFILES.DAT in the root directory. Notice that this command includes both a slash (*/v*) and a backslash (*allfiles.dat*).

- Line 18 finally searches ALLFILES.DAT for the string you specified.

Changes to FINDFILE.BAT for Version 2 Users

Line 13 in Figure 13-8 uses an If Exist command to check for the existence of ALLFILES.DAT in the root directory, but Version 2 of DOS doesn't permit a path name with the If Exist command. Enter the following command after line 1 of Figure 13-8:

```
cd \
```

With this change, FINDFILE.BAT works with either Version 2 or Version 3, but leaves the current directory set to the root when it returns to DOS (the version in Figure 13-8 leaves the current directory unchanged). If you prefer that FINDFILE.BAT leave the current directory unchanged, see "Modifying FINDFILE.BAT to Restore the Current Directory" later in this chapter.

Testing FINDFILE.BAT

FINDFILE.BAT requires no other files. First, type the command with no parameters:

```
A>findfile
```

FINDFILE.BAT should display the following instructions:

```
Command              Result
findfile STRING      Searches for file names that contain STRING.
                     STRING must be entered in uppercase.
findfile STRING new  Forces a Check Disk command.

A>_
```

The first time you use it, FINDFILE.BAT runs the Check Disk command because there is no file named ALLFILES.DAT in the root directory. You must enter the search string in uppercase because the output of the Check Disk command is uppercase. Type the following to display the names of all files whose name contains EXE:

```
A>findfile EXE
```

FINDFILE.BAT responds by telling you that it's running chkdsk, then displays the names of the files it found. Because it uses the Find command, the list of files is preceded by a line that identifies the file searched (\ALLFILES.DAT). The output might look like this:

```
Executing Check Disk command.

---------- \allfiles.dat
     C:\AUTOEXEC.BAT
     C:\DOS\ATTRIB.EXE
     C:\DOS\FIND.EXE
     C:\DOS\JOIN.EXE
     C:\DOS\SHARE.EXE
     C:\DOS\SORT.EXE
     C:\DOS\SUBST.EXE
```

Your list is different, of course, but it should include all these files (though not necessarily in the same order or directory). Notice that in addition to the files whose extension is EXE, the list also includes AUTOEXEC.BAT (it may be in a different position in the list, depending on where it appears in your root directory).

You can limit the output to just files with the extension EXE by including the period in the string to find. Enter the Findfile batch command again:

```
A>findfile .EXE
```

This time there's no message and the command takes much less time, because it doesn't have to run chkdsk. And there's no AUTOEXEC.BAT in the list of files. From now on, each search will be this fast until you specify *new* to force another Check Disk command or erase ALLFILES.DAT from the root directory.

Whenever you want to make a new copy of ALLFILES.DAT, add *new* as a second parameter following the search string.

Quick and Safe Disk Formatting

DISKFORM.BAT provides both safety and convenience in formatting disks. It replaces FORMAT.COM as the command you use to format a disk, and will format only the disk specified in the batch file—never a fixed disk. It beeps when it's ready for you to insert a floppy disk, so that you don't have to sit watching the screen while you format a new box of disks.

DISKFORM.BAT uses the program REPLY.COM, described in Chapter 7. If you have not yet created REPLY.COM, do it now, and place it in the same directory with DISKFORM.BAT.

Figure 13-9 shows the commands in DISKFORM.BAT.

```
 1:    echo off
 2:    cls
 3: :NEW_DISK
 4:    echo <Alt-7>Put the floppy disk to be formatted in drive A.
 5:    echo {ESC}[7mPress F1 to format, any other key to stop.{ESC}[m
 6:    echo <Alt-255>
 7:    reply
 8:    if errorlevel 59 if not errorlevel 60 goto OK
 9:    goto END
10: :OK
11:    cls
12:    xformat a: < \batch\formrply.dat
13:    goto NEW_DISK
14: :END
15:    echo <Alt-255>
16:    echo ** Formatting stopped.
```

Figure 13-9. DISKFORM.BAT: Quick and safe disk formatting.

The following explanations describe how DISKFORM.BAT works:

- Lines 2–6 clear the screen and display the instructions followed by a blank line. The bell (Alt-7) in line 4 is used because it's central to one of the purposes of DISKFORM.BAT.

- Line 7 waits for you to press a key.

- Line 8 proceeds with formatting if you press F1.

- Line 9 returns to DOS.

- Line 12 executes the Format command (renamed XFORMAT.COM) with input redirected to \BATCH\FORMRPLY.DAT, which contains a carriage return to start formatting and an *N* to format no more disks.

- Line 13 goes back to display the instructions again.

- Lines 15 and 16 display a blank line and tell you that the batch file has ended.

Before testing DISKFORM.BAT, change the name of FORMAT.COM to XFORMAT.COM. If you have already renamed FORMAT.COM, change *xformat* in line 12 of Figure 13-9 to the new name.

As shown in Figure 13-9, DISKFORM.BAT formats only floppy disks in drive A. If you format disks in both drive A and drive B, you could name the version shown in Figure 13-9 FORMDRVA.BAT, then change *a:* in line 12 of Figure 13-9 to *b:* and save that version as FORMDRVB.BAT. If you don't want two batch files for formatting disks, you could change *a:* in line 12 of Figure 13-9 to *%1:* and enter the drive letter with the Diskform batch command. The choice depends on whether you prefer to limit the number of files or avoid entering a parameter with the command.

Testing DISKFORM.BAT

DISKFORM.BAT requires the file FORMRPLY.DAT in the \BATCH directory. Create it by typing:

```
A>copy con \batch\formrply.dat
<Enter>
N<Enter>
<F6><Enter>
         1 File(s) copied

A>_
```

Have a disk ready that you can format and type the command:

```
A>diskform
```

DISKFORM.BAT responds by beeping, clearing the screen, and displaying its instructions:

```
Put the floppy disk to be formatted in drive A.
Press F1 to format, any other key to stop.
```

Put the disk to be formatted in drive A and press F1. FINDFILE.BAT clears the screen again, and now the DOS Format command displays its instructions and starts formatting the disk:

```
Insert new diskette for drive A:
and strike ENTER when ready

Formatting . . .
```

You don't have to press Enter because DISKFORM.BAT redirects the input of the Format command to FORMRPLY.DAT, which contains a carriage return.

When the disk is formatted, the Format command displays its message that shows how much space is available on the disk, then DISKFORM.BAT beeps and displays its instructions again.

This time press the spacebar (or any other key except F1) to stop DISKFORM.BAT.

Restoring the Current Directory

It can be disconcerting or inconvenient if a batch command leaves you in a directory different from the one in which you entered it. But even if a batch command must change the directory to carry out its mission, you can make it restore the directory before it returns to DOS.

The technique requires only four additional commands in a batch file:

1. A Change Directory (cd) command whose output (the name of the current directory) is redirected to a temporary file.

2. A Copy command that combines this temporary file with a file that contains *cd* followed by a space, creating a batch file that changes to the directory whose name was saved in step 1.

3. An Erase command that erases the temporary file created in step 1.

4. The batch command created in step 2, which must be in a directory in the command path so that it can be used from any directory.

As usual, it's more complicated in the telling than the doing. You can test it in a few moments.

The example assumes that you have a directory named \BATCH that you use for batch files; if you don't, create it or substitute the name of some other directory in your command path that you use for batch files wherever you see *batch* in the example.

To follow the example, you need the file that contains *cd* followed by a space. This isn't a temporary file; it must always be available to any batch file that restores the directory. Type the following to create CD.CMD:

```
A>copy con \batch\cd.cmd
cd ^Z
        1 File(s) copied
```

Notice that you don't press Enter after *cd*, but only after you press the spacebar and F6. That's because you're going to add the temporary file that contains the current directory to this file to create a Change Directory command; if there were a carriage return after *cd*, DOS would end the batch command at that point and simply display the current directory. If you did press Enter before you pressed F6, repeat the Copy command.

Now you're ready to test the commands required to save and restore the current directory:

1. Redirect the output of a Change Directory command to create a temporary file named CD.$$$:

```
A>cd > cd.$$$
```

2. Create the batch file that actually restores the directory by combining CD.CMD and CD.$$$ with a Copy command:

```
A>copy \batch\cd.cmd+cd.$$$ \batch\restdir.bat > nul
```

3. Erase CD.$$$:

```
A>erase cd.$$$
```

Change to the root directory (or any other directory on the current disk):

```
A>cd \
```

4. Type the RESTDIR.BAT command to return to the directory where you started:

```
A>restdir
```

To make any batch file restore the current directory, put the Change Directory, Copy, and Erase commands anywhere before the batch file changes the directory, and end the batch file with the Restdir batch command.

The Erase command isn't really required, but if you didn't erase CD.$$$, a file with that name would be left in each directory in which you used a batch command that restored the current directory. It isn't necessary to erase RESTDIR.BAT, though, because a new version is created in \BATCH (or whatever directory you use for batch files) each time.

Modifying FINDFILE.BAT to Restore the Current Directory

If you're using Version 2 of DOS and would prefer that FINDFILE.BAT not change the current directory to the root, make the following changes:

- If you added *cd* \ after line 1 (the line numbers refer to Figure 13-9), remove it.

- Insert the following commands after line 1:

```
cd > cd.$$$
copy c:\batch\cd.cmd+cd.$$$ c:\batch\restdir.bat > nul
erase cd.$$$
cd \
```

- Remove the backslash before *allfiles.dat* shown in lines 13, 16, and 18.

- Insert the following command as the last command in the file (after the label *:END*):

```
restdir
```

Save this revised version of FINDFILE.BAT.

The batch files in this chapter give you several useful ways to work with files, and may give you ideas for some others. Batch files are something like tools: They accumulate in cabinets and drawers, but it sure is handy to have the right one around.

CHAPTER
14

Putting It All Together: Your Own Menu System

I t's not all that unusual, unfortunately: You've got an hour or so to edit and print a file; enter some data into a spreadsheet, recalculate, and print it; send an electronic-mail message to your project team; and make a quick outline of your presentation at this afternoon's staff meeting. Here's a not-so-usual solution:

- Press two keys and your word processor is running in the directory that contains the document you need.

- Quit the word processor, press two more keys, and your spreadsheet program is running in the directory that contains the spreadsheet you need.

- Quit the spreadsheet, press another couple of keys, and the communications program is running.

- Quit the communications program, press a key, and your outline processor is running.

- You finish the outline, print it, and press one last key. As you head for the door the screen goes blank to protect the phosphor.

You didn't type any commands to change the directory or start a program; you just used the function keys to select options from a series of menus tailored to the programs and directories that you use. That's what this chapter is all about—in a sense, that's what this book is about: giving you control, so that your system takes care of as much housekeeping as possible, and you can concentrate on getting your work done.

The Menu System

This chapter shows you how to create a menu system that lets you run any application program, in any directory, with one or two keystrokes. The menu system requires some investment of your time, but the payoff is worth it: For most routine work using application programs, you may never again type a command to change the directory or start a program.

The menu system includes a Main Menu with sub-menus, and incorporates the Printer Setup Menu described in Chapter 11. The Main Menu includes two types of menu selections:

- A *program selection* changes the directory and starts a program that uses only one directory.

- A *sub-menu* displays a menu of several directories that contain files you use with the same program, such as a word processor or spreadsheet.

You use the same key (F10) to return from a sub-menu to the Main Menu and to return from the Main Menu to DOS. The F10 key always takes you back one level.

The chapter shows you how to enter and test the Main Menu, how to incorporate the Printer Setup Menu, and how to add your own program selections and sub-menus. It also shows you how to use the menu system with a RAM disk, and even how to customize AUTOEXEC.BAT so that the menu system runs on a RAM disk, if one is defined, or on a real disk.

Appendix F shows the contents of each file required for a menu system based on the descriptions in this chapter.

Preparing for the Menu System

The menu system needs the programs REPLY.COM, NOCURS.COM, and NORMCURS.COM. If you haven't created REPLY.COM, turn to "Making Batch Commands Interactive: REPLY.COM" in Chapter 7 and follow the instructions listed there. If you haven't created NOCURS.COM and NORMCURS.COM, turn to "Don't Curse the Cursor" in Chapter 10.

Before you start working on the menu system, type the following commands to create the directory \MENU on your system disk and change to that directory:

```
A>md \menu
A>cd \menu
```

Copy REPLY.COM to \MENU. If you entered the Printer Setup Menu in Chapter 11, copy all four files (PRNTMENU.BAT, PRNTMENU.DOC, PRNTOPT1.DOC, and PRNTOPT2.DOC) to \MENU.

Entering the Menu System

The menu system requires at least two new files: MAINMENU.DOC and MAINMENU.BAT. You'll start by entering a skeleton Main Menu, then gradually add program selections and sub-menus. Each sub-menu requires an additional file, which you create by copying and modifying the file MAINMENU.DOC.

The Text File: **MAINMENU.DOC**

MAINMENU.DOC contains the Main Menu as it appears on the screen. It contains text and ANSI.SYS commands to control display attributes, but no DOS commands. You can create it with any text editor or word processor that accepts characters in the extended character set and lets you save a file without formatting codes.

Figure 14-1 shows the contents of MAINMENU.DOC.

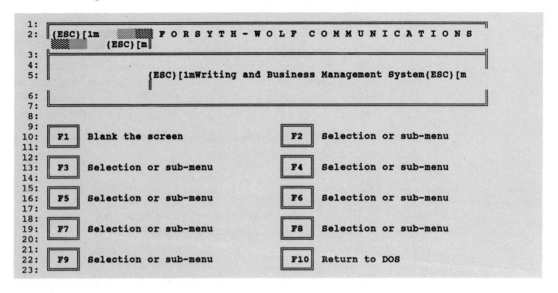

Figure 14-1. MAINMENU.DOC: The Main Menu.

If you entered the Printer Setup Menu in Chapter 11, you've already done most of the work. Copy PRNTMENU.DOC to MAINMENU.DOC and revise the copied file to match Figure 14-1.

If you haven't entered the Printer Setup Menu, you'll need it in a moment, so you might as well enter it now. Turn to "Entering PRNTMENU.DOC" in Chapter 11 and follow the instructions there; they include some hints for using the cut-and-paste capability of your word processor to simplify the process of entering the file. When you have entered the file, save it as PRNTMENU.DOC, then revise it to match Figure 14-1 and save it as MAINMENU.DOC.

If you're using a RAM disk, copy MAINMENU.DOC (and if you just entered it, PRNTMENU.DOC) to a real disk so you won't lose your work if something goes wrong.

Check your menu by displaying it with the Type command:

`A>type mainmenu.doc`

If something isn't right, correct the file and display it again. When it's finished, copy the final version to a real disk if you're using a RAM disk.

The Batch File: MAINMENU.BAT

The menu system batch file has a simple structure. It displays the file
MAINMENU.DOC and waits for you to press a key. If you press F1
through F10, it carries out the commands required by that menu selection;
it ignores any other key.

Because MAINMENU.BAT gets pretty long by the time you define all ten
selections, you'll start by entering a skeleton that includes only two selections: F1 to blank the screen and F10 to return to DOS. Guided by examples, you'll then add your program selections and sub-menus. Figure 14-2
shows the commands in MAINMENU.BAT.

```
 1:    echo off
 2: :START
 3:    cls
 4:    cd \menu
 5:    type mainmenu.doc
 6: :GET_RPLY
 7:    reply
 8:    if errorlevel 69 goto GET_RPLY
 9:    if errorlevel 68 goto F10
10:    if errorlevel 67 goto F9
11:    if errorlevel 66 goto F8
12:    if errorlevel 65 goto F7
13:    if errorlevel 64 goto F6
14:    if errorlevel 63 goto F5
15:    if errorlevel 62 goto F4
16:    if errorlevel 61 goto F3
17:    if errorlevel 60 goto F2
18:    if errorlevel 59 goto F1
19:    goto GET_RPLY
20: :F10
21:    cls
22:    goto END
23: :F9
24:    goto GET_RPLY
25: :F8
26:    goto GET_RPLY
27: :F7
28:    goto GET_RPLY
29: :F6
30:    goto GET_RPLY
31: :F5
32:    goto GET_RPLY
33: :F4
34:    goto GET_RPLY
35: :F3
36:    goto GET_RPLY
37: :F2
38:    goto GET_RPLY
39: :F1
40:    cls
41:    nocurs
42:    reply
43:    normcurs
44:    goto START
45: :END
```

Figure 14-2. MAINMENU.BAT: Skeleton of the menu-system batch file.

Use the cut-and-paste capabilities of your text editor or word processor to simplify entering MAINMENU.BAT:

1. Enter lines 1 through 9.

2. Copy line 9 nine times.

3. Change lines 10 through 18 to match Figure 14-2.

4. Enter lines 19 through 24.

5. Copy lines 23 and 24 seven times.

6. Change the labels in lines 25 through 37 to match Figure 14-2.

7. Enter lines 39 through 45.

Save MAINMENU.BAT. If you're using a RAM disk, be sure to copy MAINMENU.BAT to the directory \MENU on a real disk.

How MAINMENU.BAT Works

As you might guess from the patterns of commands in MAINMENU.BAT, its operation is fairly simple. It changes the directory to \MENU, displays the Main Menu, then waits for you to press a key. If you press a function key, it goes to the corresponding label to carry out the selection; if you press any other key, it goes back to GET_RPLY to wait for you to press another key. (In this skeleton form, it also goes back to GET_RPLY if you press F2 through F9, but you'll soon change that.)

The following explanations describe the line-by-line operation of MAINMENU.BAT:

- Lines 1–5 clear the screen, change the directory to \MENU, and display the Main Menu.

- Line 7 waits for you to press a key.

- Line 8 goes back to wait for you to press another key if the code of the key you press is 69 or greater (the highest code you're looking for is 68, which is F10).

- Lines 9–18 go to the label that corresponds to the function-key label (F10 through F1), if you press a function key.

- Line 19 goes back to wait for you to press another key if the code of the key you press is less than 59 (the lowest code you're looking for is 59, which is F1).

- Lines 21 and 22 clear the screen and return to DOS if you press F10.

- Lines 23–38 go back to wait for you to press another key if you press F9 through F2. The *goto GET_RPLY* commands in these lines are temporary; you'll replace them as you add program selections and sub-menus to the Main Menu.

- Lines 40 and 41 blank the screen if you press F1 by clearing the screen and making the cursor invisible. Line 42 waits for you to press a key. No matter what key you press, line 43 restores the cursor and line 44 goes back to display the Main Menu.

Although MAINMENU.BAT will grow as you add program selections and sub-menus, this basic structure remains unchanged. The labels are descriptive enough to remain accurate landmarks even when you have completed all ten choices.

Testing MAINMENU.BAT

If the current directory contains MAINMENU.DOC, MAINMENU.BAT, NOCURS.COM, and NORMCURS.COM—and, if you're using a RAM disk, you have copied MAINMENU.DOC and MAINMENU.BAT to a real disk—you're ready to test the Main Menu. Type the menu-system command:

```
A>mainmenu
```

The screen should clear and then display the Main Menu. If it does, skip the next topic and go on to "Testing the Main Menu."

What If It Doesn't Work?

Troubleshooting your creation can be frustrating, so use the clues that DOS gives you. In the remainder of this chapter, if the menu system doesn't behave as it should, watch for error messages that DOS may display:

- *Bad command or file name* could mean that MAINMENU.BAT or some other command or batch file isn't in the current directory, or that you misspelled its name either when you created it or when you typed a command. Some possible remedies:

  - Make sure that you spelled *mainmenu* correctly when you typed the command to start the menu system.

  - Make sure that the current directory is set to \MENU (or the directory you're using for your menu system, if it's different).

  - Display the directory to make sure that the required batch files are there and that their names are spelled correctly.

- If a batch command is used in another batch file, make sure the name of the batch command is spelled correctly. If the batch command isn't the last command in the batch file, make sure the Command command is used with the /C parameter (for example, *command /c prntmenu mainmenu* in MAINMENU.BAT).

- *File not found* could mean that MAINMENU.DOC or some other text file isn't in the current directory, or that you misspelled its name either when you created it or when you entered it in a batch file. Some possible remedies:

  - Make sure that the current directory is set to \MENU (or the directory you're using for your menu system, if it's different).

  - Display the directory to make sure that the required text files are there and that their names are spelled correctly.

  - Check the Type command in the batch file that displays the text file (for example, *type mainmenu.doc* in MAINMENU.BAT) to make sure that the name of the text file is spelled correctly.

If you make sure this skeleton form of the menu system works correctly, then add program selections and sub-menus one at a time, testing each as you add it, you shouldn't have to do much troubleshooting.

Testing the Main Menu

For the rest of this chapter, if the menu system doesn't react as it should and the reason isn't readily apparent, go back to the heading "What If It Doesn't Work?" for suggestions about solving the problem.

If you're looking at the Main Menu, press F1. After a short delay, the screen should go blank. It takes a moment because MAINMENU.BAT checks to see which key you pressed in high-to-low order (see lines 9–18 of Figure 14-2); F1 is the last key it checks for. You'll find that the higher the function-key number, the more quickly the menu responds.

Press any key; the screen should display the Main Menu again.

Now press F2 through F9. None of those keys should have any effect, other than to cause MAINMENU.BAT to load REPLY.COM from disk again. When you press F10, the screen should clear and DOS should display the system prompt.

Adding a Program Selection to the Main Menu

Adding a program selection to the Main Menu requires few changes. This topic describes the general technique, then gives an example. Use the example as a guide to adding your programs to the Main Menu.

To add a program selection to the Main Menu:

- Make the program name a Main Menu selection by changing the appropriate line in MAINMENU.DOC.

- Insert two commands at the appropriate label in MAINMENU.BAT to change the directory and start the program.

- Change the *goto GET_RPLY* command in MAINMENU.BAT that follows the two commands you insert to *goto START*.

Figure 14-3 shows the steps required to make F8 in the Main Menu run MaxThink (an outline processor); it also shows how the affected portion of MAINMENU.BAT would look after the addition:

1. Change the legend for F8 (the second occurrence of *Selection or submenu* in line 19 of MAINMENU.DOC) to *MaxThink*.

2. Insert the following two commands after the label *:F8* in MAINMENU.BAT (line 25 of Figure 14-2):

```
cd \max
max
```

3. Change the command *goto GET_RPLY* after the label *:F8* in MAINMENU.BAT (line 26 of Figure 14-2) to *goto START*.

   The affected portion of MAINMENU.BAT is shown below; the numbered lines are the existing lines in MAINMENU.BAT shown in Figure 14-2:

```
23: :F9
24:     goto GET_RPLY
25: :F8
        cd \max
        max
26:     goto START
27: :F7
```

Figure 14-3. Adding a program selection to the Main Menu.

To add a program of your own, choose a function key and a program you use with a single directory (you'll add a sub-menu a bit later to handle programs that you use with more than one directory). Using Figure 14-3 as a guide, change the function key legend in MAINMENU.DOC and insert the commands in MAINMENU.BAT.

Fire up the Main Menu by typing *mainmenu*, and press the function key you chose; the program you selected should start. End the program, and the Main Menu should be on the screen again. Press F10 to return to DOS. If something went awry, go back to "What If It Doesn't Work?" for help.

Incorporating the Printer Setup Menu Into the Menu System

If you haven't yet entered the Printer Setup Menu and want to include it in the menu system, turn to "The Printer Setup Menu" in Chapter 11. Follow the instructions there, then continue with this topic. If you don't want to include the Printer Setup Menu, skip this topic and continue with "Adding a Sub-menu to the Main Menu."

To incorporate the Printer Setup Menu, copy PRNTMENU.BAT, PRNTMENU.DOC, PRNTOPT1.DOC, and PRNTOPT2.DOC to \MENU (if they aren't there already). Make the following changes to MAINMENU.DOC and MAINMENU.BAT:

1. Change the legend for F9 in MAINMENU.DOC (the first occurrence of *Selection or sub-menu* in line 22 of Figure 14-1) to *Printer Setup Menu*. This is the only change to MAINMENU.DOC.

2. Insert the following command after the label *:F9* of MAINMENU.BAT (line 23 of Figure 14-2):

    ```
    command /c prntmenu mainmenu
    ```

3. Change the command *goto GET_RPLY* after the label *:F9* in MAINMENU.BAT (line 24 of Figure 14-2) to *goto START*.

4. Insert the following command after *type prntmenu.doc* in PRNTMENU.BAT (line 3 of Figure 11-15):

    ```
    if "%1"=="mainmenu" echo {ESC}[23;24HMain Menu
    ```

    This command changes the F10 legend to read *Return to Main Menu* instead of *Return to DOS* if PRNTMENU.BAT is called by MAINMENU.BAT.

The Printer Setup Menu should work as it did before; if you haven't used it yet, see "Using the Printer Setup Menu" in Chapter 11. To use the Printer Setup Menu from the Main Menu, type:

`A>mainmenu`

When the Main Menu is displayed, press F9. The Printer Setup Menu should be displayed, and the legend for F10 should read *Return to Main Menu*. Try some of the selections—F9 to reset the printer, for example, will tell you right away whether the menu is working—then press F10 to return to the Main Menu, and press F10 again to return to DOS.

If your system prompt is long or colorful, you may have noticed it flash briefly after the Main Menu cleared and before the Printer Setup Menu was displayed. DOS displays the system prompt because MAINMENU.BAT uses the Command command to run PRNTMENU.BAT. Minimize this distraction by adding two commands to MAINMENU.BAT, but it's only an aesthetic problem. If it doesn't bother you, go on to the next section.

You can't avoid the system prompt, but you can make it shorter; insert the following two commands in MAINMENU.BAT:

- *prompt* (with no parameter) immediately before *command /c prntmenu mainmenu* (the Command command you just entered).

- *promptrs* as the last line (after the label *:END*).

These two commands define the standard system prompt (A>) before displaying the Printer Setup Menu, then restore your system prompt before returning to DOS. If you haven't yet created a batch file named PROMPTRS.BAT that restores your system prompt (as described earlier in Chapter 8), do it now. (You could just make the last command of MAINMENU.BAT a Prompt command that restores your standard system prompt, but there may be places where you'll have to restore your system prompt, and it's simpler to use the same batch file everywhere).

Adding a Sub-menu to the Main Menu

If you frequently use a word processor or spreadsheet program, you may keep the program itself in one directory and store the document or spreadsheet files in several directories that identify a particular project, department, or client. A sub-menu displays all the directories that you use with one program; no matter what you choose from the sub-menu, the same program is started. The choice determines only which directory becomes the current directory.

Adding a sub-menu involves a bit more work than adding a program selection, but significantly expands the usefulness of your menu system. This topic describes the general technique, then shows an example; use the example as a guide to adding your sub-menus to the menu system.

To add a sub-menu to the menu system:

- Create a text file that contains the sub-menu. This is fairly simple: Copy MAINMENU.DOC to the new text file, then change the title and menu selections. If the sub-menu has fewer than ten selections, delete the function-key symbols that aren't required, but leave blank lines in their place, so that the F10 symbol—which returns you to the Main Menu— always appears in the same place on the screen. Save the file under the new sub-menu name.

- Put the sub-menu name in the Main Menu by changing the legend of the associated function key in MAINMENU.DOC.

- Delete the *goto GET_REPLY* command that follows the label of the associated function key in MAINMENU.BAT.

- Insert the commands that display and manage the sub-menu following the label of the associated function key in MAINMENU.BAT. These commands are a miniature version of MAINMENU.BAT that:

  –Display the sub-menu with a Type command.

  –Wait for a response with REPLY.COM.

  –Check the response with a series of If Errorlevel commands. If a valid key is pressed, change the directory. If any other key is pressed, go back to wait for a response.

  –Start the application program.

  –Display the sub-menu again when the program ends.

To illustrate, suppose you use Microsoft Word. You store document files in four directories— \WORD\LETTERS, \WORD\MEMOS, \WORD\REPORTS, and \WORD\PROPOSAL—and you want F3 on the Main Menu to display a sub-menu called *Word Processing Directories*.

First, you would create WORDMENU.DOC, the text file that contains the menu, shown in Figure 14-4. Create it by copying MAINMENU.DOC to WORDMENU.DOC, then change WORDMENU.DOC to match Figure 14-4. Notice that both files contain the same number of lines. The symbols for F5 through F9 are deleted, but the blank lines remain.

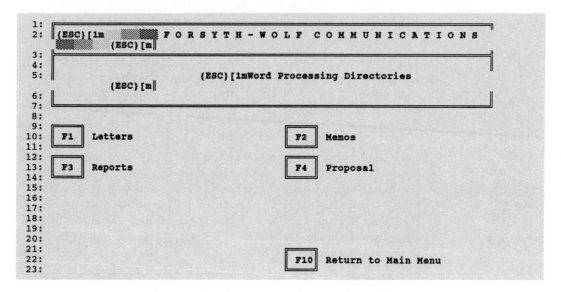

Figure 14-4. WORDMENU.DOC: The Word Processing sub-menu.

Next, you would modify MAINMENU.BAT to make F3 display and manage the Word Processing sub-menu:

1. Change the legend for F3 (the first occurrence of *Selection or sub-menu* in line 13 of Figure 14-1) to *Word Processing Menu*.

2. Change the command *goto GET_RPLY* after the label *:F3* (line 36 of Figure 14-2) to *goto F3*.

3. Insert the following commands after the label *:F3* (line 35 of Figure 14-2), and before the *goto F3* command you just entered.

```
 1:     cls
 2:     type wordmenu.doc
 3: :RPLY_WRD
 4:     reply
 5:     if errorlevel 69 goto RPLY_WRD
 6:     if errorlevel 68 goto START
 7:     if errorlevel 63 if not errorlevel 68 goto RPLY_WRD
 8:     if errorlevel 62 if not errorlevel 63 cd \word\proposal
 9:     if errorlevel 61 if not errorlevel 62 cd \word\reports
10:     if errorlevel 60 if not errorlevel 61 cd \word\memos
11:     if errorlevel 59 if not errorlevel 60 cd \word\letters
12:     if errorlevel 0 if not errorlevel 59 goto RPLY_WRD
13: :WORD
14:     word
```

- Lines 1 and 2 clear the screen and display the Word Processing menu.

- Line 4 waits for you to press a key.

- Lines 5 through 12 check which key you pressed and take the appropriate action:

  – Line 5 goes back to wait for you to press another key if the code of the key you pressed was 69 or greater (the highest code you're looking for is 68, which is F10).

    – Line 6 displays the Main Menu if you press F10 (code 68).

    – Line 7 goes back to RPLY_WRD to wait for you to press a key if you press F5 (code 63) through F9 (code 67), because only F1 through F4 are valid choices).

    – Lines 8 through 11 change to the directory that corresponds to the selections shown in Figure 14-4 if you press F4 (code 62) through F1 (code 59).

    – Line 12 goes back to RPLY_WRD if the code of the key you press is less than 59.

- Line 14 starts Microsoft Word.

Figure 14-5 shows the affected portion of MAINMENU.BAT after adding the Word Processing sub-menu; the numbered lines are existing lines in MAINMENU.BAT as shown in Figure 14-2.

```
33: :F4
34:    goto GET_RPLY
35: :F3
       cls
       type wordmenu.doc
    :RPLY_WRD
       reply
       if errorlevel 69 goto RPLY_WRD
       if errorlevel 68 goto START
       if errorlevel 63 if not errorlevel 68 goto RPLY_WRD
       if errorlevel 62 if not errorlevel 63 cd \word\proposal
       if errorlevel 61 if not errorlevel 62 cd \word\reports
       if errorlevel 60 if not errorlevel 61 cd \word\memos
       if errorlevel 59 if not errorlevel 60 cd \word\letters
       if errorlevel 0 if not errorlevel 59 goto RPLY_WRD
       word
       goto F3
37: :F2
38:    goto GET_RPLY
```

Figure 14-5. MAINMENU.BAT after adding the Word Processing sub-menu.

The line numbers in MAINMENU.BAT will change as you add commands (your text editor or word processor may not even show line numbers) but the labels remain accurate landmarks.

To add a sub-menu of your own, choose a function key and a program you use with several directories. Using the example as a guide, create the text file that contains the menu, change the function-key legend, and insert the commands in MAINMENU.BAT.

Testing Your First Sub-menu

Make sure that the text file you created that contains the sub-menu is in the current directory. To test your sub-menu, start the Main Menu:

A>mainmenu

You have tested the other selections, so press the function key that selects the sub-menu. The screen should clear and display the sub-menu. Press a function key on the sub-menu; the application program should start in the directory that corresponds to the choice you made from the sub-menu.

End the application program; the screen should display the sub-menu again. Press F10, and the screen should display the Main Menu. Press F10 once again to return to DOS.

Tailoring the Menu System

You've seen how to add a program selection and a sub-menu to the Main Menu. Now it's time to customize the menu for the programs that you use. But before you start, take the time to plan your selections and sub-menus. Sketch the Main Menu with its ten choices and write in the selections you want. On the same piece of paper, write the names of the directories and programs that each selection requires, so that you have all the information in one place when you start to revise the files.

In the same way, sketch the sub-menus you want; the most likely candidates are word processing and spreadsheets, but you might include business graphics, database, telecommunications, CAD/CAM, or some other application program you use with several directories for data files. Again, write in each selection and the names of the programs and directories that each selection requires.

It will be tempting to add all the selections at once. Resist this temptation. It takes a bit longer to add the menu selections one at a time, but it's much easier to track down a mistake. It could take much longer if you filled out the entire menu all at once, then couldn't find one small, elusive error.

And don't forget to change the title lines of MAINMENU.DOC, PRNTMENU.DOC, and all the sub-menu DOC files, so that each menu announces that you didn't buy this menu system, you *wrote* it. The purpose isn't to amaze your friends—although a little bit of that might not hurt—but to remind you that you're in charge of this computer.

Adding Color to the Menus

The DOC files that contain the Main Menu, Printer Setup Menu, and Word Processing sub-menu include a few ANSI.SYS commands to highlight the titles. You can add more ANSI.SYS commands to make the screens more attractive, especially if you use a color display.

One particularly effective technique is to make each sub-menu selection on the Main Menu a different color, then use that color for the selections on the sub-menu. However, it takes a lot of ANSI.SYS commands to make the function-key boxes different colors, so you might want to experiment with a copy of the DOC file until you decide on how to use color.

Remember, by the way, that if you add color to PRNTMENU.DOC, you'll have to match those colors in PRNTOPT1.DOC and PRNTOPT2.DOC. Again, it might be prudent to experiment with copies of these files before you commit yourself to a particular use of color.

If you have defined your own standard colors as described in Chapter 10, the menus may not always look right. You can remedy that by inserting *{ESC}[m*—the ANSI.SYS command that turns off all display attributes— right after *echo off* at the beginning of MAINMENU.DOC. To restore your standard colors (and your system prompt), make *promptrs* the last command in MAINMENU.BAT, as described earlier in this chapter and under "Watch Out for Those Batch Files" in Chapter 10.

MAINMENU.DOC and WORDMENU.DOC in Appendix F include ANSI.SYS commands to set foreground colors.

Eliminating a Distraction

When a menu is on the screen, the cursor remains in the row and column position following the last item displayed. The cursor doesn't mark the location of something to be typed (there's nothing to be typed), it just blinks at you until you press a function key. This is another minor aesthetic blemish—like the system prompt flashing between the Main Menu and Printer Setup Menu—that you can correct, if you wish, with a few commands. If it doesn't bother you, skip the next paragraph.

To make the cursor invisible, insert the command *nocurs* after the label *:START* in MAINMENU.BAT (line 2 of Figure 14-2). To restore it, insert the command *normcurs* after the label *:END* in MAINMENU.BAT (line 45 of Figure 14-2). If you added *promptrs* as the last command to restore the system prompt, make sure it remains the last command because PROMPTRS.BAT returns to DOS.

Starting the Menu System with One Keystroke

Even though the menu system handles most of your routine work with application programs, you'll return to DOS to copy or erase files, display directories, and take care of miscellaneous or infrequent chores. Rather than typing *mainmenu* each time you want to start the menu system again, you can assign the command to a key.

Alt-F10 is a fairly easy combination to type; its key code is *0;113*. If another program uses that combination, or you prefer another key, substitute a different key code in the following command. Type the following to assign the menu–system command to Alt-F10:

```
A>prompt $e[0;113;"mainmenu";13p
```

Press Alt-F10. The screen should display the Main Menu; press F10 to return to DOS.

Type *promptrs* to restore your system prompt (if you haven't yet created PROMPTRS.BAT, type just *prompt* to restore the standard system prompt).

To make this assignment permanent, put an Echo command that makes the key assignment in AUTOEXEC.BAT. To start the menu system with Alt-F10, as the previous example did, put the following command in AUTOEXEC.BAT:

```
echo {ESC}[0;113;"mainmenu";13p
```

Again, if another program uses that combination or you prefer another key, substitute a different key code in the Echo command. From now on, the menu-system command is assigned to the key each time you start DOS.

Using the Menu System with a RAM Disk

If you're using Version 2 of DOS and don't have a RAM disk program, you can skip this topic and go on to "A Complete Sample Menu System." But the benefits of using a RAM disk are significant enough that you should consider upgrading to Version 3 of DOS—which includes VDISK.SYS, a RAM disk program—or getting some other RAM disk program. If you do, come back and read this topic.

If you have a RAM disk program and haven't yet read Chapter 9, do so before continuing with this topic.

Every time DOS runs a batch file or program, it must load the batch file or program from disk into memory. The menu system uses several batch files and programs; you can eliminate the disk activity and speed up the menu system substantially by running the menu system from your RAM disk. If you always use a RAM disk, you can run your menu system from the RAM disk by simply adding a few commands to AUTOEXEC.BAT and MAINMENU.BAT.

These suggestions use an environment variable; if you aren't familiar with their use, read "Using Environment Variables in a Batch File" and "Creating Your Own Environment Variables" in Chapter 8. The suggestions also assume that your RAM disk is drive D and your normal system disk is drive C; if your RAM disk and system disks are on different drives, substitute the correct letters.

First, add the commands shown in Figure 14-6 to AUTOEXEC.BAT.

```
1:   echo off
2:   echo {ESC}[7m*** Copying Menu System files to RAM disk ***{ESC}[0m
3:   md d:\menu
4:   copy \menu d:\menu > nul
5:   set path=d:\menu;<remainder of your command path>
6:   set dr=d:
7:   echo {ESC}[0;113;"d:mainmenu";13p
     <Existing AUTOEXEC.BAT commands go here.>
8:   mainmenu
```

*Figure14-6. An AUTOEXEC.BAT file that always runs the menu system from
a RAM disk.*

The commands added to AUTOEXEC.BAT copy the files to the RAM disk
and guarantee that the menu system will be executed from the RAM disk:

- Line 2 tells you that the menu-system files are being copied to the
  RAM disk.

- Line 3 creates the directory MENU in the root directory of the RAM
  disk. This matches the \MENU directory on the real disk.

- Line 4 copies the menu-system files to the RAM disk.

- Line 5 puts the menu-system directory on the RAM disk at the beginning of your command path; you may want it in some other position,
  but be sure to include it and *not* to include C:\MENU. Add the directories in your current command path after *d:\menu*.

- Line 6 creates an environment variable named DR and sets its value to *d:*.
  DR represents the drive from which the menu system runs; it is used in
  MAINMENU.BAT to change the current drive. If your RAM drive uses
  a different letter, substitute its drive letter for *d*. Don't forget the colon:
  It makes the value of DR a valid command to change the current drive.

- Line 7 assigns the menu-system command to Alt-F10. If another
  program uses Alt-F10 or you prefer another key, substitute a different
  key code in the Echo command.

- Line 8 starts the Main Menu. It runs from the RAM disk because the first directory in the command path is D:\MENU, and C:\MENU wasn't included in the command path.

Put the existing commands in AUTOEXEC.BAT between lines 6 and 7 of Figure 14-6.

Changes to MAINMENU.BAT

Add the following commands to MAINMENU.BAT to change the current drive:

- Insert %dr% after the label :START (line 2 of Figure 14-2). DOS replaces %dr% with the value of the environment variable DR, and AUTOEXEC.BAT sets DR to d:, so this command changes the current drive to D.

- Insert c: (or the drive letter of your system disk, if it's not C) after each label that represents a program selection that uses a directory or program on a real disk. For example, if F8 is a program selection, as shown in Figure 14-3, you would insert c: after the label :F8 (line 25 in Figure 14-3).

- Insert c: (or the drive letter of your system disk, if it's not C) after each label that waits for a reply to a sub-menu that uses a directory or program on a real disk. For example, if F3 selects a sub-menu, as shown in Figure 14-5, you would insert c: after the label :RPLY_WRD.

- Insert %dr% after the label :END (line 45 of Figure 14-2).

The next time you start or restart DOS, the menu system should run much more quickly; you'll appreciate the speed, and your disk drives will appreciate the rest.

What If You Don't Always Use a RAM Disk?

You may not always want to use a RAM disk; the purpose of VDISK.BAT (described in Chapter 9), in fact, is to make it easy for you to use whatever sort of RAM disk you like—including none at all. This uncertainty complicates things a bit for your menu system, because you can't count on the RAM disk always being there; the AUTOEXEC.BAT file shown in Figure 14-6 won't work properly if there isn't a RAM disk.

But if you use VDISK.BAT to change your RAM disk configuration, AUTOEXEC.BAT can set up your menu system correctly whether or not there's a RAM disk, because the root directory contains a file named VDISK.LOG if a RAM disk is defined. Add the commands shown in Figure 14-7 to AUTOEXEC.BAT.

```
 1:      echo off
 2:      if not exist vdisk.log goto NO_VDISK
 3:      echo {ESC}[7m*** Copying Menu System files to RAM disk ***{ESC}[0m
 4:      md d:\menu
 5:      copy \menu d:\menu > nul
 6:      set path=d:\menu;<remainder of your command path>
 7:      set dr=d:
 8:      goto END
 9:  :NO_VDISK
10:      set path=c:\menu;<remainder of your command path>
11:      set dr=c:
12:  :END
13:      echo {ESC}[0;113;"mainmenu";13p
         <Commands always to be carried out in AUTOEXEC.BAT go here.>
14:      mainmenu
```

Figure 14-7. Sample AUTOEXEC.BAT to run file system with or without a RAM disk.

AUTOEXEC.BAT now contains two alternate setup routines: One runs the menu system from a RAM disk if there is one, and the other runs the menu system from the real disk if there isn't a RAM disk. Line 2 of AUTOEXEC.BAT selects the appropriate routine based on whether or not the root directory contains VDISK.LOG:

● Line 2 goes to set up for the real disk if VDISK.LOG doesn't exist in the root directory.

● Lines 3–8 are carried out if VDISK.LOG is in the root directory (which means that there is a RAM disk):

– Line 3 tells you that the menu-system files are being copied to the RAM disk.

– Line 4 creates the directory MENU in the root directory of the RAM disk. This matches the \MENU directory on the real disk.

– Line 5 copies the menu-system files to the RAM disk.

– Line 6 puts the menu-system directory on the RAM disk at the beginning of your command path. You may want it in some other position, but be sure to include it and *not* to include C:\MENU. Add the directories in your current command path after *d:\menu.*

– Line 7 creates an environment variable named DR and sets its value to *d:.* DR represents the drive from which the menu system runs; it is used in MAINMENU.BAT to change the current drive. If your RAM drive uses a different letter, substitute its drive letter for *d.* Don't forget the colon: It makes the value of DR a valid command to change the current drive.

- –Line 8 goes to carry out the commands in AUTOEXEC.BAT that are always carried out, whether or not there is a RAM disk.

- The commands in lines 10 and 11 are carried out if VDISK.LOG is not in the root directory (which means that there is not a RAM disk):

  - –Line 10 puts the menu-system directory on the *real* disk at the beginning of your command path. You may want it in some other position, but be sure to include it and *not* to include D:\MENU. Add the directories in your current command path after *c:\menu*.

  - –Line 11 creates the environment variable named DR and sets its value to *c:* (see the explanation of line 7). If your system disk isn't in drive C, substitute the correct drive letter.

- The commands in lines 13 and 14—and any other commands between them—are always carried out:

  - –Line 13 assigns the menu-system command to Alt-F10. If another program uses Alt-F10 or you prefer another key, substitute a different key code in the Echo command.

  - –Line 14 starts MAINMENU.BAT.

Put the existing commands in AUTOEXEC.BAT between lines 13 and 14 of Figure 14-7.

The commands to be added to MAINMENU.BAT, which change the current drive, are the same as those listed in the previous section, under "Changes to MAINMENU.BAT." If you already made those changes to run from a RAM disk, you're through. If you didn't make those changes, return to that section and make them now.

Now you can use the menu system whether or not a RAM disk is defined. The next time you start or restart DOS, AUTOEXEC.BAT will automatically run the menu system from the proper disk.

A Word About Performance

Because COMMAND.COM must read and carry out each command in a batch file, batch files don't operate as quickly as programs. Version 3 of DOS, for example, responds to the first choice in MAINMENU.BAT about 8 times faster than Version 2. If you're dissatisfied with the performance of MAINMENU.BAT (or any other batch file), you might consider buying the most recent version of DOS.

A Complete Sample Menu System

Appendix F shows the contents of all the files needed for a menu system with sub-menus (including the Printer Setup Menu). It doesn't explain the files line-by-line—that would be mostly a repeat of this chapter—but it gives you a complete set of files to use as a reference. By comparing the menus and their selections with the commands in the batch files, you can see how to handle just about any situation.

CHAPTER
15

The Care and Feeding
of Your Computer

I t wasn't so long ago that computers had to be isolated in their own, expensive environment: temperature and humidity controlled within a narrow range, a false floor to keep all the cables out of harm's way. Occasional windows afforded fleeting glimpses of what went on inside the computer room, but the entrances were usually guarded. One of the more liberating qualities of personal computers is their tolerance of a more realistic environment. They require little more care than other electronic appliances, such as a VCR.

But there are still a few things to keep in mind. This chapter suggests ways to keep your computer healthy, and ideas on how to keep yourself comfortable while using it. It's not DOS, but it's all part of using a computer.

Pushing Back the Limits

You may have read that the uses for some piece of hardware or software are "limited only by your imagination." View any such claim with a severely jaundiced eye, not only because it raises the suspicion that the writer couldn't think of any good uses in time for deadline, but also because it simply isn't true. The uses of your computer are also limited, among other things, by the capacity and speed of its memory, the capacity and speed of the disk drives, and the capacity and speed of the microprocessor.

Capacity and Speed

Too little memory or disk capacity may mean you can't even load a program, let alone run it; or maybe you can load it, but *run* is much too generous a term to describe its progress. More insidiously, a program may run just slowly enough to discourage you from making that last change to the spreadsheet or report that's due this afternoon.

You're also limited by the reliability and availability of your system—it's hard to be productive on a system that occasionally lapses into psychotic behavior, or one that you have to share with several other people. And there are times when you're limited simply by the number of hours in a day.

You may not be able to do much about sharing a system, and you can't change the hours in a day, but you can improve both capacity and speed. If you haven't yet done the following, each will help:

- Add memory to bring your system to the 640K maximum. It shouldn't cost more than $200, and you'll probably get another serial or parallel port in the bargain.

- Buy a fixed disk; you can get a 20-megabyte drive for less than $500. Once you have used one, you'll never want to use a floppy disk-only system again.

- Use a RAM disk, especially if you don't have a fixed disk. If you use so many resident programs that you don't have enough memory, consider eliminating enough resident programs to use at least a 64K RAM disk, or buy an expanded memory board.

- If you're using Version 2 of DOS, upgrade to Version 3. Not only does it include VDISK.SYS (a RAM disk program), Version 3.1 adds the Join and Substitute commands, lets you use a path name when you type a command or check the existence of a file with the If command, and is slightly faster for some disk operations. Version 3.2 includes all that, plus two new commands for copying files (Xcopy and Replace) and a device driver (DRIVER.SYS) that lets you assign a second drive letter to an existing disk drive.

Give the Big Red Switch a Rest

A computer, like a light bulb or a stereo amplifier, experiences a bit of extra electrical stress each time you turn it on. You can prolong the life of your computer by turning it on and off as infrequently as possible. Because computers require so little electricity—about the same as a 100-watt light bulb—leaving the system on doesn't cost much and will probably save you money over the life of the system by reducing maintenance costs.

Once you turn your system on, don't turn it off until you're through with it for the day. Don't, however, leave something displayed on the screen for hours at a time; this runs the risk of burning whatever is displayed into the phosphor coating on the inside of the screen. For the same reason that you don't turn the computer off, however, don't turn the display off; instead, turn down the brightness control or use a program that blanks the screen.

There's one exception to this practice: When you start using a brand-new computer, leave it on day and night for the first week or two. If an electrical component—especially an integrated circuit—is going to fail, chances are it will fail early in its life (chip manufacturers have given this characteristic the macabre name *infant mortality*). If something is going to fail, you want it to fail as quickly as possible so it can be repaired while still under warranty.

Keep It Clean!

Cleanliness is the best preventive maintenance you can perform on your computer. But don't be a fanatic about it; remember, personal computers are fairly hardy, so don't try for an antiseptic environment.

The normal home or office environment is usually fine for your computer, but do keep your floppy disks in their envelopes and store them in some sort of closed container. The stray dust mote is much more likely to garble the data on a floppy disk than damage part of the computer.

Moving parts are most susceptible to dirt, and almost all the moving parts in your computer are in one device: the keyboard. And with rare exception, if your keyboard stops working, you stop working, so take some pains to keep it healthy.

The biggest enemy of keyboards is liquid, especially liquid that contains sugar. If you spill a soft drink, coffee, tea, or 100-percent-natural fruit juice on the keyboard, it will almost certainly stop working properly within a few days; maybe just a few keys will stick, or fail to make contact, or otherwise misbehave, but the problem almost always renders the computer unusable. And unless you're exceptionally adept mechanically and have a good supply of small tools, there's a better-than-even chance that taking the keyboard apart to clean it will create even worse problems.

The only sure way to avoid this is *never* to drink while you're using the computer. But you probably will. So give yourself every chance: Find or make a place to put your glass, cup, or can at least a foot away from the keyboard. Never put it anywhere else. Put it down on your work, if necessary; better to spill something on that final copy you just spent an hour printing than on the keyboard. Don't put your drink above the keyboard; put it below the keyboard if possible, on the same level if necessary, but never above. And *look* when you reach; if you keep your eyes glued to the screen (or the keyboard) while you reach for your drink, sooner or later you'll tip your drink over on the keyboard.

If there's a noticeable amount of dust where you work, you can reduce the chance of a problem by putting a dustcover over the keyboard when you're not using it. One of those expensive, custom-fitted numbers isn't really necessary; a piece of plastic or tightly woven nylon will do nicely.

Smoking is far more dangerous to you than your computer or disks. Dire warnings you may have heard to the contrary, computers, like old-time politicians, operate just fine in a smoke-filled room. But make it a habit to go to another room or, better yet, outside to smoke. You'll smoke less, the office or house will smell better, people won't yell at you for smoking, and your computer will stay cleaner. Everybody wins.

Static Electricity Is a Killer

But if the danger of dirt and smoke is exaggerated, the danger of static electricity may be underrated. If your computer freezes or behaves erratically at random moments, the cause may be small static-electricity charges transmitted from you through the keyboard. If you sometimes feel a slight zap when you touch a doorknob or filing cabinet, you're carrying around enough static electricity to disturb or even destroy one or more of the integrated circuits that make up your computer.

Low humidity is the chief cause of static electricity; the condition is made worse by carpeting and clothing made of synthetic fibers. Low humidity is the norm in the mountain and desert states, but it can be a problem anywhere in the winter, especially in buildings with forced-air heating systems. It can be a year-round problem in a building whose climate-control system reduces the humidity too much.

Back to the symptom: If you feel a slight zap when you touch metal, the static electricity situation is serious enough that you should do something about it. You can try two approaches: Dissipate any accumulated charge before you touch the computer, or reduce the potential for accumulating static electricity; you may want to try both.

Dissipating the charge is the more direct method. Develop the habit of touching something metal before you touch the computer, such as a chair frame, table leg, or lamp. If you're surrounded by plastic, put a substantial metal object—a large pewter ashtray, perhaps, or a bronze bowling trophy—near the computer and touch it. These methods are by no means foolproof, because the metal isn't grounded, but they provide substantially more protection than doing nothing. Static-dissipation devices are available that provide a grounded metal plate to touch; some attach to the keyboard, others are part of a power-distribution device that fits between the system unit and display. These units are more effective than merely touching something metal, and may be necessary if static electricity is a serious problem in your office.

You can buy an anti-static mat—a small carpet with metallic threads woven through it. Be sure to get one large enough to cover the area where your chair moves about on the floor and the area under the table where you rest your feet. Anti-static sprays—to spray on your existing carpet—are also available, but the effect is temporary.

To reduce the accumulation of static electricity, you must increase the humidity, change or get rid of the carpeting, or both. Although a small room-sized humidifier may help, these steps often are too expensive to be practical. A less expensive (and correspondingly less effective) step is to avoid wearing leather-soled shoes or clothes made of synthetic fibers. Whether you take any of these steps, you should still touch metal to dissipate the charge before you touch the computer.

Power-Line Conditioners

The electric power from your wall plug isn't perfect; sometimes the voltage is a bit higher than it should be, sometimes it's a bit lower, and occasionally there might be a brief burst of high voltage called a spike. Most of these go unnoticed, but a severe irregularity can cause your computer to reset, perhaps losing some work. If this happens while the computer is reading from or writing to a disk, data on the disk can be damaged.

You can buy a device called a *surge suppressor* to smooth out the variations in the power, but seek some advice before buying one. Some of the cheaper ones don't offer much more than a false sense of security. And you may not need one at all; the power supplies in most IBM and IBM-compatible computers are remarkably tolerant of power fluctuations. If you have used your computer for several months and haven't noticed any errant behavior, chances are that you won't need one. But if there are large industrial users of electricity in your neighborhood, or a power-hungry device such as an air conditioner or refrigerator is on the same circuit as your computer, or electrical storms are common in your part of the country, it might be a good idea to get a surge suppressor. A good one costs from $60 to $100.

A surge suppressor won't help when the power goes off. If you want protection from power outages, you need something that continues to provide electricity itself. Such a device is called an *uninterruptible power supply,* or UPS; it switches to a battery when the utility company power fails, and will run your computer for 10 to 20 minutes. A UPS isn't meant to be an alternate source of power, but simply keeps you running long enough to save files and shut the system down in an orderly fashion. They are rated in watts; 200 watts should be sufficient for a floppy disk-based system, and 300 or 350 watts for a system with a fixed disk. A UPS of this capacity costs from $300 to $500.

If you want to keep working when the power is off, get both a UPS and a gasoline-powered 110-volt generator. The generator, too, is rated in watts. If you use it just for the computer, 400 watts is plenty. You can get one for less than $500. When the power fails, save your files and turn the system off. Unplug the computer from the UPS, start the portable generator, plug the computer into the portable generator, and turn the computer back on.

Do not plug the portable generator into the wall socket; you could send electricity back into the power lines and injure or kill a repair worker trying to fix the power lines.

Read the instructions carefully for a surge suppressor, UPS, or portable electric generator before you use it. If you have any questions about its operation, ask the person who sold it to you. If you're still in doubt, especially about the portable generator, get the advice of an experienced electrician or your electric utility.

Treat Yourself Right, Too

You spend as much time working in your office as the computer does, so don't neglect your own comfort or convenience.

Leave plenty of work space on either side of the keyboard. Keep a pad and pencil handy; no matter how many pop-up programs you have for taking notes and keeping track of telephone numbers and appointments, you're still going to want to write something down once in a while.

The proper distance and height of the display varies from person to person, but take the time to try several positions until you find the most comfortable for you. Make sure there are no windows or bright lights directly behind you or the monitor.

The quality of the lighting can have a dramatic effect on your comfort and efficiency. Bright overall lighting usually means glare on the display, and fluorescent lights often flicker; both situations can cause tension and eyestrain. Try to keep the lighting directed to your work area; swing-arm lamps are especially good, but watch out for heat from incandescent bulbs: It can damage floppy disks or even the plastic case of your computer. If you use swing-arm lamps, limit the bulbs to 60 watts. If you must have overall lighting, try to keep it indirect and not bright.

Put a telephone close by; you don't want to get up to answer the phone, and you'll probably consult with someone from time to time while you're sitting at the keyboard. If there isn't a phone jack close to the computer, use a long extension cord. If you use a modem, check whether it has two telephone jacks on the rear panel: If it does, plug the cord from the wall jack into one and the telephone into the other; if it doesn't, put a splitter on the end of the cord from the wall jack and plug one cord into the modem and the other into the phone.

Depending on the time of year, don't hesitate to open windows, turn on a fan or air conditioning, or turn on the heat to control the temperature. In most cases, if it's comfortable for you, your computer will be just fine.

Things to Buy (or Make)

If your system includes a printer and a color display, you have to turn three switches on or off (four if there's a lamp nearby). Save yourself the trouble, and save wear and tear on the switches, by plugging everything into a multiple-outlet box. You can get a six-outlet box at a hardware store with a master switch and circuit breaker for $15 to $20; either attach it to the underside of your desk or work table, or just put it on the floor. If you wish, you can get a fancy one with an individual switch for each outlet that fits between the system unit and display for $100 or so. Some include a surge suppressor; be sure the surge suppressor is a good one before spending the extra money.

If you're still putting the stack of fresh paper behind your printer and letting the finished pages fold up on top of the fresh, buy or make a printer stand. There isn't much to one—just something that holds the printer several inches above the tabletop to make room for the stack of fresh paper. You can buy one for $15 to $30, or make one from a piece of ½-inch plywood and a couple of lengths of 1x4 or 1x6. (If you haven't thrown away your college furniture, you could use bricks and boards.)

If you enter a lot of text or data, buy or make a copy stand. Again, it's fairly simple: just something to hold papers, magazines, or books at a comfortable reading angle. The adjustable kind on a spring-loaded arm are handy, but cost $25 to $40 and won't handle anything very heavy. All you need is something that's about a foot high, with a front sloped at about a 15-degree angle, that you can keep from sliding under the weight of whatever you prop against it.

Buy one of those mini vacuum cleaners that's about the size of a small flashlight. It's perfect for cleaning the keyboard, air vents, fans, disk drives, and other parts of the computer. Every three months or so—more often if your office has a lot of dust—remove the cover from your computer and vacuum the inside; clean every surface you can see. This tool is great for cleaning cameras, calculators, VCRs, and other appliances and instruments, too. The vacuum cleaner goes through a 9-volt battery in less than an hour, so get the AC adapter, too. You can get both the vacuum cleaner and AC adapter for less than $25.

Where Not to Save Money

For reasons described earlier, don't turn your computer off each time you're going to be gone for an hour or two.

Don't buy bargain-basement floppy disks. The money you saved loses all meaning the first time you put an archive disk in drive A to do some more work to that masterpiece and DOS blandly responds *General Failure error reading drive A*.

Don't save money on a chair. The more hours a day you spend at the computer, the more important it is to have a proper chair. Get one with good, high back support, and make sure it's deep enough to support the underside of your thighs all the way to the knee. The padding at the front edge should be rounded and padded well enough so it won't cut off the circulation in your legs after several hours of sitting.

Don't waste much time trying to conserve printer paper. It's fairly cheap, and recycling centers love it; just separate it from the newsprint and pasteboard, if you recycle those.

Keep at least one brand-new, name-brand printer ribbon stored away, because when you're ready to print the final copy of that masterpiece and discover that the ribbon in the printer is worn out, it's usually 3:30 a.m. or Sunday afternoon. Generic ribbons and re-inkers save substantial amounts of money, but that last re-inking may not have worked, and this generic ribbon may be the one that sneaked through Quality Control; spare no expense on your ace in the hole.

SECTION

III

Quick

Reference

A Quick Reference to ANSI.SYS Commands

Each ANSI.SYS command begins with {ESC}[, the Escape character (code 27) followed by a left bracket.

The terms shown in angle brackets (<>) in the following list are used in the command descriptions later in this appendix. They are grouped here to provide you with a quick reference.

<attr> specifies a display attribute such as high intensity, blink, or color.

<col> is a number from 1 through 80 that specifies the column to which the cursor is to be moved.

<cols> is a number from 1 through 79 that specifies how many columns the cursor is to be moved.

<key code> specifies the key to be defined. If the key is one of the standard ASCII characters, <key code> is a number from 1 through 127. If the key is a function key, keypad key, or a combination of the Shift, Ctrl, or Alt key and some other key, <key code> is two numbers separated by a semicolon, the first of which is always 0 and the second taken from the table in Appendix D.

<mode> specifies the display mode. It can be a digit from 0 through 7.

<result> is the character or characters to be produced when a key is pressed. It can be specified as an ASCII code, an extended key code, a string enclosed in quotation marks, or any combination of codes and strings separated by semicolons.

<row> is a number from 1 through 25 that specifies the row to which the cursor is to be moved.

<rows> is a number from 1 through 24 that specifies how many rows the cursor is to be moved.

Cursor Commands

Cursor Up	{ESC}[<rows>A
	Moves the cursor up the specified number of rows without changing the column.
	<rows> is a number from 1 through 24 that specifies how many rows the cursor is to be moved up. If you omit <rows>, DOS moves the cursor up one row.
Examples	{ESC}[13A Move the cursor up 13 rows.
	{ESC}[A Move the cursor up one row.

Figure A-1. Cursor commands.

(continued)

Cursor Commands

Cursor Down	{ESC}[<rows>B Moves the cursor down the specified number of rows without changing the column. <*rows*> is a number from 1 through 24 that specifies how many rows the cursor is to be moved down. If you omit <rows>, DOS moves the cursor down one row.
Examples	{ESC}[8B Move the cursor down eight rows. {ESC}[B Move the cursor down one row.
Cursor Right	{ESC}[<cols>C Moves the cursor right the specified number of columns without changing the row. <*cols*> is a number from 1 through 79 that specifies how many columns the cursor is to be moved right. If you omit <cols>, DOS moves the cursor right one column.
Examples	{ESC}[40C Move the cursor right 40 columns. {ESC}[C Move the cursor right one column.
Cursor Left	{ESC}[<cols>D Moves the cursor left the specified number of columns without changing the row. <*cols*> is a number from 1 through 79 that specifies how many columns the cursor is to be moved left. If you omit <cols>, DOS moves the cursor left one column.
Examples	{ESC}[10D Move the cursor left ten columns. {ESC}[D Move the cursor left one column.
Move Cursor	{ESC}[<row>;<col>H or {ESC}[<row>;<col>f Moves the cursor to the specified row and column. <*row*> is a number from 1 through 25 that specifies the row to which the cursor is to be moved. If you omit <row>, DOS moves the cursor to row 1. To omit <row> but specify <col>, enter the semicolon to show that <row> is omitted. <*col*> is a number from 1 through 80 that specifies the column to which the cursor is to be moved. If you omit <col>, DOS moves the cursor to column 1. If you omit both <row> and <col>, DOS moves the cursor to the home position (row 1, column 1—the upper left corner of the screen).
Examples	{ESC}[;10H Move the cursor to column 10, row 1. {ESC}[H Move the cursor to row 1, column 1.
Save Cursor Position	{ESC}[s Stores the current row and column position of the cursor. You can later move the cursor to this location with a Restore Cursor Position command.
Example	{ESC}[s Save the current cursor position.

Figure A-1 continued.

Cursor Commands

Restore Cursor Position	{ESC}[u
	Moves the cursor to the row and column position most recently saved with a Save Cursor Position command.
Example	{ESC}[u Move the cursor to the row and column last saved with a Save Cursor Position command.

Figure A-1 continued.

Erase Commands

Erase Display	{ESC}[2J
	Erases the entire display (equivalent to the DOS Clear Screen, or cls, command).
Example	{ESC}[2J Erase the screen.
Erase to End of Line	{ESC}[K
	Erases from the current cursor position through the end of the line that contains the cursor.
Example	{ESC}[K Erase from the cursor to the end of the line.

Figure A-2. Erase commands.

Display Attribute and Mode Commands

Set Attribute   {ESC}[<attr>m

Turns on a characteristic, or *attribute,* of the display, such as high intensity, blink, or foreground and background color.

<attr> specifies the display attribute to be turned on. More than one attribute can be specified by using a semicolon to separate the attribute numbers. <attr> can be any of the following:

Attribute		Color	Foreground	Background
0	None	Black	30	40
1	High intensity	Red	31	41
4	Underline	Green	32	42
5	Blink	Yellow	33	43
7	Reverse	Blue	34	44
8	Invisible	Magenta	35	45
		Cyan	36	46
		White	37	47

Figure A-3. Display attribute and Mode commands.

(continued)

Display Attribute and Mode Commands

	If you omit <attr>, all attributes are turned off (equivalent to specifying <attr> as 0).
Examples	{ESC}[1m High intensity.
	{ESC}[1;5m High intensity and blink.
	{ESC}[30;46m Black foreground, cyan background.
	{ESC}[m Turn off all attributes.
	{ESC}[0m Turn off all attributes.
	{ESC}[0;1;36m Turn off all attributes, then turn on high-intensity cyan foreground.
Set Display Mode	{ESC}[= <mode>h
	Sets the width and color capability of the display (generally equivalent to the DOS Mode command). This command can also be used to cause lines longer than 80 characters to be broken at the 80th character and continued on the next line, rather than truncated at the 80th column; this is called *line wrap*. It can be turned off with the Turn Off Line Wrap command. Note the equal sign (=) that precedes <mode>.
	<mode> specifies the display mode. It can be one of the following:
	Value *Display Mode*
	0 40 columns by 25 rows, black and white
	1 40 columns by 25 rows, color on
	2 80 columns by 25 rows, black and white
	3 80 columns by 25 rows, color on
	4 320 by 200 graphics, color on
	5 320 by 200 graphics, black and white
	6 640 by 200 graphics, black and white
	7 Turn on line wrap
Examples	{ESC}[= 1h Set the display to 40 by 25 color on.
	{ESC}[= 7h Continue lines longer than 80 characters, don't truncate them.
Turn Off Line Wrap	{ESC}[= 7l Causes lines longer than 80 characters to be truncated at the 80th character, rather than continued to the next line.
Example	{ESC}[= 7l Truncate lines longer than 80 characters.

Figure A-3 continued.

Keyboard Commands

Define Key	{ESC}[<key code>;<result>p
	Assigns one or more characters to be produced when you press a key.
	<key code> specifies the key to be defined. If the key is one of the standard ASCII characters, <key code> is a number from 1 through 127. If the key is a function key, keypad key, or a combination of the Shift, Ctrl, or Alt key and some other key, <key code> is two numbers separated by a semicolon, the first of which is always 0 and the second taken from the figures in Appendix D.
	<result> is the character or characters to be produced when a key is pressed. It can be specified as an ASCII code, an extended key code, a string enclosed in quotation marks, or any combination of codes and strings separated by semicolons. To restore a key to its original meaning, enter a Define Key command that sets <result> equal to <key code>.
Examples	{ESC}[126;92p Redefine the tilde (~) key as a backslash (\ ).
	{ESC}[126;126p Restore the tilde (~) key to its original meaning.
	{ESC}[0;112;"dir ¦ sort";13p Redefine Alt-F9 as a Directory command piped to a Sort command, followed by a Carriage Return.
	{ESC}[0;112;0;112p Restore Alt-F9 to its original meaning.

Figure A-4. Keyboard commands.

Epson–Compatible Printer Commands

T his appendix briefly describes some of the more common commands accepted by Epson and Epson-compatible printers. Most printers accept more commands than are shown here; check your printer's manual for a complete list of the commands it accepts.

Figures B-1 through B-3 summarize three groups of printer commands:

- *Typeface* commands, shown in Figure B-1, control the type of print to be used, which may include normal, bold, extended, compressed, elite, and italic.

- *Format* commands, shown in Figure B-2, control such characteristics as the space between lines, skip to a new line or page, page size, margins, and tabs.

- *Printer Control* commands, shown in Figure B-3, reset the printer to its standard settings, sound the bell, cause the paper-out detector to be ignored, set the direction and speed of printing, and control other machine-related functions.

The command descriptions use these conventions:

^E represents holding down the Ctrl key and pressing the key shown by the uppercase letter. Figure C-4 in Appendix C shows the codes and corresponding DOS echo for characters 1 through 31.

<*Alt-5*> represents holding down the Alt key and typing the digits on the numeric keypad (*not* the upper row of keys on the main keyboard). <Alt-5> and ^E both represent character 5; no matter how you enter it, DOS echoes character 5 as ^E; your word processor or other programs may echo it as ♣.

<*0*>, which represents character 0 (zero). You cannot enter character 0 with the Alt-key technique; most printers accept Alt-128 in its place.

{ESC}, which represents character 27 (called *Escape*). You cannot type this character with the Esc key; either use the Alt-key technique or, if you're using Edlin, type Ctrl-V followed by a left bracket ([).

Typeface Commands

Boldface Start	{ESC}E	
Boldface Stop	{ESC}F	
Condensed Start	^O or <Alt-15>	
Condensed Stop	^R or <Alt-18>	
Double Print Start	{ESC}G	
Double Print Stop	{ESC}H	
Elite	{ESC}M	12 characters per inch.
Expanded Start	^N or <Alt-14> {ESC}W1	One line only. Until stopped.
Expanded Stop	^T or <Alt-20> {ESC}W0	Stops ^N only. Stops both {ESC}W1 and ^N.
Italic Start	{ESC}4	
Italic Stop	{ESC}5	
NLQ (Near Letter Quality)	{ESC}n	
Pica	{ESC}P	10 characters per inch.
Subscript Start	{ESC}S1	
Superscript Start	{ESC}S0	
Sub/superscript Stop	{ESC}T	
Underline Start	{ESC} – 1	
Underline Stop	{ESC} – 0	

Figure B-1. Typeface commands.

Format Commands

Form Feed	^L or <Alt-12> Advances the paper to the top of the next page.
Left Margin	{ESC}l<col> Sets the left margin to the specified column.
Line Spacing 6 lpi	{ESC}2 Sets the line spacing to six lines per inch.
Line Spacing 8 lpi	{ESC}0 Sets the line spacing to eight lines per inch.
Line Spacing in 1/72″	{ESC}A<units> Sets the line spacing to the specified number of 1/72″.

Figure B-2. Format commands.

(*continued*)

Format Commands

Line Spacing in 1/216"	{ESC}3<units> Sets the line spacing to the specified number of 1/216".
Page Length	{ESC}C<0><inches> Sets the page length to the specified number of inches.
Right Margin	{ESC}Q<col> Sets the right margin to the specified column.
Skip Perforation	{ESC}N<lines> Skips the specified number of lines at the bottom of each page. If you start printing at the top of a page, this leaves top and bottom margins equal to half the perforation skip.
Tab Set	{ESC}D<col> . . . <0> Sets a tab at the column specified by <col>, up to 32. Specify each tab with the character whose code is the column number: Column 1 is <Alt-1>, for example, and column 10 is <Alt-10>. End the list with character 0.
Tab Set (repeating)	{ESC}e<0><cols> Sets a tab position every specified number of <cols> across the entire line. {ESC}e<character 0><character 5>, for example, sets a tab at columns 5, 10, 15, and so on. Most printers accept <character 128> as well as <character 0>. Some printers call this command *Set Tab Unit*.

Figure B-2. continued.

Printer Control Commands

Bell	^G or <Alt-7> Sounds the beep on the printer.
Reset	{ESC}@ Resets the printer to its standard settings.
Disable Paper-Out Detector	{ESC}8 Makes the printer ignore the paper-out detector. Necessary to print close to the bottom of single sheets of paper.
Enable Paper-Out Detector	{ESC}9 Makes the printer stop when it nears the bottom of a sheet of paper. Prevents printing on the platen when you run out of continuous-form paper.

Figure B-3. Printer Control commands.

APPENDIX

C

The ASCII
and IBM Extended
Character Sets

Figures C-1 and C-2 show all 256 characters of the IBM extended character set supported by most computers that run MS-DOS. The figures show the characters in four columns; each character is followed by its corresponding code in decimal and hexadecimal. Many compatible printers print the full character set; if you're not sure about your printer, check its manual. Figure C-1 shows the first 128 characters (codes 0 through 127) of the ASCII standard character set; Figure C-2 shows the IBM extended character set (codes 128 through 255). Figure C-3 shows the four sets of box-drawing characters in the IBM extended character set. Figure C-4 shows the names and codes for the *control characters*, the first 32 ASCII characters (codes 0 through 31).

ASCII	Dec	Hex	ASCII	Dec	Hex	ASCII	Dec	Hex	ASCII	Dec	Hex
	0	00	\<space\>	32	20	@	64	40	`	96	60
☺	1	01	!	33	21	A	65	41	a	97	61
☻	2	02	"	34	22	B	66	42	b	98	62
♥	3	03	#	35	23	C	67	43	c	99	63
♦	4	04	$	36	24	D	68	44	d	100	64
♣	5	05	%	37	25	E	69	45	e	101	65
♠	6	06	&	38	26	F	70	46	f	102	66
•	7	07	'	39	27	G	71	47	g	103	67
◘	8	08	(	40	28	H	72	48	h	104	68
○	9	09	)	41	29	I	73	49	i	105	69
◙	10	0A	*	42	2A	J	74	4A	j	106	6A
♂	11	0B	+	43	2B	K	75	4B	k	107	6B
♀	12	0C	,	44	2C	L	76	4C	l	108	6C
♪	13	0D	–	45	2D	M	77	4D	m	109	6D
♫	14	0E	.	46	2E	N	78	4E	n	110	6E
☼	15	0F	/	47	2F	O	79	4F	o	111	6F
►	16	10	0	48	30	P	80	50	p	112	70
◄	17	11	1	49	31	Q	81	51	q	113	71
↕	18	12	2	50	32	R	82	52	r	114	72
‼	19	13	3	51	33	S	83	53	s	115	73
¶	20	14	4	52	34	T	84	54	t	116	74
§	21	15	5	53	35	U	85	55	u	117	75
▬	22	16	6	54	36	V	86	56	v	118	76
↨	23	17	7	55	37	W	87	57	w	119	77
↑	24	18	8	56	38	X	88	58	x	120	78
↓	25	19	9	57	39	Y	89	59	y	121	79
→	26	1A	:	58	3A	Z	90	5A	z	122	7A
←	27	1B	;	59	3B	[	91	5B	{	123	7B
∟	28	1C	<	60	3C	\	92	5C	|	124	7C
↔	29	1D	=	61	3D	]	93	5D	}	125	7D
▲	30	1E	>	62	3E	^	94	5E	~	126	7E
▼	31	1F	?	63	3F	_	95	5F	Δ	127	7F

Figure C-1. The ASCII standard character set.

ASCII	Dec	Hex	ASCII	Dec	Hex	ASCII	Dec	Hex	ASCII	Dec	Hex
Ç	128	80	á	160	A0	└	192	C0	α	224	E0
ü	129	81	í	161	A1	┴	193	C1	β	225	E1
é	130	82	ó	162	A2	┬	194	C2	Γ	226	E2
â	131	83	ú	163	A3	├	195	C3	π	227	E3
ä	132	84	ñ	164	A4	─	196	C4	Σ	228	E4
à	133	85	Ñ	165	A5	┼	197	C5	σ	229	E5
å	134	86	ª	166	A6	╞	198	C6	µ	230	E6
ç	135	87	º	167	A7	╟	199	C7	τ	231	E7
ê	136	88	¿	168	A8	╚	200	C8	Φ	232	E8
ë	137	89	⌐	169	A9	╔	201	C9	Θ	233	E9
è	138	8A	¬	170	AA	╩	202	CA	Ω	234	EA
ï	139	8B	½	171	AB	╦	203	CB	δ	235	EB
î	140	8C	¼	172	AC	╠	204	CC	∞	236	EC
ì	141	8D	¡	173	AD	═	205	CD	φ	237	ED
Ä	142	8E	«	174	AE	╬	206	CE	ε	238	EE
Å	143	8F	»	175	AF	╧	207	CF	∩	239	EF
É	144	90	░	176	B0	╨	208	D0	≡	240	F0
æ	145	91	▒	177	B1	╤	209	D1	±	241	F1
Æ	146	92	▓	178	B2	╥	210	D2	≥	242	F2
ô	147	93	│	179	B3	╙	211	D3	≤	243	F3
ö	148	94	┤	180	B4	╘	212	D4	⌠	244	F4
ò	149	95	╡	181	B5	╒	213	D5	⌡	245	F5
û	150	96	╢	182	B6	╓	214	D6	÷	246	F6
ù	151	97	╖	183	B7	╫	215	D7	≈	247	F7
ÿ	152	98	╕	184	B8	╪	216	D8	°	248	F8
Ö	153	99	╣	185	B9	┘	217	D9	∙	249	F9
Ü	154	9A	║	186	BA	┌	218	DA	·	250	FA
¢	155	9B	╗	187	BB	█	219	DB	√	251	FB
£	156	9C	╝	188	BC	▄	220	DC	η	252	FC
¥	157	9D	╜	189	BD	▌	221	DD	²	253	FD
₧	158	9E	╛	190	BE	▐	222	DE	∙	254	FE
ƒ	159	9F	┐	191	BF	▀	223	DF		255	FF

Figure C-2. The IBM extended character set.

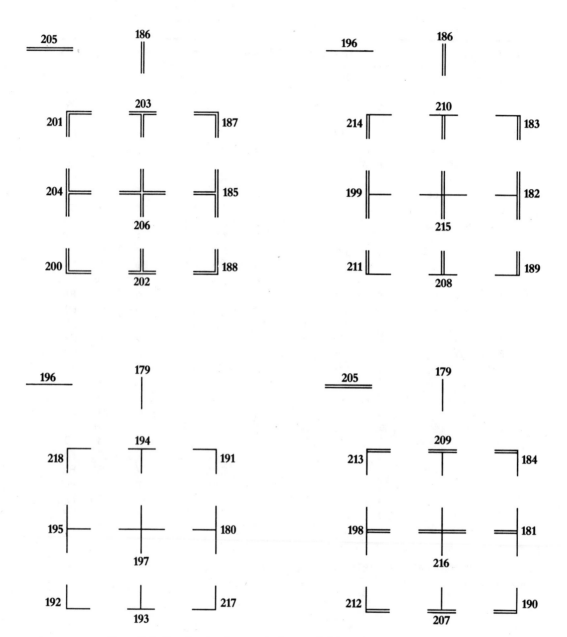

Figure C-3. Box-drawing characters in the extended-character set.

Abbreviation and Full Name		Code		To enter with		
		Dec	Hex	Alt-Key	Ctrl-Key	Echoes as
NUL	Null	0	0	none	none	nothing
SOH	Start of heading	1	1	Alt-1	Ctrl-A	^A
STX	Start of text	2	2	Alt-2	Ctrl-B	^B
ETX	End of text	3	3	Alt-3	Ctrl-C	^C
EOT	End of transmission	4	4	Alt-4	Ctrl-D	^D
ENQ	Enquiry	5	5	Alt-5	Ctrl-E	^E
ACK	Acknowledge	6	6	Alt-6	Ctrl-F	^F
BEL	Bell	7	7	Alt-7	Ctrl-G	^G
BS	Backspace	8	8	Alt-8	Ctrl-H	^H
HT	Horizontal tab	9	9	Alt-9	Ctrl-I	^I
LF	Line feed	10	A	Alt-10	Ctrl-J	^J
VT	Vertical tab	11	B	Alt-11	Ctrl-K	^K
FF	Form feed	12	C	Alt-12	Ctrl-L	^L
CR	Carriage return	13	D	Alt-13	Ctrl-M	^M
SO	Shift out	14	E	Alt-14	Ctrl-N	^N
SI	Shift in	15	F	Alt-15	Ctrl-O	^O
DLE	Data link escape	16	10	Alt-16	Ctrl-P	^P
DC1	Device control 1	17	11	Alt-17	Ctrl-Q	^Q
DC2	Device control 2	18	12	Alt-18	Ctrl-R	^R
DC3	Device control 3	19	13	Alt-19	Ctrl-S	^S
DC4	Device control 4	20	14	Alt-20	Ctrl-T	^T
NAK	Negative acknowledge	21	15	Alt-21	Ctrl-U	^U
SYN	Synchronous idle	22	16	Alt-22	Ctrl-V	^V
ETB	End transmission block	23	17	Alt-23	Ctrl-W	^W
CAN	Cancel	24	18	Alt-24	Ctrl-X	^X
EM	End of medium	25	19	Alt-25	Ctrl-Y	^Y
SUB	Substitute	26	1A	Alt-26	Ctrl-Z	^Z
ESC	Escape	27	1B	Alt-27	Ctrl-[	^[
FS	File separator	28	1C	Alt-28	Ctrl-\	^\
GS	Group separator	29	1D	Alt-29	Ctrl-]	^]
RS	Record separator	30	1E	Alt-30	Ctrl-^	^^
US	Unit separator	31	1F	Alt-31	Ctrl-_	^_

Figure C-4. ASCII control-code names (characters 0–31).

APPENDIX

D

ANSI.SYS Key and Extended Key Codes

F igures D-1 and D-2 show the identifying codes used with the
ANSI.SYS Define Key command for all keys and key combinations
that can be redefined. The first column shows the key legend. The column
headed *Alone* shows the code for pressing just the key; the next three columns show the code for holding down the key at the top of the column
(*Shift, Ctrl,* or *Alt*) and pressing the key shown in the first column. A
dash (—) means the key or key combination cannot be redefined.

Where one number is shown, it is the ASCII code for the key; where
two numbers are shown, they are the extended code whose first number
is always 0.

Figure D-1 shows the extended codes for the function keys (F1 through
F10), keypad keys, and PrtSc; an extended code is two numbers, the first of
which is always 0. Figure D-2 shows the single-number codes for the standard ASCII characters (letters, numbers, hyphen, equal sign, and tab), plus
the extended codes for combinations.

The extended code for including a null character (ASCII 0) in the result
code of the Define Key command is 0;3.

Key	Alone	Shift	Ctrl–	Alt–
F1	0;59	0;84	0;94	0;104
F2	0;60	0;85	0;95	0;105
F3	0;61	0;86	0;96	0;106
F4	0;62	0;87	0;97	0;107
F5	0;63	0;88	0;98	0;108
F6	0;64	0;89	0;99	0;109
F7	0;65	0;90	0;100	0;110
F8	0;66	0;91	0;101	0;111
F9	0;67	0;92	0;102	0;112
F10	0;68	0;93	0;103	0;113
Home	0;71	55	0;119	—
Cursor Up	0;72	56	—	—
Pg Up	0;73	·57	0;132	—
Cursor Left	0;75	52	0;115	—
Cursor Right	0;77	54	0;116	—
End	0;79	49	0;117	—
Cursor Down	0;80	50	—	—
Pg Dn	0;81	51	0;118	—
Ins	0;82	48	—	—
Del	0;83	46	—	—
PrtSc		—	0;114	—

Figure D-1. Extended codes for function and numeric-keypad keys.

Key	Alone	Shift	Ctrl-	Alt-
A	97	65	1	0;30
B	98	66	2	0;48
C	99	67	3	0;46
D	100	68	4	0;32
E	101	69	5	0;18
F	102	70	6	0;33
G	103	71	7	0;34
H	104	72	8	0;35
I	105	73	9	0;23
J	106	74	10	0;36
K	107	75	11	0;37
L	108	76	12	0;38
M	109	77	13	0;50
N	110	78	14	0;49
O	111	79	15	0;24
P	112	80	16	0;25
Q	113	81	17	0;16
R	114	82	18	0;19
S	115	83	19	0;31
T	116	84	20	0;20
U	117	85	21	0;22
V	118	86	22	0;47
W	119	87	23	0;17
X	120	88	24	0;45
Y	121	89	25	0;21
Z	122	90	26	0;44
1	49	33	—	0;120
2	50	64	—	0;121
3	51	35	—	0;122
4	52	36	—	0;123
5	53	37	—	0;124
6	54	94	—	0;125
7	55	38	—	0;126
8	56	42	—	0;127
9	57	40	—	0;128
0	48	41	—	0;129
–	45	95	—	0;130
=	61	43	—	0;131
Tab	9	0;15	—	—

Figure D-2. Extended codes for standard ASCII characters.

APPENDIX

E

Converting Hexadecimal Numbers to Decimal

H exadecimal numbers, like decimal numbers (or any other number base) represent powers of the base number—in this case, 16. The rightmost digit represents the instances of 16 to the zero power, or 1; the second digit from the right represents the instances of 16 to the first power, or 16; the third digit from the right represents the instances of 16 to the second power, or 256; the fourth digit from the right represents the instances of 16 to the third power, or 4,096; and so on.

Figure E-1 simplifies converting hexadecimal numbers up to FFFF to decimal. Each section of the table lists the decimal value of each hexadecimal digit in the corresponding digit of a number.

Fourth Digit		Third Digit		Second Digit		First Digit	
Hex	*Dec*	*Hex*	*Dec*	*Hex*	*Dec*	*Hex*	*Dec*
0	0	0	0	0	0	0	0
1	4,096	1	256	1	16	1	1
2	8,192	2	512	2	32	2	2
3	12,288	3	768	3	48	3	3
4	16,384	4	1,024	4	64	4	4
5	20,480	5	1,280	5	80	5	5
6	24,576	6	1,536	6	96	6	6
7	28,672	7	1,792	7	112	7	7
8	32,768	8	2,048	8	128	8	8
9	36,864	9	2,304	9	144	9	9
A	40,960	A	2,560	A	160	A	10
B	45,056	B	2,816	B	176	B	11
C	49,152	C	3,072	C	192	C	12
D	53,248	D	3,328	D	208	D	13
E	57,344	E	3,584	E	224	E	14
F	61,440	F	3,840	F	240	F	15

Figure E-1. Hexadecimal-to-decimal conversion table.

To use Figure E-1 to convert a hexadecimal number to decimal, find the decimal value of each hexadecimal digit and add the decimal values to find the decimal equivalent of the hexadecimal number. For example, to convert 7F3 hexadecimal to decimal:

- The hexadecimal number has three digits, so start with the section of Figure E-1 labeled *Third Digit*. Find 7 in the column labeled *Hex*; the corresponding entry in the column labeled *Dec* is 1,792.

- In the section of the table labeled *Second Digit,* find F; its decimal equivalent is 240.

- Use the section labeled *First Digit* for the rightmost digit; the decimal equivalent of 3 hexadecimal in this digit position is 3.

- Add the decimal equivalents of each digit to find the decimal equivalent of the number: 1,792 plus 240 plus 3 is 2,035.

A few more examples of using Figure E-1 to convert a hexadecimal number to decimal:

Hexadecimal Number	Fourth Digit		Third Digit		Second Digit		First Digit		Decimal Equivalent
9								=	9
D							13	=	13
1B					16	+	11	=	27
64					96	+	4	=	100
100			256	+	0	+	0	=	256
C5A			3,072	+	80	+	10	=	3,162
1000	4,096	+	0	+	0	+	0	=	4,096
FFFF	61,440	+	3,840	+	240	+	15	=	65,535

APPENDIX

F

A Sample
Menu System

igures F-1 through F-9 show the BAT and DOC files required for a menu system with four sub-menus. Although the program and directory names are different from yours, seeing the menus and corresponding batch files may help you put your menu system together.

The Main Menu batch file (MAINMENU.BAT) shown in Figure F-5 assumes that an environment variable named DR contains the letter of the drive from which the menu system is to be run and that the application programs are on drive C.

The Main Menu (MAINMENU.DOC) and Word Processing sub-menu (WORDMENU.DOC) shown in Figures F-1 and F-3 include ANSI.SYS commands that set various foreground colors for the title frame and menu selections. Each selection of WORDMENU.DOC is cyan, which matches the color of the Word Processing selection in MAINMENU.DOC.

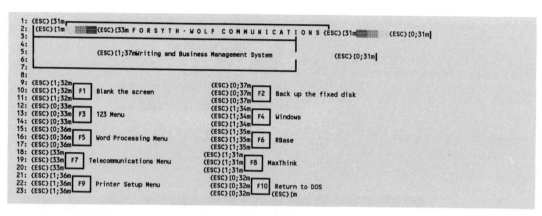

Figure F-1. The sample Main Menu (MAINMENU.DOC).

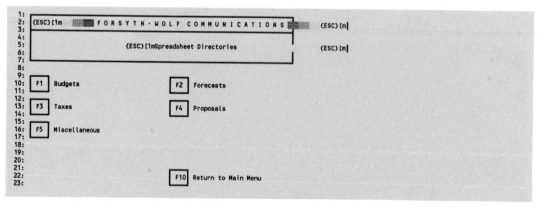

Figure F-2. The sample Spreadsheet Menu (123MENU.DOC).

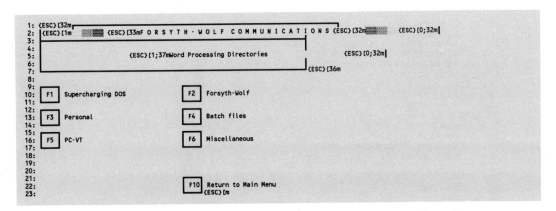

Figure F-3. The sample Word Processing sub-menu (WORDMENU.DOC).

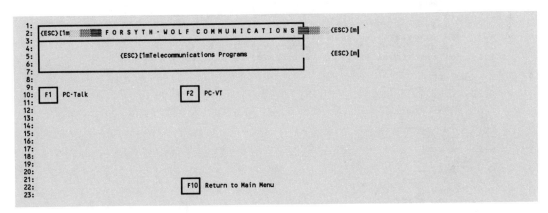

Figure F-4. The sample Telecommunications Menu (TELEMENU.DOC).

```
 1:     echo off
 2:     echo {ESC}[m
 3:     prompt
 4: :START
 5:     cls
 6:     nocurs
 7:     %dr%
 8:     cd \menu
 9:     type mainmenu.doc
10: :GET_RPLY
11:     reply
12:     if errorlevel 69 goto GET_RPLY
13:     if errorlevel 68 goto F10
14:     if errorlevel 67 goto F9
15:     if errorlevel 66 goto F8
16:     if errorlevel 65 goto F7
17:     if errorlevel 64 goto F6
```

(continued)

Figure F-5. The sample Main Menu batch program (MAINMENU.BAT).

```
18:    if errorlevel 63 goto F5
19:    if errorlevel 62 goto F4
20:    if errorlevel 61 goto F3
21:    if errorlevel 60 goto F2
22:    if errorlevel 59 goto F1
23:    goto GET_RPLY
24: :F10
25:    cls
26:    goto END
27: :F9
28:    cls
29:    prompt
30:    command /c prntmenu mainmenu
31:    goto START
32: :F8
33:    c:
34:    cd \max
35:    max
36:    goto START
37: :F7
38:    cls
39:    type telemenu.doc
40: :RPLY_COM
41:    c:
42:    reply
43:    if errorlevel 68 goto START
44:    if errorlevel 60 if not errorlevel 61 goto F2_COMM
45:    if errorlevel 59 if not errorlevel 60 goto F1_COMM
46:    goto RPLY_COM
47: :F1_COMM
48:    cd \pc-talk
49:    pc-talk
50:    goto F7
51: :F2_COMM
52:    cd \pc-vt
53:    pc-vt
54:    goto F7
55: :F6
56:    cls
57:    cd \rbase
58:    rbase
59:    goto START
60: :F5
61:    cls
62:    type wordmenu.doc
63: :RPLY_WRD
64:    reply
65:    if errorlevel 69 goto RPLY_WRD
66:    if errorlevel 68 goto START
67:    if errorlevel 65 if not errorlevel 68 goto RPLY_WRD
68:    c:
69:    if errorlevel 64 if not errorlevel 65 cd \word\misc
70:    if errorlevel 63 if not errorlevel 64 cd \pc-vt
71:    if errorlevel 62 if not errorlevel 63 cd \batch
72:    if errorlevel 61 if not errorlevel 62 cd \word\pers
73:    if errorlevel 60 if not errorlevel 61 cd \word\for-wolf
74:    if errorlevel 59 if not errorlevel 60 cd \word\super
75:    if errorlevel 0 if not errorlevel 59 goto RPLY_WRD .
76:    word
77:    %dr%
78:    cd \menu
79:    goto F5
80: :F4
81:    c:
```

Figure F-5 continued.

```
82:    cd \windows
83:    win
84:    goto START
85: :F3
86:    cls
87:    type 123menu.doc
88: :RPLY_123
89:    reply
90:    if errorlevel 69 goto RPLY_123
91:    if errorlevel 68 goto START
92:    if errorlevel 64 if not errorlevel 68 goto RPLY_123
93:    c:
94:    if errorlevel 63 if not errorlevel 64 cd \123\misc
95:    if errorlevel 62 if not errorlevel 63 cd \123\proposal
96:    if errorlevel 61 if not errorlevel 62 cd \123\taxes
97:    if errorlevel 60 if not errorlevel 61 cd \123\forecast
98:    if errorlevel 59 if not errorlevel 60 cd \123\budget
99:    if errorlevel 0 if not errorlevel 59 goto RPLY_123
100:   123
101:   %dr%
102:   cd \menu
103:   goto F3
104: :F2
105:   command /c bakup
106:   goto START
107: :F1
108:   cls
109:   reply
110:   goto START
111: :END
112:   %dr%
113:   normcurs
114:   promptrs
```

Figure F-5 continued.

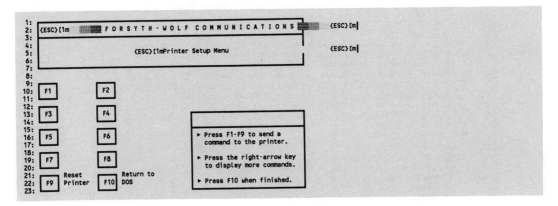

Figure F-6. The Printer Setup Menu (PRNTMENU.DOC).

```
1: {ESC}[14;49H{ESC}[1m Typeface Commands      {ESC}[m
2: {ESC}[9;8H            {ESC}[9;24H
3: {ESC}[10;8HExpanded {ESC}[10;24HCompressed
4: {ESC}[12;8H            {ESC}[12;24H
5: {ESC}[13;8HElite      {ESC}[13;24HProportional
6: {ESC}[15;8H            {ESC}[15;24H
7: {ESC}[16;8HBold       {ESC}[16;24HItalic
8: {ESC}[18;8H            {ESC}[18;24H
9: {ESC}[19;8HUnderline{ESC}[19;24HNLQ
```

Figure F-7. The Typeface commands (PRNTOPT1.DOC).

```
1: {ESC}[14;49H{ESC}[1mPage Format Commands{ESC}[m
2: {ESC}[9;8H            {ESC}[9;24H
3: {ESC}[10;8H1½ space {ESC}[10;24HDouble space
4: {ESC}[12;8HTriple     {ESC}[12;24H8 lines
5: {ESC}[13;8HSpace      {ESC}[13;24HPer inch
6: {ESC}[15;8HTiny       {ESC}[15;24H
7: {ESC}[16;8HPrint      {ESC}[16;24H11-inch page
8: {ESC}[18;8HAddress    {ESC}[18;24HDisable
9: {ESC}[19;8Hlabels     {ESC}[19;24Hpaper out
```

Figure F-8. The Page Format commands (PRNTOPT2.DOC).

```
 1:     echo off
 2:     cls
 3:     type prntmenu.doc
 4:     if "%1"=="mainmenu" echo {ESC}[22;24HMain Menu
 5: :CHOICE_1
 6:     type prntopt1.doc
 7: :REPLY_1
 8:     reply
 9:     if errorlevel 77 if not errorlevel 78 goto CHOICE_2
10:     if errorlevel 69 goto REPLY_1
11:     if errorlevel 68 goto END
12:     if errorlevel 67 echo {ESC}@> prn
13:     if errorlevel 66 if not errorlevel 67 echo {ESC}n> prn
14:     if errorlevel 65 if not errorlevel 66 echo {ESC}-1> prn
15:     if errorlevel 64 if not errorlevel 65 echo {ESC}4> prn
16:     if errorlevel 63 if not errorlevel 64 echo {ESC}E> prn
17:     if errorlevel 62 if not errorlevel 63 echo {ESC}p1> prn
18:     if errorlevel 61 if not errorlevel 62 echo {ESC}M> prn
19:     if errorlevel 60 if not errorlevel 61 echo <Alt-15>> prn
20:     if errorlevel 59 if not errorlevel 60 echo {ESC}W1> prn
21:     goto REPLY_1
22: :CHOICE_2
23:     type prntopt2.doc
24: :REPLY_2
25:     reply
26:     if errorlevel 77 if not errorlevel 78 goto CHOICE_1
27:     if errorlevel 69 goto REPLY_2
28:     if errorlevel 68 goto END
29:     if errorlevel 67 echo {ESC}@> prn
30:     if errorlevel 66 if not errorlevel 67 echo {ESC}8> prn
31:     if errorlevel 65 if not errorlevel 66 echo {ESC}C0<Alt-7>> prn
32:     if errorlevel 64 if not errorlevel 65 echo {ESC}C<Alt-128>{ESC}N
        <Alt-6>> prn
```

Figure F-9. The Printer Setup Menu batch file (PRNTMENU.BAT).   (continued)

```
33:    if errorlevel 63 if not errorlevel 64 echo <Alt-15>{ESC}S0{ESC}3
       <Alt-15>> prn
34:    if errorlevel 62 if not errorlevel 63 echo {ESC}0> prn
35:    if errorlevel 61 if not errorlevel 62 echo {ESC}3l> prn
36:    if errorlevel 60 if not errorlevel 61 echo {ESC}3H> prn
37:    if errorlevel 59 if not errorlevel 60 echo {ESC}36> prn
38:    goto REPLY_2
39: :END
40:    cls
```

Figure F-9 continued.

Glossary

A

ANSI.SYS: A program (called a device driver) that tells DOS how to manage the display and keyboard. ANSI stands for American National Standards Institute. *See also* ANSI.SYS command.

ANSI.SYS command: A command recognized by ANSI.SYS that controls the cursor, display attributes, and keyboard assignments. Each ANSI.SYS command begins with Escape (character 27) followed by a left bracket. If you want to use ANSI.SYS commands, the file ANSI.SYS must be on your system disk, and the file CONFIG.SYS must be in the root directory of the system disk and contain the configuration command *device = ansi.sys*.

ASCII: The code that most computers use to represent letters, numbers, and symbols. ASCII stands for American Standard Code for Information Interchange.

Attribute: *See* Display attribute.

B

Batch command: The name of a batch file. When a batch command is typed while DOS is at the command level, DOS carries out the commands in the batch file.

Batch file: A text file with the extension BAT that contains DOS commands. When you type the name of the batch file, DOS carries out the commands in the file.

Binary: The base-2 numbering system whose only digits are 0 and 1. Computers use the binary system because the digits can be represented by the presence (1) or absence (0) of a voltage.

Bit: The smallest quantity a computer can measure or detect; corresponds to a binary digit (either 0 or 1). Eight bits make up a byte.

Buffer: An area of memory that DOS uses as an intermediate storage area when it reads from or writes to a disk. You can control the number of buffers with the Buffers configuration command.

Byte: The unit of measure for computer memory and disk storage. One byte contains eight bits and can store one character (a letter, number, or symbol).

C

Command: An instruction you give to a program such as DOS, ANSI.SYS, Debug, Edlin, or an application program.

Command path: The list of path names that tells DOS where to look for command files that aren't in the current directory.

COMSPEC: A configuration command that tells DOS where to find the program that interprets what is typed in response to the system prompt. Except in unusual circumstances, the program is COMMAND.COM. *COMSPEC* stands for *command specification*.

CONFIG.SYS: A file of configuration commands that DOS reads each time it starts.

Configuration: The makeup of a computer system, as described to DOS in the file CONFIG.SYS. The configuration includes devices that require special programs, such as a mouse; memory set aside for special use, such as file buffers; and some aspects of system operation, such as how often to check whether Ctrl-C has been typed.

Configuration command: An instruction in the file CONFIG.SYS that tells DOS some detail of the system configuration, such as the name of a device driver (*device = ansi.sys*) or how many buffers to use for disk operations (*buffers = 20*).

Control character: One of the first 32 characters (codes 0 through 31) that, in the ASCII code, represent an action—such as tab or backspace—rather than a character.

D

Debug: A DOS program that lets you examine memory, alter memory, load sectors of data from a disk, and create assembly-language programs.

Device driver: A program that tells DOS how to operate, or *drive,* a device. It can be a separate program with the extension SYS, such as ANSI.SYS, or part of another program (many application programs include device drivers for printers, for example). A device driver may give instructions for a device that DOS considers uncommon (such as MOUSE.SYS), or it may give instructions for handling a common device in an uncommon way (such as ANSI.SYS). *See also* Configuration command.

Display attribute: A feature of the display that can be controlled, such as high intensity, blinking, or color. One way to control display attributes is with ANSI.SYS commands.

E

Environment: An area of memory in which DOS stores definitions of system-wide features such as the command path or system prompt.

Environment variable: A description that is stored in the environment. It consists of a name and value separated by an equal sign, such as *PROMPT = [$p]*. In addition to the environment variables created by DOS and other programs, you can create your own with the Set command.

Errorlevel: A numeric value set by some programs that you can test with the ERRORLEVEL option of the If batch command.

Escape character: An ASCII control character—code 27—often used to mark the beginning of a series of characters that represent a command rather than data. So called because it escapes from the usual meaning of the ASCII code and allows commands to be interspersed in a file of data, especially for data transmission.

Escape sequence: A series of characters, usually beginning with the Escape character, that is to be interpreted as a command and not as data.

Extended character set: The characters assigned to codes 128 through 255 on IBM and IBM-compatible computers. These characters are not defined by the ASCII standard.

Extended key code: The two-number code that represents pressing a key outside the typewriter portion of the keyboard, such as a function key, cursor-control key, or combinations of the Ctrl and Alt keys with another key. The first number is always 0, and is separated from the second number by a semicolon. *See also* Key code.

F

FCB (File Control Block): An area of memory used by DOS to describe the name, size, location, and other information about a file that is being used by a program.

H

Hexadecimal: The base-16 numbering system whose digits are 0 through F (the letters A through F represent the decimal numbers 10 through 15). Often used in computer programming because hexadecimal is a convenient shorthand for working with binary, the base-2 numbering system used by computers.

K

Key code: The number that represents pressing a key in the typewriter portion of the keyboard (a letter, number, or punctuation mark). The key code is the ASCII code for the corresponding character. *See also* Extended key code.

P

Path: The list of directory names that defines the location of a directory.

Printable character: Sometimes used to describe characters 32 through 127, the ASCII codes for characters to be printed, as opposed to characters 0 through 31, the ASCII codes for control characters.

Printer command: A series of characters that cause a printer to take some action, such as changing the typeface or line spacing, rather than printing a character. Most printer commands are *escape sequences*.

R

RAM: Short for *random access memory*, the memory that a computer uses for programs and data. The content of RAM changes often and is lost when the computer is turned off.

RAM disk: An area of memory that behaves like a disk drive under the control of a device driver such as VDISK.SYS.

Redirection symbol: The greater-than (>), less-than (<), and vertical bar (|) symbols used to redirect input or output and pipe the output of one program to another.

Register: An area of memory on the microprocessor chip used to hold one- or two-byte values.

ROM: Short for *read-only memory.* A type of memory whose content is permanently recorded and not lost when the computer is turned off. This type of memory is normally used to store a program or data that never changes, such as the shape of the characters used on the display.

S

Script file: A text file that contains a complete sequence of commands, or a *script,* for a program so that input can be redirected from the console to the file. Used to automate the operation of application programs such as Debug.

V

VDISK.SYS: A device driver that tells DOS to treat an area of memory as a disk drive.

Virtual disk: *See* RAM disk.

Index

A

ADD.BAT, 201
Address part of Dump command output, 52
Advanced Batch File Techniques, 71–87
ALLFILES.DAT, 211, 218
Alt key, 10
ANSI.SYS, 18, 285
   changing the keyboard layout, 186
   commands, 19, 285
      Cursor Down, 254
      Cursor Left, 255
      Cursor Right, 255
      Cursor Up, 254
      Define Key, 31, 185, 187, 234, 258, 270
      Erase Display, 256
      Erase to End of Line, 256
      Move Cursor, 24, 134, 255
      putting in a file, 27
      Restore Cursor Position, 136, 256
      Save Cursor Position, 136, 255
      sending to the console, 20
      Set Attribute, 22, 135, 256
      Set Display Mode, 257
      Turn Off Line Wrap, 257
   device command in CONFIG.SYS, 18
   key and extended key codes, 269
   redefining the keyboard, 185
ANSI.SYS Key and Extended Key Codes, 269–71
Anti-static devices, 245
Appending to a file with redirection, 84
ASCII, 6, 285
   code, 5, 48
   table of characters, 264
   translation part of Dump command output, 51–52
ASCII and IBM Extended Character Sets, 263–67
Assemble command, 67
Assigning a Command to a Key, 33–34, 185–86
Attribute command, 74, 115, 195
Attributes
   display, 23, 25, 286
   file, 74, 115, 195
AUTOEXEC.BAT, 74, 110
   defining standard colors in, 146
   environment variables in, 235
   with RAM disk and menu system, 237

B

Background color, 143
   changing, 145
Bad command or file name, 75, 225
Batch command, 285
   redirecting output, 83
   using in other batch files, 78
Batch file, 285
   ADD.BAT, 201
   advanced techniques, 71
   AUTOEXEC.BAT, 74, 110
   BLANK.BAT, 142, 147
   BLANKSEC.BAT, 143
   BOX.BAT, 186
   calling, 78
   calling itself, 82
   chaining, 78
   changing colors with, 147
   changing display and behavior, 98
   conventions for entering, 73
   debugging, 75
   designing, 72
   DISKFORM.BAT, 214
   entry conventions, 73
   ENV.BAT, 108
   erasing part of the display with, 97
   error messages, 75
   FINDFILE.BAT, 211, 218
   FILE.BAT, 198
   FIRST.BAT, 81
   for files and disks, 194
   FORMDRVA.BAT, 215
   FORMDRVB.BAT, 215
   GO.BAT, 196
   hints for writing, 74
   MAINMENU.BAT, 221, 279
      how it works, 224
      testing, 225
   MAINMENU.DOC, 221, 278
   MEMO.BAT, 206
   MENU-1.BAT, 93
   MENU-2.BAT, 94
   MENU-3.BAT, 95
   MENU-4.BAT, 96

Batch file *(continued)*
   MENU-5.BAT, 97
   MENU-6.BAT, 98
   NOTE.BAT, 204
   PRNT.BAT, 157, 178
   PRNTMENU.BAT, 166, 170, 282
   PRNTMENU.DOC, 166, 170, 222, 281
   PRNTOPT1.DOC, 166, 169, 282
   PRNTOPT2.DOC, 166, 169, 282
   PROMPTRS.BAT, 108, 147
   redirecting the output of, 83
   RESTDIR.BAT, 217
   SECOND.BAT, 81
   SELF.BAT, 82
   SHOWPATH.BAT, 109
   STAMP.BAT, 209
   TIMER.BAT, 86
   TINY.BAT, 161
   to define system prompt, 108
   to display command paths, 109
   UNBOX.BAT, 186
   useful techniques, 77
     echoing a blank line, 77
   using batch commands in, 78
   using environment variables in, 107
   VDISK.BAT, 121
Bell printer command, 262
BIGCURS.COM, 138
BIGCURS.SCR, 138
Binary, 285
Bit, 285
BLANK.BAT, 142, 147
Blanking the screen, 141
BLANKSEC.BAT, 143
Bold Print Start command, 152, 261
Bold Print Stop command, 261
BOX.BAT, 186
Box-drawing characters, 13, 43, 158, 168, 186, 266
Break command
   configuration, 74, 114
   DOS, 74
Buffer, 285
   file, 112
   print, 153
   printer, 153
Buffers configuration command, 112
Byte values part of Dump command output, 51–52
Bytes, 4, 6, 48, 285
   changing a series of, 56
   changing a single, 56
Bytes, ASCII, and Hexadecimal, 3–7, 48

C

Capacity and Speed, 242
Care and Feeding of Your Computer, 241–49
Carriage return, 53

Character
   ASCII set, 5, 48, 264
   box- and line-drawing, 13, 43, 158, 168, 186, 266
   carriage-return, 53
   control, 11, 12, 267, 286
   escape, 19
     entering in a file, 27
     in printer commands, 152
   extended set, IBM, 9, 40, 265
   international, 11
   line-feed, 53
   non-keyboard, 10
   zero (null), 77, 157, 270
Check Disk (chkdsk) command, 81, 211, 216
Chkdsk. *See* Check Disk command
Cleanliness, computer environment, 243
Color
   adding to menus, 233
   background, 143
   changing, 143–45
   combinations, 145
   defining your own standard, 146
   foreground, 143
   monitor, 26, 29
COM files
   BIGCURS.COM, 138
   COMMAND.COM, 78, 106, 114
   DEBUG.COM, 50
   FAST.COM, 189
   FLASH.COM, 63
   NOCURS.COM, 140
   NORMCURS.COM, 139
   PRNTREST.COM, 163
   REPLY.COM, 90
   RESET.COM, 121
Command command, 78
Command path, 109, 286
Command processor, 78
COMMAND.COM, 78, 106, 114
Command-line editing keys, 182
Commands
   ANSI.SYS, 19
     Cursor Down, 254
     Cursor Left, 255
     Cursor Right, 255
     Cursor Up, 254
     Define Key, 31, 185, 187, 234, 258, 270
     Erase Display, 256
     Erase to End of Line, 256
     Move Cursor, 24, 134, 255
     putting in a file, 27
     Restore Cursor Position, 136, 256
     Save Cursor Position, 136, 255
     sending to the console, 20
     sending to the printer, 37
     Set Attribute, 22, 135, 256
     Set Display Mode, 257
     Turn Off Line Wrap, 257

Commands (*continued*)
  assigning to a key, 33, 185, 234
  configuration, 111
    Break, 74, 114
    Buffers, 112
    CONFIG.SYS, 106
    Device, 112, 119
    FCBS, 114
    Files, 114
    Lastdrive, 129
    Shell, 114
  Debug
    Assemble, 68
    Dump, 50, 54
    Enter, 55
    Name, 57
    Quit, 58
    Register, 60
    Unassemble, 68
    Write, 57
  DOS
    Attribute, 74, 115
    Break, 74
    Check Disk (chkdsk), 81, 211, 216, 218
    Command, 78
    Copy, 217, 218
    Echo, 37, 75, 142
    Erase, 217, 218
    Exit, 80
    For, 78
    Format, 215
    If, 77, 243
    Join, 243
    Print, 153, 155
    Prompt, 21, 132
    Replace, 243
    Substitute, 243
    Set, 106
    Xcopy, 243
  editing with function keys, 182
  printer, 36, 151
    bell, 262
    copying from the console, 39
    Disable Paper-out Detector, 262
    Enable Paper-out Detector, 262
    form-feed, 156, 261
    putting in a file, 39
    Reset, 44, 262
    Set Left Margin, 156, 261
    Set Line Spacing 6 per inch, 261
    Set Line Spacing 8 per inch, 261
    Set Line Spacing in 1/72", 262
    Set Line Spacing in 1/216", 161, 262
    Set Page Depth command, 156, 262
    Set Repeating Tab Positions, 156, 262
    Set Right Margin, 156, 262
    Set Tab Positions, 156, 262

Commands (*continued*)
    Skip Perforation, 156, 262
    Start Bold Print, 152, 261
    Start Compressed Print, 152, 261
    Start Double Print, 261
    Start Elite, 261
    Start Expanded Print, 261
    Start Italics, 152, 261
    Start NLQ (near letter quality), 261
    Start Pica, 261
    Start Subscript, 261
    Start Superscript, 161, 261
    Start Underline, 261
    Stop Bold Print, 261
    Stop Compressed Print, 152, 261
    Stop Double Print, 261
    Stop Expanded Print, 261
    Stop Italics, 152, 261
    Stop Sub/superscript, 261
    Stop Underline, 261
    using the Echo command, 37
  Prompt, 21
COMSPEC, 106, 286
Compressed Print Start command, 152, 261
Compressed Print Stop command, 152, 261
CONFIG.SYS, 18, 106, 111, 286
Configuration
  command, 106, 111, 286
    Break, 74, 114
    Buffers, 112
    Device, 112
    FCBS, 114
    Files, 114
    Lastdrive, 129
    Shell, 114
Console, copying from
  to send commands to the printer, 39
Control character, 286
  entering, 11
  searching for, with word processor, 12
  table, 267
Controlling the Display. *See also* ANSI.SYS commands
  Move Cursor command, 24
  Set Attribute command, 22
Controlling the Environment and
    CONFIG.SYS, 105–15
Controlling the Environment with the Set Command, 107
Controlling the Keyboard, 30–34. *See also* ANSI.SYS
    commands
  Define Key command, 31, 185, 187, 234, 258, 270
Converting Hexadecimal Numbers to
    Decimal, 273–75
Copy command, 217
Copying from the console
  to send commands to the printer, 39
CR.DAT, 84, 205
Ctrl-Z, 129

Current drive
    setting, 110
    setting with environment variable, 235
Cursor. *See also* ANSI.SYS commands
    BIGCURS.COM, 138
    block, 138
    commands
        Cursor Down, 254
        Cursor Left, 255
        Cursor Right, 255
        Cursor Up, 254
    form of, 137
    invisible, 140
    NOCURS.COM, 140
    NOCURS.SCR, 140
    NORMCURS.COM, 139
    NORMCURS.SCR, 139
    restoring the normal, 139

D

Date command, 84
Date stamp, 84, 209
DATE.$$$, 85
DATE.TMP, 84
Debug, 47, 286
    adding to a file using, 59
    BIGCURS.COM, 138
    commands
        Assemble, 68
        Dump, 50, 54
        Enter, 55
        Name, 57
        Quit, 58
        Register, 60
        Unassemble, 68
        Write, 57
    creating a program with, 63, 68, 91
    DEBUG.COM, 50
    FAST.COM, 189
    FLASH.COM, 63
    NOCURS.COM, 140
    NOCURS.SCR, 140
    NORMCURS.COM, 139
    NORMCURS.SCR, 139
    PRNTREST.COM, 163
    redirecting input to a script file, 65
    REPLY.COM, 91
    RESET.COM, 121
    searching an area of memory, 67
    verifying your work, 58
    working with files, 48, 50
Debug: A Special Sort of Editor, 47–69
DEBUG.COM, 50
Define Key command, 31, 185, 187, 234, 258, 270

Defining a RAM Disk, 118–20
Defining Your Own Standard Colors, 146
Designing batch files, 72
Designing an Interactive Menu System, 89–101
Device configuration command, 112, 119
Device driver, 286
    ANSI.SYS, 18
    VDISK.SYS, 118
Directory
    displaying in the command path, 109
    GO.BAT, 196
    moving around through, 195
    restoring the current, 216
    setting up, 194
Disk, RAM
    contents lost, 74, 120
    defining, 118
    formatting, 214
    VDISK.SYS, 118
DISKFORM.BAT, 214
Display
    attributes, 23, 286
    blanking, 141
    changing the colors, 143
    color combinations, 145
    controlling with ANSI.SYS commands, 22
    defining your own standard colors, 146
    erasing with batch file, 97
Display It Your Way, 131–48
Displaying Additional Information with a Batch
    File, 95–97
Displaying the Directories in the Command Path, 109
Displaying a File with the Dump Command, 50–54
Displaying the Help Screen, 30
    with one keystroke, 33
Displaying Something at a Specific Location, 25
Displaying at a Specific Location with Attributes, 25–26
DOS commands
    Attribute, 74
    Break, 74
    Check Disk (chkdsk), 81, 211, 216, 218
    Command, 78
    Copy, 217, 218
    Echo, 37, 75
    Erase, 217, 218
    Exit, 80
    Format, 215
    If, 77, 243
    Join, 243
    Print, 153, 155
    Prompt, 21, 132
    Replace, 243
    Substitute, 243
    Set, 106
    Xcopy, 243
Double Print Start command, 261
Double Print Stop command, 261

Drive
    increasing number of, 129
    setting current, 110
    setting current with environment variable, 235
Drive letter, 129
Dump command, 50, 54
    changing an area of memory, 55
    output, 53
        address, 51–52
        ASCII translations, 51–52
        byte values, 51–52

E

Echo command
    debugging a batch file, 75
    echoing a blank line, 77
    sending commands to the printer, 37, 162
    using programs instead of redirecting, 177
Editing keys, 182
Edlin
    adds Ctrl-Z, 129
    entering character 0 (null), 77
    entering the Escape character, 28
Elite Start command, 261
Enable Paper-out Detector command, 262
Enter command, 55
    changing a series of bytes, 56
    changing a single byte, 56
ENV.BAT, 108
Environment
    changing, 80
    increasing size of, 114
    out of space, 111, 135
    variable, 106, 287
        changing, 107
        controlling with Set command, 107
        creating, 110
        COMSPEC, 106, 286
        creating your own, 110
        PATH, 107
        PROMPT, 107
        using in a batch file, 107
        using with menu system, 235
    size limit, 110
Epson-Compatible Printer Commands, 259–62
Erase command, 217
Erase Display command, 256
Erase to End of Line command, 256
Erasing Part of the Display with a Batch File, 97–98
Error messages
    batch file, 75, 225
    environment space, 111, 135
Errorlevel, 90, 287

Escape
    character, 19, 287
        entering using Alt-key, 27
        entering with Edlin, 28
        entering in a file, 27
        in printer commands, 152
    sequence, 287
Exit command, 80
Expanded Print Start command, 261
Expanded Print Stop command, 261
Extended character set, 9, 287
    printing, 40
    table, 265
Extended key code, 287
    table, 270
    using, 32, 90

F

FAST.COM, 189
FAST.SCR, 189
FCB (file control block), 114, 287
FCBS configuration command, 114
File not found, 75, 226
FILE.BAT, 198
FILE1.DOC, 85
Files
    123MENU.DOC, 279
    ADD.BAT, 201
    ALLFILES.DAT, 211, 218
    AUTOEXEC.BAT, 74, 110, 146
    adding to, 59
    batch
        advanced techniques, 71
        conventions for entering, 73
        error messages, 75
        hints for writing, 74
    BIGCURS.COM, 138
    BIGCURS.SCR, 138
    BLANK.BAT, 142, 147
    BLANKSEC.BAT, 143
    BOX.BAT, 186
    buffer, 112
    COMMAND.COM, 78, 106, 114
    CONFIG.SYS, 106
    CR.DAT, 84, 205
    DATE.TMP, 84
    date-stamping, 84, 209
    DEBUG.COM, 50
    DISKFORM.BAT, 214
    displaying with the Dump command, 50
    ENV.BAT, 108
    examining and changing with Debug, 50

Files *(continued)*
FAST.COM, 189
FAST.SCR, 189
FILE.BAT, 198
FILE1.DOC, 85
FINDFILE.BAT, 211, 218
finding on a fixed disk, 211
FIRST.BAT, 81
FLASH.COM, 63
FLASH.SCR, 64
FORMDRVA.BAT, 215
FORMDRVB.BAT, 215
FORMRPLY.DAT, 215
GO.BAT, 196
MAINMENU.BAT, 221, 279
    how it works, 224
    testing, 225
MAINMENU.DOC, 221, 278
MEMO.BAT, 206
MEMOFROM.DAT, 206
MEMOSUBJ.DAT, 206
MEMOTO.DAT, 206
MENU-1.BAT, 93
MENU-2.BAT, 94
MENU-3.BAT, 95
MENU-4.BAT, 96
MENU-5.BAT, 97
MENU-6.BAT, 98
naming, 194
naming with the Name command, 57
NOCURS.COM, 140
NOCURS.SCR, 140
NORMCURS.COM, 139
NORMCURS.SCR, 139
NOTE.BAT, 204
printing in pages, 155
PRNT.BAT, 157, 178
PRNTMENU.BAT, 166, 170, 282
PRNTMENU.DOC, 166, 170, 222, 281
PRNTOPT1.DOC, 166, 169, 282
PRNTOPT2.DOC, 166, 169, 282
PROMPTRS.BAT, 108, 147
protecting with Attribute command, 74
putting printer commands in, 39
read-only attribute, 74, 115, 195
REPLY.COM, 90
RESET.COM, 121
RESET.SCR, 121
RESTDIR.BAT, 217
sample chart, 40
SECOND.BAT, 81
SELF.BAT, 82
separate for large menus or displays, 76
SHORT.DOC, 161
SHOWPATH.BAT, 109
specifying length with the Register
    command, 60

Files *(continued)*
STAMP.BAT, 209
storing with the Write command, 57
storing with a different name, 57
TELEMENU.DOC, 279
TEMP.$$$, 210
TEST.DOC, 159
time-stamping, 84, 209
TIMER.BAT, 86
TINY.BAT, 161
UNBOX.BAT, 186
VDISK.BAT, 121
VDISK.LOG, 124
working with, 49
WORDMENU.DOC, 230, 279
XFORMAT.COM, 215
Files configuration command, 114
FINDFILE.BAT, 211, 218
FIRST.BAT, 81
FLASH.COM, 63
FLASH.SCR, 64
For command, 78
Foreground color, 143
    changing, 144
Form feed, 156, 261
Format command, 215
Format commands, printer, 260
FORMDRVA.BAT, 215
FORMDRVB.BAT, 215
FORMRPLY.DAT, 215
Function keys
    editing the command line, 182
    extended key codes, 270

G

Glossary, 285–89
GO.BAT, 196
Graphic characters, 13, 43, 158, 168, 186

H

Help screen
    displaying, 30
        with one keystroke, 33
    entering, 28
Hex dump mode of printer, 152
Hexadecimal, 6, 48, 287
Hexadecimal numbers, 6
    converting to decimal, 274
Humidity, 245

I

If command, 77
Increasing the Size of the Environment, 114–15
Increasing Your Keyboard's IQ, 181–91
Infant mortality, 243
Intermediate file error during pipe, 75
International characters, 11
Italic Print Start command, 152, 261
Italic Print Stop command, 152, 261

K

Key code, 288
    extended, 287
    table, 270
    using, 32
Keyboard
    changing the layout, 186
    controlling with ANSI.SYS commands, 30
        Define Key command, 31, 185, 187, 234, 258, 270
    redefining, 185
    speeding up the IBM PC/AT, 189
    using the DOS editing keys, 182
Keys, editing, 182

L

Labels, 73
    duplicate, 75
Lastdrive configuration command, 129
Learning Your Printer's Language, 36–45
Left Margin Set printer command, 156, 261
Line-drawing characters, 13, 43, 158, 168, 186, 266
Line feed, 53
Line Spacing commands
    6 per inch, 261
    8 per inch, 261
    in ½₂″, 262
    in ½₁₆″, 161, 262

M

Main Menu, 222
    adding color, 233
    adding a program selection, 226
    adding a sub-menu, 229
    tailoring, 233
    testing, 226
    using with a RAM disk, 235

MAINMENU.BAT, 221, 279
    adding a program selection, 226
    adding a sub-menu, 229
    how it works, 224
    RAM disk, changes for, 237
    tailoring, 233
    testing, 225
MAINMENU.DOC, 221, 278
    adding color, 233
    adding a program selection, 227
    adding a sub-menu, 229
MEMO.BAT, 206
MEMOFROM.DAT, 206
MEMOSUBJ.DAT, 206
MEMOTO.DAT, 206
Memory
    changing an area of, 55
    searching an area of, 67
Menu, Printer Setup, 164
    changing a menu item, 176
    combining the DOC files with
        PRNTMENU.BAT, 177
    combining with PRNT.BAT, 178
    Page Format commands, 165, 175
    PRNTMENU.BAT, 166, 170, 282
    PRNTMENU.DOC, 166, 222, 281
    PRNTOPT1.DOC, 166, 169, 176, 282
    PRNTOPT2.DOC, 166, 169, 176, 282
    Typeface Commands, 165
Menu system
    entering, 221
    Main Menu, 221
    program selection, 220
    RAM disk, using with, 235
    sample, 239
    starting, 234
    sub-menu, 220
    tailoring, 233
    testing, 226
MENU-1.BAT, 93
MENU-2.BAT, 94
MENU-3.BAT, 95
MENU-4.BAT, 96
MENU-5.BAT, 97
MENU-6.BAT, 98
Microprocessor
    registers, 60
Microsoft Word, 231
Modem, 247
Monitor
    color, 26, 29
    monochrome, 25, 28
Move Cursor command, 24, 134, 255

N

Name command
    storing a file with a different name, 57
Naming Your Files, 194
NLQ (near letter quality) Start command, 261
Non-keyboard characters, 10
NOCURS.COM, 140
NOCURS.SCR, 140
NORMCURS.COM, 139
NORMCURS.SCR, 139
NOTE.BAT, 204
Null character
    entering, 77
    extended key code for, 270
    substituting character 128, 156
Null parameter, checking for, 77

O

Out of environment space, 111, 135
Output of batch file, redirecting, 83
Output of Dump command, 51, 53

P

Page Depth printer command, 156, 262
Page Format commands, 165, 175
Paper-out Detector Disable command, 262
Paper-out Detector Enable command, 262
Parameter
    checking for null, 77
    checking whether typed, 77
Path, 107, 288
PATH environment variable, 107
Pica Start command, 261
Playing It Smart with Files and Disks,
    193–218
Power-line conditioners, 245
Print buffer, 153
Print command, 153, 155
Print It Your Way, 149–79
Printable character, 288
Printer
    buffer, 153
    caring for, 151
    commands, 36, 151, 288
        bell, 262
        Disable Paper-out Detector, 262
        Enable Paper-out Detector, 262
        form feed, 156, 261
        putting in a file, 39
        Reset, 44, 262
        Set Left Margin, 156, 261
        Set Line Spacing 6 per inch, 261, 262

Printer *(continued)*
    Set Line Spacing 8 per inch, 261
    Set Line Spacing in ½″, 262
    Set Line Spacing in ½₁₆″, 161
    Set Page Depth command, 156, 262
    Set Repeating Tab Positions, 156, 262
    Set Right Margin, 156, 262
    Set Tab Positions, 156, 262
    Skip Perforation, 156, 262
    Start Bold Print, 152, 261
    Start Compressed Print, 152
    Start Double Print, 261
    Start Elite, 261
    Start Expanded Print, 261
    Start Italics, 152, 261
    Start NLQ (near letter quality), 261
    Start Pica, 261
    Start Subscript, 261
    Start Superscript, 161
    Start Underline, 261
    Stop Compressed Print, 152, 261
    Stop Double Print, 261
    Stop Expanded Print, 261
    Stop Italics, 152, 261
    Stop Sub/superscript, 261
    Stop Underline, 261
    using the Echo command, 37
    Epson-compatible, 150
    experimenting with, 45
    hex dump mode, 152
    learning the language, 36
    not compatible, 42
    operating, 151
    Print command, 153
    resetting with a program, 163
    ribbon, 248
    self test, 151
    sending commands to, 37
        by copying from the console, 39
        with the Echo command, 37
        with a program, 162
Printer control commands, 260
    in a file, 39
Printer Setup Menu, 163, 174
    changing a menu item, 176
    combining the DOC files with PRNTMENU.BAT,
        177
    combining with PRNT.BAT, 178
    incorporating into menu system, 228
    Page Format commands, 165, 175
    PRNTMENU.BAT, 166, 170, 282
    PRNTMENU.DOC, 166, 222, 281
    PRNTOPT1.DOC, 166, 169, 176, 282
    PRNTOPT2.DOC, 166, 169, 176, 282
    Typeface Commands, 165
Printing
    file in pages, 155
    IBM extended character set, 40
    small, 160

PRNT.BAT, 157
  combining with the Printer Setup Menu, 178
PRNTMENU.BAT, 166, 170, 282
  changing, 176
  combining with DOC files, 177
PRNTMENU.DOC, 166, 177, 233, 281
PRNTOPT1.DOC, 166, 282
  changing, 176, 233
  combining with PRNTMENU.BAT, 177
  entering, 169
PRNTOPT2.DOC, 166, 282
  changing, 176, 233
  combining with PRNTMENU.BAT, 177
  entering, 169
PRNTREST.COM, 163
Program
  creating with Debug, 68
    BIGCURS.COM, 138
    FAST.COM, 189
    FLASH.COM, 63
    NOCURS.COM, 140
    NORMCURS.COM, 139
    REPLY.COM, 91
    RESET.COM, 121
  to restart DOS, 121
  to reset the printer, 163
  stay-resident, 110
Program selection, 220
  adding to the Main Menu, 226
Prompt. *See* System prompt
Prompt command, 132
  to carry out ANSI.SYS commands, 21
PROMPT environment variable, 107
PROMPTRS.BAT, 108, 147, 234
Putting ANSI.SYS Commands in a File, 27–30
Putting It All Together: Your Own Menu System, 219–39

Q

Quick Reference to ANSI.SYS Commands, 254–57
Quit command, 58

R

RAM, 118, 288
RAM disk, 288
  contents lost, 74, 120
  creating with a batch file, 121
  defining, 118
  menu system, using with, 235
  using, 120
  VDISK.BAT, 121
  VDISK.SYS, 118, 243
Read-only, 74, 115, 195
Redefining a Key, 31

Redefining the Keyboard, 185
Redirecting Debug's Input to a Script File, 65–67
Redirecting the Output of a Batch Command, 83
Redirection symbol, 288
Register, 60, 288
Register command, 60
Replace command, 243
REPLY.COM,
  creating, 91
  description, 90
  testing, 92
  using to accept any key, 92
  using to accept only certain keys, 94
  using to isolate a single key, 95
Reset printer command, 44, 262
RESET.COM, 121
RESET.SCR, 121
Resetting the printer with a program, 162
Restarting DOS with a Program, 121–22
RESTDIR.BAT, 217
Restore Cursor Position command, 136, 256
Restoring the Current Directory, 216–18
Restoring the system prompt, 108, 147, 234
Reverse video, 23, 135
Ribbon, printer, 248
Right Margin printer command, 156, 262
ROM, 288

S

Sample chart
  changing with one command, 44
  creating, 40
Sample menu system, 277–83
Save Cursor Position command, 136, 255
Screen
  attributes, 23
  blanking, 141
  changing the colors, 143
  color combinations, 145
  controlling with ANSI.SYS commands, 22
  defining your own standard colors, 146
Script file, 63, 289
  BIGCURS.SCR, 138
  FAST.SCR, 189
  FLASH.SCR, 64
  NOCURS.SCR, 140
  NORMCURS.SCR, 139
  PRNTREST.SCR, 163
  redirecting Debug's input to, 65
  RESET.SCR, 121
SECOND.BAT, 81
SELF.BAT, 82
Set Attribute command, 22, 135, 256
Set command, 106
Set Display Mode command, 257

Set Left Margin printer command, 156, 261
Set Line Spacing 6 per inch command, 261
Set Line Spacing 8 per inch command, 261
Set Line Spacing in $\frac{1}{72}''$ command, 262
Set Line Spacing in $\frac{1}{216}''$ command, 161, 262
Set Page Depth printer command, 156, 262
Set Repeating Tab Positions printer command, 156, 262
Set Right Margin command, 156, 262
Set Tab Positions printer command, 156, 262
Setting Up and Using a RAM Disk, 117–29
Shell
    COMMAND.COM, 114
    configuration command, 115
SHORT.DOC, 161
SHOWPATH.BAT, 109
Size
    of environment, 110
    of file buffer, 112
    increasing environment, 114
Skip Perforation printer command, 156, 262
Small printing, 160
Speeding Up the IBM PC/AT Keyboard, 189
STAMP.BAT, 209
Start Bold Print command, 152, 261
Start Compressed Print command, 152, 261
Start Double Print command, 261
Start Elite command, 261
Start Expanded Print command, 261
Start Italics printer command, 152, 261
Start NLQ (near letter quality) command, 261
Start Pica command, 261
Start Subscript command, 261
Start Superscript command, 161, 261
Start Underline command, 261
Stay-resident program, 110
Stop Bold Print command, 261
Stop Compressed Print command, 152, 261
Stop Expanded Print command, 261
Stop Italics printer command, 152, 261
Stop Sub/superscript command, 261
Stop Underline command, 261
Sub-menu, 220
    adding to main menu, 229
    testing, 232
Sub/superscript Stop command, 261
Subscript Start command, 261
Superscript Start command, 161, 261
Surge suppressor, 246
System prompt
    batch file to define, 108
    changing, 107
    part of environment, 80
    restoring, 108, 147, 234
    samples, 132
    simplifying for menu system, 229

T

Taking Control of Your Screen and Keyboard
    with ANSI.SYS, 17–34
TELEMENU.DOC, 279
TEST.DOC, 159
Text files, batch files to create
    ADD.BAT, 201
    FILE.BAT, 198
    MEMO.BAT, 206
    NOTE.BAT, 204
Tick, 153
Time command, 84
Time stamp, 84, 209
Timer tick, 153
TIMER.BAT, 86
TINY.BAT, 161
Turn Off Line Wrap command, 257
Typeface commands
    printer commands, 260
    Printer Setup Menu, 165, 174

U

Unassemble command, 68
UNBOX.BAT, 186
Underline Start command, 261
Underline Stop command, 261

V

Variable, environment, 287
    changing, 107
    COMSPEC, 106, 286
    creating your own, 110
    PATH, 107
    PROMPT, 107
    using in a batch file, 107
    using with menu system, 235
VDISK.BAT, 121
    entering, 122
    testing, 126
VDISK.LOG, 124
VDISK.SYS, 118, 242, 289
Virtual disk. *See* RAM disk

W, X

Word Processing sub-menu, 230–32
WORDMENU.DOC, 230, 279
Write command, 57
Xcopy command, 243
XFORMAT.COM, 215

VAN WOLVERTON

A professional writer since 1963, Van Wolverton has had bylines as a newspaper reporter, editorial writer, political columnist, and technical writer. He wrote his first computer program—one that tabulated political polls—for the *Idaho State Journal* in Pocatello, Idaho, in 1965. His interest in computers and writing have been intertwined ever since. As a computer professional, Wolverton has worked at IBM and Intel, and has written software documentation for the major national software companies, including Microsoft Corporation. His book, **RUNNING MS-DOS**, is a classic with more than 300,000 copies in print. Van and his wife Jeanne live in Alberton, Montana.

The manuscript for this book was prepared and submitted to Microsoft Press in electronic form. Text files were processed and formatted using Microsoft Word.

Cover design by Greg Hickman

Interior text design by The NBBJ Group

Principal typographer: Lisa Iversen

Principal production artist: Gloria Sommer

Text composition by Microsoft Press in Bembo with display in Bembo bold, using the CCI composition system and the Mergenthaler Linotron 202 digital phototypesetter.

Other Titles from Microsoft Press

Running MS-DOS, 2nd Edition
The Microsoft guide to getting the most out of its standard
operating system
Van Wolverton $21.95

Advanced MS-DOS
The Microsoft guide for assembly language and C programmers
Ray Duncan $21.95

The Peter Norton Programmer's Guide to the IBM PC
The ultimate reference guide to the entire family of IBM personal
computers
Peter Norton $19.95

Command Performance: Lotus 1-2-3
The Microsoft desktop dictionary and cross-
reference guide
Eddie Adamis $24.95

Command Performance: dBASE III
The Microsoft desktop dictionary and cross-
reference guide
Douglas Hergert $22.95

Variations in C
Programming techniques for developing efficient professional
applications
Steve Schustack $19.95

Word Processing Power with Microsoft Word, 2nd edition
Peter Rinearson $19.95

Programmers at Work
Interviews with 19 of today's most brilliant
programmers
Edited by Susan Lammers $14.95

XENIX at Work
*Edited by JoAnne Woodcock and
Michael Halvorson* $21.95

Balance of Power
International politics as the ultimate global game
Chris Crawford $10.95

Available wherever fine books are sold.